Abstracts of
Charles County Maryland
Court and Land Record
Volume 2
1665-1695

Taken From Microfilm of Proceedings of the
Charles County Circuit Court Records
From the Archives of Maryland

1666-1668	C 1, i.	CR 35,689-3	1682-1684	K 1. i.	CR 35,691-2
1668-1670	D 1	CR 35,689-4	1684-1685	L 1, i.	CR 35,691-3
1669-1670	D 1	CR 35,689A	1685-1686	M 1, i.	CR 35,692-1
1671-1674	E 1	CR 35,690-1	1686-1688	N 1, i.	CR 35,692-2
1674-1676	F1,i.	CR 35,690-2	1687	O 1, i.	CR 35,692-3
1677-1678	F 1, i.	CR 35,690-3	1688-1690	P 1, i.	CR 35,692-4
1678-1689	G 1, i.	CR 35,690-4	1690-1693	R 1, i.	CR 35,693-1
1680-1682	I 1,i.	CR 35-691-1	1693-1694	S 1, i.	CR 35,693-2

Elise Greenup Jourdan

HERITAGE BOOKS
2007

HERITAGE BOOKS
AN IMPRINT OF HERITAGE BOOKS, INC.

Books, CDs, and more—Worldwide

For our listing of thousands of titles see our website
at
www.HeritageBooks.com

Published 2007 by
HERITAGE BOOKS, INC.
Publishing Division
65 East Main Street
Westminster, Maryland 21157-5026

Copyright © 1994 Elise Greenup Jourdan

All rights reserved. No part of this book may be reproduced or transmitted in any form or by any means, electronic or mechanical, including photocopying, recording or by any information storage and retrieval system without written permission from the author, except for the inclusion of brief quotations in a review.

International Standard Book Number: 978-1-58549-285-5

FOREWORD

The first volume of this series covers the 8-year period from 1658 to 1666, including abstracts of all the court records, which gives the reader a glimpse of the many facets of life of the colony.

However, since the primary interest of most researchers is in the land records, the decision was made to abstract only the indentures, deeds of gift, records relating to birth, death, marriage and presentation of bonded servants while not including the court cases.

All persons mentioned in the following pages were identified as living in Charles County and all land was located in Charles County unless otherwise noted. All designations of acreage were followed by "more or less." Most tobacco was described as "good and merchantable" and usually followed by "and cask."

Elise Greenup Jourdan
Knoxville, Tennessee
January, 1994

Table of Contents

Liber C	Page	1
Liber D	Page	8
Liber E	Page	19
Liber F	Page	38
Liber G	Page	50
Liber H	Page	55
Liber I	Page	63
Misc. Relationships (Libers C-L)	Page	69
Liber K	Page	72
Liber L	Page	80
Cattle Marks (Libers C-L)	Page	85
Servants (Libers C-L)	Page	90
Liber M	Page	103
Liber N	Page	110
Liber O	Page	114
Liber P	Page	114
Births, Burials and Marriages to 1687	Page	121
Liber R	Page	132
Liber S	Page	144
Index	Page	156

Abstracts
of
Charles County Land Records
from
County Court Proceedings

All land and persons mentioned are located in Charles County unless otherwise stated.
Most tobacco mentioned is described as "good and merchantable in cask."
All acreage is described as "more or less" the number of acres mentioned.
Indentures may cover several pages of text. The page number given is only the first page on which the indenture appears.

Liber C & D
1665-1670

Liber C, Page 1

24 Jun 1665; Indenture from **Henry Moore** and **Elisabeth**, his wife, to **Johannah Nevil**, widow; a parcel of land lying on the west side of Zachia Swamp; 500 acres according to patent; now occupied by Johannah Nevill; /s/ Henry Moore, Elisabeth Moore; wit. William Price, Thomas Hussey

Liber C, Page 10

20 Oct 1665; Indenture from **George Thompson** to **John Caine**, planter; a parcel of land called *Bewplayne* on the east side of Anacostia River in a creek called St. John's; bounded by John Meekes, William Middleton; containing 1,000 acres; /s/ George Thompson; wit. Thomas Allcoks (mark), William Williams (mark)

Liber C, Page 14

20 Sep 1665; Indenture from **Henry Moore** and **Elisabeth**, his wife, to **Jacob Peeterson**, planter; for 1,200# of tobacco; a parcel of land called *Moore's Branch* lying on the west side of a branch of Zachia Swamp; containing 50 acres according to patent; /s/ Henry Moore, Elizabeth Moore; wit. Benjamin Rosier, Daniell Johnson

Liber C, Page 18

30 Mar 1665; Indenture from **Thomas Allonson**, Gent., to **William Boyden**, planter; for 16,000# of tobacco a parcel of land of 450 acres according to patent called *Doage's Neck*; bounded by the

river, Chingamuxon Creek; /s/ Thomas Allonson; wit. William Price, Garrard Browne

Liber C, Page 22

8 Jan 1665; Indenture from **Owen Joanes** to **Humphery Joanes** and **Richard Joanes**; for 3,500# of tobacco; a parcel of land on the east side of the main fresh of the Avon River; containing 400 acres; purchased from Mr. James Lendsey; and a parcel of 250 acres; /s/ Owen Joanes, Joanne Joanes (mark), Humphery Joanes (mark), Richard Joanes (mark); wit. John Wheeler (mark), Leo Greene

Liber C, Page 26

13 Mar 1665; Indenture from **William Boyden**, planter, to **James Hussey**, planter; a parcel of land called *River's Spring* on the east side of the Avon River; adjoining land of James Lendsey; containing 250 acres; /s/ William Boyden; wit. George Thompson

Liber C, Page 31

9 Jun 1666; Indenture from **Thomas Baker** to **Richard Dod**; a parcel of land in a valley; bounded by Thomas Baker; containing 40 acres; /s/ Thomas Baker (mark); wit. Sa. Cressey, Richard Lambe (mark)

Liber C, Page 39

9 Jun 1666; Indenture from **Walter Beane**, planter, to **James Walker**, planter; a parcel of land on the south side of Wicomico River; James Walker formerly sold to Christopher Carnell, dec'd; then owned by several others until Mr. Francis Doughty, late Minister to the County, owned it; he sold to Walter Beane; bounded by Thomas Michels land now in possession of John Cage; /s/ Walter Beane(mark), Elenor Beane (mark); wit. Richard Foukes, Jonathan Marler

Liber C, Page 43

19 Apr 1666; Indenture from **George Thompson**, Gent., to Mr. **Robert Prous** and **Charles Hill**, merchants of New England; a parcel of land called *Gift* lying on the north side of Piscataway River and south side of Chingamuxon Creek; bounded by John Hatch; containing 300 acres; /s/ George Thompson; wit. Walter Hall, Thomas Hussey

Liber C, Page 54
11 Aug 1666; Indenture from **John Courts**, planter, to **Edward Philpot**, wheelwright; a parcel of land called *Courts Palace* on the north side of the Potomac and west side of the main fresh of Wicomico River; containing 100 acres; /s/ John Courts, Margaret Courts (mark); wit. Edward Swan (mark), Thomas Hopkins (mark)

Liber C, Page 58
11 Aug 1666; Indenture from **Edward Swane**, planter, to **Gilbert Corner**, tailor; for 4,000# of tobacco; a parcel of land called *Chestnut Poynt* on the west side of Wicomico River; bounded by Edward Philpot, William Marshall and Francis Pope; containing 200 acres and now in possession of Gilbert Corner; /s/ Edward Swan (mark), Susannah Swan (mark); wit. John Courts, Thomas Pope, Hen Cole

Liber C, Page 61
13 Aug 1666; Indenture from **William Nevill**, planter, and **Thomas Hussey**, Gent., and **Johanna** his wife, the relict of John Nevill, dec'd, to **Thomas Wentworth**, planter; for 2,600# of tobacco; a tract on the north side of the Piscataway River called *Wheeler's Palme*; containing 150 acres; /s/ William Nevill, Thomas Hussey, Johanna Hussey (mark); wit. Gerrard Fouke, John Wright, John Lewgar

Liber C, Page 64
13 Aug 1666; Indenture from **John Lewgar**, Gent., and **Martha** his wife, to **John Wright**, Gent.; for £50 from specialty now in England; a parcel of 150 acres out of his manor of 1,000 acres on the north side of a beaver dam bounding on the east with a branch called St. Elisabeth's; bounded by Deep Swamp; /s/ John Lewgar, Martha Lewgar (mark); wit. Gerrard Fouke, Thomas Wentworth, Wm. Price

Liber C, Page 79
Court of 13 Sep 1666; **Dan. Makhenie** formerly mortgaged a parcel of land to **Mathias Obryan**; Obryan acknowledged return of the land upon payment of debt

Liber C, Page 80
8 Aug 1665; Indenture **Daniel Johnson** did acknowledge conveyance of land to Mr. **Sam. Fendall;** confirmed in this court by his wife, **Elisabeth Johnson**

24 Oct 1666; Indenture from **William Allen** to **Jeremiah Dickenson**; for 20,000# of tobacco a tract of land lying on the north side of the easternmost branch of the Avon River; bounded by Joseph Harrison; containing 300 acres; /s/ William Allen, Mary Allen (mark); wit. Joseph Harrison, William Price, Stephen Mountague

Liber C, Page 100
Court of 27 Nov 1666; **John Lambert** and **Ellinor** his wife acknowledge the ensuing conveyance to **Richard True** in consideration that the said True and his wife **Anne** acknowledge all his right and title to a parcel of 150 acres of land at the head to Stone Creek to the said Lambert; wit. Edmund Lambert, John Boyden; conveyance to be acknowledged at the next court

Liber C, Page 101
12 Nov 1666; Indenture from **John Lambert** to **Richard True**; for 150 acres of land conveys a parcel of land called *Nonesuch* in the woods on the west side of the main fresh of Poynton Creek; /s/ John Lambert (mark), Eleanor Lambert (mark); wit. Luke Greene, John Stone, Geo. Powell (mark); John Ashbrooke

Liber C, Page 105
14 Jun 1665; Indenture from **Thomas Stone** of *Poynton*, Gent., to **John Mun**, planter; a parcel of 150 acres of land on the north side of Mathew Stone's land on *Poynton Manor*; /s/ Thomas Stone; wit. Will. Boyden (mark), Luke Green

7 Dec 1665; **John Mun**, planter, assigns his rights in the above indenture to **John Lambert**; /s/ John Mun (mark); wit. Luke Greene, William Boyden

Liber C, Page 109
12 Nov 1666; **John Lambert**, planter, assigns his rights in the above indenture to **Richard True**, boatwright; /s/ John Lambert (mark); wit. Luke Greene, John Stone

13 Mar 1665; Indenture from **William Boyden**, planter, to **James Hussey** a parcel of land called *River's Spring* on the east side of

Avon River; bounded by James Lindsey; containing 250 perches (?acres); /s/ William Boyden; wit. George Thompson, John Hatch
Liber C, Page 112

8 Jan 1666/7; **John Glosse** binds his son to **Owen Jones** to age 21 years; /s/ George Glosse (mark); wit. William Price, Thomas Allanson
Liber C, Page 114

8 Jan 1666; Indenture from **Richard True** to **John Lambert**; for 100 acres of land and lease of 150 acres made over to him by Lambert; True acknowledges sale of a parcel of land on the easternmost branch of Nangemy Creek; containing half of 300 acres; /s/ Richard True (mark); wit. John Boyden, Edmund Lambert (mark)
Liber C, Page 120

10 Nov 1658; Indenture from **William Boarman** of St. Mary's Co., Gent., to **Richard True**, boatwright, 300 acres of land on the east side of the easternmost branch of Nangemy Creek; /s/ William Boarman, Sarah Boarman; wit. William Williams, Theophilus Aldred
Liber C, Page 121

8 Jan 1666/7; Indenture from **Jeremiah Dickenson** to **Richard Stone**; for 9,000# of tobacco; a tract of land on the north side of Avon River adjoining the land of Capt. William Stone called *Poynton Manor*; first possessed by James Lindsey, later by Jeremiah Dickenson, now by Richard Stone; laid out for 500 acres; /s/ Jeremiah Dickenson; wit. William Price, Stephen Montague
Liber C, Page 130

18 Jan 1666; Bond from **Will. Boyden** to **Walter Peake** obliging himself under penalty of 20,000# of tobacco; assuring conveyance of 150 acres of *Doegs Neck* and 300 acres *Wheeler's Choice*; acknowledged this court
Liber C, Page 136

12 Mar 1666; Indenture from **Roger Dickinson**, planter, to **John Lambert**, planter; for 7,000# of tobacco; a parcel of land on the north side of the Potomac River and the east side of Avon River; containing 100 acres; bounded by Edmund Lindsey late in the possession of Roger Dickenson but now in possession of John

Lambert; /s/ Rog. Dickenson (mark); wit. Will Price, Thomas Allanson

Liber C, Page 143

12 Mar 1666; Indenture from **Thomas Hussey**, Gent., to **Wll. Boyden**, planter; for delivery of a mare; a parcel of land called *Whitland* located on the north side of Piscataway River and the south side of Mattawoman River or St. Thomas Creek; containing 450 acres; /s/ Thomas Hussey; wit. William Price, Luke Green

Liber C, Page 150

17 Aug 1666; Indenture from **William Nevill** of Portobacco to **Thomas Mathews**, Gent.; for 3,000# of tobacco, a parcel of land called *Huckle Berry Swamp* laid out for 300 acres; located in the woods back of the land of Thomas Baker; /s/ William Nevill, Joane Nevill (mark); wit. Samuell Cressey, Ignatius Causeen

Liber C, Page 171

10 Jun 1667; Indenture from **Morgan Jones**, planter, to **John Hutchinson**, Gent.; a parcel of land on the north side of the Potomac River about 2 miles from the mouth of Nangemy; bounded by land formerly laid out for Daniell Gordian now in possession of Robert Slye; /s/ Morgan Jones (mark); wit. Geo. Thompson, James Lindsey

Liber C, Page 177

11 Jun 1667; Indenture from **Jeremiah Dickinson** and **Stephen Montague**; for 3,200# of tobacco; a parcel of land called *Batchelor's Harbour* lying on the east side of Piscataway River about 2 miles from Piscataway Creek at the mouth of St. George's Creek; bounded by Jerome's Creek and Ashe Creek; containing 800 acres by patent granted jointly to Jeremiah Dickenson and Stephen Montague 26 May 1663; /s/ Jeremiah Dickinson (mark); wit. Rich. Randall, William Allen

Liber C, Page 185

30 May 1667; Indenture from **Oliver Balfe** of Stafford Co., Virginia, planter, to **George Harris** of Maryland, planter; for 10,000# of tobacco; a tract of land called *Troope's Rendezvous* lying on the east side of Avon River; bounded by land of Andrew Watson, Edward Deane and James Lindsey; containing 350 acres; /s/ Oliver Baulfe (mark); wit. Stephen Montague, Alexander Synett

Liber C, Page 192

11 Jun 1667; Indenture from **George Harris**, planter, to **John Robinson** and **Elizabeth** his wife; for 11,000# of tobacco; a parcel of land called *Troope's Rendezvous*; [see above indenture]; /s/ George Harris (mark); wit. Richard Randall, Gerrard Browne

Liber C, Page 198

8 Jun 1667; Indenture from **John Robinson**, planter, and **Elizabeth** his wife; to Richard Randall; for 10,000# of tobacco; a tract of land called *Troope's Rendezvous*; [see above indenture]; /s/ John Robinson (mark), Elizabeth Robinson (mark); wit. Gerrard Browne, William Allen, Geo. Harris (mark)

Liber C, Page 204

11 Jun 1667; Indenture from **John Charman** to **Alexander White**; a tract of land called *Charman's Purchase* lying on the north side of the Potomac next to land of John Tompkison called *Maryland Point*; first in possession of John Charman and now in possession of Alexander White; containing 200 acres; /s/ John Charman; wit. Stephen Montague, Richard Randall

Liber C, Page 223

13 Aug 1667; Indenture from **William Boyden**, planter, and **Walter Peake**, innholder of St. Mary's County; for 10,000# of tobacco; a parcel of land of 150 acres being part of a grant from Thomas Allanson, Gent., to Boyden; called *Doges Neck*; bounded by the Potomac; /s/ William Boyden; wit. Fran. Swanson, Geo. Thompson, Jonathan Marler

Liber C, Page 229

13 Aug 1667; Indenture from **William Boyden** to **Walter Peake**, innholder of St. Mary's County, for 12,000# of tobacco; a parcel of land called *Wheeler's Choice* on the east side of Piscataway River between Nattyn and Pamunkey; about a mile from the exterior line of land laid out for Luke Gardiner; bounded by John Ward; containing 400 acres; /s/ William Boyden; wit. Geo. Thompson, Francis Swanston, Jonathan Marler

Liber C, Page 247

13 Nov 1667; Patent from Mr. **Stephen Montague**, admn. of estate of Capt. **Robert Troop**, dec'd; for 500 acres of land called *Scotland Yard* lying on the Anacostia which Capt. Troope bequeathed to

Lyndsey and Macoy; discharge to Montague given; /s/ James Lyndsey, James Macoy (mark); wit. Richard Boughton, Thomas Allanson

Liber C, Page 270

24 Jun 1668; Trust by **Verlinda Burdit**, admn. of **Thomas Burdit**, dec'd, before her marriage to **Richard Boughton**; for children, **Elizabeth Burdit, Francis Burdit, Parthenia Burdit,** and **Sarah Burdit**; her brothers, **Samuel Eaton** and **Nathaniel Eaton**, to be trustees for part of her late husband's estate including 1,000 acres of *Burdit's Rest* and *Burdit's Neast*; /s/ Verlinda Burdit; wit. Gerrard Fowke, Richard Boughton

Liber D, Page 7

6 Mar 1667; Indenture from **Henry Hawkins**, planter, to **Nathan Barton**, planter; for 2,000# of tobacco and a mare; a parcel of 300 acres on the north side of Potomac and west side of the main fresh of Wicomico River; bounded by land formerly laid out to John Clerk; now occupied by Henry Hawkins and lately occupied by Francis Wine, and lately by Daniel Johnson and Richard Morrice; /s/ Henry Hawkins, Nathan Barton; wit. William Barton, Jr., John Walters, John Smyth (mark)

Liber D, Page 9

10 Mar 1667; Indenture from **John Lambert**, planter, to **John Godshall**, planter; a parcel of land called *Hogge Quarter*; located on the east side of the fresh of Avon River; adjoining *Poynton Manor*; containing 100 acres by patent to John Lambert dated 29 Jul 1664; /s/ John Lambert (mark), Eleanor Lambert (mark); wit. Owen Jones, Richard Joyod (mark)

Liber D, Page 10

30 Jan 1667; Indenture from **George Harris**, planter, to **Robert Robbins**, planter; for 5,600# of tobacco; a parcel of land on the north side of the Potomac and east side of the easternmost branch of Avon River; containing 150 acres; part of a divident called *Lyndsey* which Harris purchased of Edward Deane; formerly taken up by James Lyndsey, patent bearing date 2 Sep 1659; /s/ George Harris (mark); wit. Owen Jones, John Couffer (mark)

Liber D, Page 13

21 Jan 1667; Conveyance from **Walter Pake** of great St. Lawrence of St. Mary's Co. to **Henry Aspinall** and **Mary** his wife; 350 acres of land called *Doags Neck* bought of William Boyden conveyance dated 13 Aug 1667; /s/ Walter Pake; wit: William Price, Rupert Berkenhead, John Tarkington (mark)

Liber D, Page 14

26 Apr 1668; Conveyance from **Hugh Thomas**, planter, to **Thomas Lomax**, merchant of St. Mary's Co.; for 3,500# of tobacco; half of a 600 acre parcel of land on the west side of the main fresh of Wicomico River call *Rich Hill*; patent granted Thomas 19 Apr 1666; /s/ Hugh Thomas (mark); wit. Rich. Morrice (mark), Tho. Hopper (mark)

Liber D, Page 16

9 Jun 1668; Indenture from **Henry Frankam**, planter, to **Thomas Allanson**, Gent.; for 2,000# of tobacco; a parcel called *How-Land* on the north side of Piscataway River and south side of Mattawoman Creek; bounded by swamp and Indian field; containing 200 acres; /s/ Henry Frankam, Amie Frankam (mark); wit. William Allen, Gerrard Browne

Liber D, Page 18

9 Jun 1668; Indenture from **Henry Frankam** to **William Allen**; for 4,500# of tobacco; a tract of land called *Maisemore*; near Mattawoman Creek; bounded by Daniel Mathenas and George Howse; containing 200 acres; /s/ Henry Frankome, Amee Frankome (mark) wit. Thomas Allanson, Gerrard Browne

Liber D, Page 20

7 Apr 1668; Indenture from **Thomas King**, planter, to **Gerrard Breeden**, planter; for 11,200# of tobacco; a parcel of land called *Rivers' Spring* on the east side of the fresh of Avon River; adjoining James Lindsey; containing 250 acres; patented to Christopher Rivers 22 Jun 1663; /s/ Thomas King (mark); Gerrard Breeden (mark); wit. Owen Jones, George Bankes

Liber D, Page 21

6 Apr 1668; Indenture from **Humphery Jones** to **George Bankes** of St. Mary's Co., planter; for 3,000# of tobacco; a parcel of land on the east side of the main fresh of Avon River; adjoining land of

Humphrey Jones; being part of the 400 acres which Owen Jones purchased of James Lyndsey; patent dated 27 Jun 1662; containing 100 acres; /s/ Humphrey Jones (mark); George Bancks (mark); wit. Owen Jones, Gerrard Breeden (mark)
Liber D, Page 24

8 Mar 1667; Indenture from **Richard Jones**, planter, to **Humphrey Jones**, planter; for 2,400# of tobacco; a parcel of land of 250 acres which Richard and Humphrey Jones bought of Owen Jones; lying on the east side of the main fresh of Avon River; part of the 400 acres Owen Jones bought of James Lindsey; /s/ Rich. Jones (mark), Humphrey Jones (mark); wit. Owen Jones, Francis Addames
Liber D, Page 26

28 May 1668; Deed of Gift from **William Boyden**, planter, to his brother, **John Boyden**; a tract of land in Mattawoman or St. Thomas Creek where William now lives; /s/ William Boyden; wit. Will. Allen, Luke Greene
Liber D, Page 27

11 Aug 1668; Indenture from **John Tompkinson**, carpenter, to **James Mackey**; for 6,000# of tobacco; a tract of land called *Thompkinson's Long Looked For* containing 200 acres; patent dated 27 May 1667; /s/ John Tompkinson; wit. William Price, George Thompson
Liber D, Page 28

11 Aug 1668; Indenture from **Thomas Baker**, planter, to **Edward Powell**, sawyer; for 4,000# of tobacco; a parcel of land on the north side of Potomac; bounded by a hill going from Francis Pope's to Thomas Baker's; /s/ Thomas Baker (mark); wit. Benjamin Rozer, Jonathan Marlar
Liber D, Page 30

8 Aug 1668; Indenture from **Thomas Stone** and **John Stone**, Gent., to **Thomas King**; Jeremy Dickenson sold a parcel of land 8 Jan 1667; possessed by Thomas and John Stone after the death of Richard Stone; for 7,000# of tobacco; a tract lying on the north side of Avon River adjoining Capt. Wm. Stone's *Poynton Manor*; first in possession of Jeremiah Dickenson, then Richard Stone; containing 500 acres; /s/ Thomas Stone, John Stone; wit. Stephen Montague, John Godshall

Liber D, Page 32

10 Aug 1668; Indenture from **Thomas Allanson**, Gent., to **Nicholas Emason**, innholder; for 5,000# of tobacco; a parcel of land of 200 acres on the south side of Mattawoman Creek called *Howland*; belonging to George Howe, dec'd, then Thomas Allanson by conveyance from Henry Frankam; /s/ Thomas Allanson; wit. George Thompson, Ignatius Causeen

Liber D, Page 34

7 Sep 1668; Indenture from **George Harris** of Kent Co. to **James Littlepage** and **Robert Littlepage**, planters; for 10,000# of tobacco; a parcel of land called *Effton Hills* on the north side of Burdit's Creek; bounded by Mrs. Verlinda Stone, Samuel Palmer; patent to George Harris dated 5 Feb 1666; now possessed by James and Robert Littlepage; /s/ George Harris (mark); wit. Owen Jones, William James (mark)

Liber D, Page 37

10 Nov 1668; Indenture from **Andrew Watson** of Stafford Co., VA, planter, to **Gerrard Browne**; for 4,500# of tobacco; 75 acres, part of a larger tract sold by Richard Trew, boatwright, to Andrew Watson, and formerly belonging to Capt. William Boarman; bounding Nangemy Creek; /s/ Andrew Watson (mark); wit. John Harris, Samuel Rower (mark)

Liber D, Page 39

8 Sep 1668; Indenture from **John Caen**, Gent., to **Robert Casleton**, cooper; for 3,500# of tobacco; a tract of land called *Napping*; on the west side of Portobacco Creek; bounded by Archibald Wayhop and Garret Synnets; laid out for 150 acres; /s/ John Caen (mark); wit. Samuel Cressey, John Stone

Liber D, Page 44

9 Jan 1668; Indenture from **John Munne** and **Will Allen**, planters, to **Henry Aspinoll**, planter; for 2,300 acres formerly belonging to Davy Prichard and 150 acres formerly surveyed for Thom. Cole adjoining Prichard's land in Mattawoman and 4,500# of tobacco; a parcel of land called *Dog's Neck* on the east side of Piscataway River; containing 300 acres; /s/ John Munn (mark), Wm. Allen; wit. Richard Edehen (Edelen), Tho. Allanson

Liber D, Page 48
12 Jan 1668; Indenture from **Henry Aspinoll** and **John Munn**, planters, to Henry Aspinoll; acknowledges sale of the land laid out from David Prichard adjoining land laid out for David Thomas on Mattawoman Creek; /s/ Henry Aspinoll (mark); wit. Richard Edelen, Thomas Allanson

Liber D, Page 56
22 Mar 1668/9; Deed of Gift from **Amey Frankcum**, widow and admn. of **Henry Frankcum**, dec'd gives to her children **Henry Frankcum** and **Elizabeth Frankcum**; gift of cattle and mares; /s/ Amey Franckum (mark); wit. Richard Fowke, Thomas Wentworth, Joannes Wrighte

Liber D, Page 68
6 Apr 1669; Deed of Gift from **William Barton** to **William Barton**, son of **Nathan Barton**, a cow calf; /s/ William Barton; wit. John Wallter (mark) James Peart

24 Apr 1669; Deed of Gift from **Edee Hills**, widow of **Wm. Hills**, lately dec'd, to dau. **Susanna Marea Hills** 2 yearling heifers; /s/ Edee Hills (mark); wit. John Helme, Ben. Marchygay

Liber D, Page 69
10 Nov 1668; Indenture from **Francis Pope**, Gent., to **Richard Pinnar**; a parcel of land on the north side of the Potomac containing 1/2 of 600 acres granted to John Tompkinson and Andrew Watson by patent 13 Jan 1654; /s/ Francis Pope; wit. Rich. Boughton, Henry Bonner

Liber D, Page 75
Acknowledgment by **Edward Swan** and **Susanna Swan** to **Wm. Ward**:
17 Aug 1658; **John Lugar**, late sec'y to the Province, for transporting several persons, due land which was granted to James Walker, assignee of John Lugar, son of John Lugar; a parcel of land on the west side of Wicomico; called *Walker's Runn*; containing 200 acres; /s/ Josias Fendall; recorded, Philip Calvert, Sec'y
James Walker assigns his rights in above 27 Jan 1658; /s/ James Walter; wit. Robert Hiscok (mark), Richard Grayner (mark)
John Piper and Sam. Dobson acknowledge ownership of the 200 acres by Edward Swan; /s/ John Piper (mark), Sam. Dobson; wit. Susanna Swan (mark)

Liber D, Page 79

9 Mar 1668; Indenture from **Edward Swan** to **William Ward**; for 15,000# of tobacco; a parcel of land formerly granted to James Walker; /s/ Edward Swane (mark); wit. John Morren (mark), Jonathan Marly

Liber D, Page 88

8 Jun 1669; Indenture from **Wm. Allen & John Munn** to **Thomas Bennett** of St. Mary's Co.; for 9,000# of tobacco; a tract of land on the north side of the Potomac on the high cliffs; bounded by Sam. Cressey formerly belonging to Wm. Robinson; bounded by Thomas Baker; being 1/2 of patent granted Jo. Jarbo for 300 acres on 14 Apr 1653; assigned to John Nevill 21 Xber 1655; to Allen and Mann by Wm. Nevill, son of John Nevill dec'd 10 9br 1667; excepting a small tract; /s/ Wm. Allen, John Munn (mark); wit. Joseph Harrison, John Charman

Liber D, Page 90

11 Aug 1668; Indenture from **Thomas Baker**, planter, to **Edward Powell**, sawyer; for 4,000# tobacco; a parcel of land on the north side of the Potomac; /s/ Tho. Baker (mark); wit. Ben. Rozer, Jonathan Marler

Liber D, Page 92

8 Jun 1669; Indenture from **Thomas King** to **Archibald Wahop**; for 14,000# a parcel of 400 acres of land sold to King by Thomas and John Stone; first taken up by James Lendsey who sold to Jeremiah Dickenson who sold to Richard Stone, brother to Thomas and John Stone; bounded by Alex. Davies, George Thompson, and John Wheeler; /s/ Thomas King (mark); wit. Rich. Boughton, Stephen Mountague

Liber D, Page 93

8 Jun 1669; Indenture from **John Munn**, planter, to **William Nevill**; for 2,700# of tobacco; a parcel laid out for Thomas Cotes on the south side of the Piscataway River on the east side of St. Thomas Creek; adjoining land laid out for David Prichard; containing 150 acres; /s/ John Munn (mark); wit. Tho. Bennet, Stephen Mountague

Liber D, Page 95

8 Jun 1669; Indenture from **Francis Adames** to **Richard Jones**; a parcel called *Batchelor's Hope* of 100 acres on the south side of St. Francis Branch; bounded by Mathias Bryan; /s/ Francis Adames; wit. Tho. Bennett, Wm. Nevill, Henry Bonner

Liber D, Page 97

John Bond's Deed of Gift to **John Robinson**: all his moveables, goods and whatsoever else belong to him

16 Jul 1669; Deed of Gift from **Francis Dowty**, minister, to **Daniell** and **Joy Oneale**, children of Capt. **Hugh Oneale**; /s/ Francis Dowty; wit. Tho. Hensy, Gyles Tomkins

Liber D, Page 98

10 Aug 1669; Deed of Gift from Capt. **Hugh Oneale** to his daughter **Wenifrett**; cow; 10 Aug 1669; /s/ Hugh Oneale; wit. Henry Bonner

Oct 1668; Deed of Gift from **John Keane** to **Tho. Ashbrouke**; heifer; /s/ John Keane (mark); wit. James Lendsey, John Hitchinson

6 Oct 1669; Request of **Ann Fouke**; division of land between **Job Chandler** and **Simon Oversee** bought of Wm. Lewis; containing 2,000 acres; /s/ Alex. Simpson (mark); wit. Henry Adames

Liber D, Page 99

2 Aug 1669; Indenture from **Tho. Bennet** of St. Mary's Co. to **Tho. Wardner**; for 10,000# of tobacco; a parcel of land on the north side of Potomac two leagues above Caedar Point; bounded on the side of a hill by Sam Cressey's fence (formerly belonging to Wm. Robinson); bounded by Thom. Baker and land formerly belonging to John Nevill. dec'd; being 1/2 the parcel of land granted John Gerbo (Jarbo); 300 acres dated 14 Apr 1653; assigned to Nevill 21 Xbr 1655; to Allen and Munn by Wm. Nevill, son of John Nevill 9br 1667; /s/ Thomas Bennet; wit. George Thompson, Henry Moore, Henry Bonner

Liber D, Page 100

29 Jul 1669; Indenture from **Nicholas Emanson** to **Stephen Mountague**; for 5,000# of tobacco; a parcel of land called *Howland* on the north side of Piscataway River and south side of Mattawoman Creek; containing 200 acres; /s/ Nich. Emanson; wit. Robert Robins, Gerrard Browne

Liber D, Page 101

30 Mar 1668; Indenture from **John Wheeler**, planter, to **Wm. Dickson**; for 2,100# of tobacco; a parcel of land adjoining *Planter's Delight* surveyed by George Thompson; containing 65 acres; assigned by patent granted to Wheeler 2 of 9br 1668 called *Stoke Hill*; /s/ John Wheeler (mark); wit. Richard Fowke, Rich. Edehen (Edelen)

Liber D, Page 105

14 Sep 1669; Indenture from **Henry Aspinall**, planter, to **Henry Fletcher**, planter; for 2,400# of tobacco; a parcel on the east side of Piscataway River on Goose Bay; containing 150 acres; /s/ Henry Aspinall (mark); wit. Geo. Thompson, Tho. Golden, John Meredith

4 Sep 1669; Indenture from **Owen Jones** to **Ed. Knight**; a parcel of land called *Adventure* on the east side of the main fresh of Avon River; bounded by Andrew Watson; containing 70 acres; /s/ Owen Jones; wit. Wm. Thomas, John Robinson (mark)

Liber D, Page 107

8 Nov 1669; Indenture from **Henry Moore**, planter, to **Francis Heydon** and **John Alword**, planters; for 3,500# tobacco; a parcel called *Moore's Hope*; bounded by George Goodrick's 600 acres and land of Thomas Hussey at head of one of the northernmost branches of Zachia Swamp; containing 100 acres; /s/ Henry Moore; wit. Henry Bonner, Wm. Baker, Garvis Crumpe

Liber D, Page 109

15 Aug 1669; Indenture from **Alex. Davies**, planter, to **William Love**, planters; for 3,900# of tobacco; a tract of land being part of the land formerly taken up by James Lindsey now occupied by Thom. King; bounded by *Poynton* of William Stone; containing 100 acres; /s/ Alex. Davies (mark); wit. Benja. Rozer, Tho. Jenkins

Liber D, Page 110

14 Sep 1669; Indenture from **Wm. Diccason**, planter, to **Edmund Taylor**, planter; for 3,000# of tobacco; a parcel of land bounded by *Planter's Delight* formerly surveyed by George Thompson; containing 65 acres; now occupied by Wm. Diccason and lately occupied by John Wheeler called *Stoake Hill*; granted Wheeler 2nd 7br 1668; wit. [blank]

William Diccasson assigns his rights in *Stoake Hill* to Edmond Taylor 11 Nov 1669; /s/ Willi Diccasson
Liber D, Page 111
8 Jun 1669; Indenture from **William Allen**, planter, to **Henry Moore**, planter; parcel called *Maysmoore*; bounded by Daniell Mathenias land standing by Mattawoman Creek and land of Geo. How; containing 200 acres; /s/ Wm. Allen, Martha Allen (mark); wit. Thomas Jenkins, Samuell Price (mark)
Liber D, Page 113
9 9br 1669; Indenture from **Tho. King**, planter, to **Alex Davies**, planter; for 4,000# of tobacco; a tract on the easternmost branch of Avon River; bound by Cap. Wm. Stone's *Poynton*; containing 100 acres; part of land taken up by James Lendsy now in possession of Thomas King; /s/ Thomas King (mark); wit. Thomas Jenkins, Benjamin Rozer
Liber D, supplement Page 1
2 Jul 1670; Deed of Gift from **William Marshall** of Piquasquo, planter, unto the inhabitants of Charles County and the Protestant Minister and inhabitants; 30 head of cattle in custody of Francis Pope and Bridgett Legatt; for use of minister Mathew Hill; overseers Mathew Hill, Humph. Warren of Hatton's Point, and John Bowles at Pickywaxen; /s/ Wm. Marshall (mark); wit. Mathew Hill, Alex. Gallant, John Long (mark)
Liber D, supplement Page 8
1 Jul 1670; Indenture from **Stephen Mountague**, planter, to **Hugh French**, planter; for 10,000# of tobacco; a parcel of land called *Batchelor's Harbour* on the east side of Piscataway River about 2 miles from Piscataway Creek at the mouth of St. Georgio Creek and goes to mouth of Jecomo Creek; containing 800 acres; /s/ Stephen Mountague; wit. Henry Bonner, Phillip Lines
Liber D, supplement Page 16
Edmund Lindsay acknowledges right in following lease to **Benjamin Rozer**:
Jan 1663; Lord Baltimore grants to **Isaack Allerton**, Gent. and Dame **Elizabeth** his wife, relict and admx. of **Symon Oversee**, late of St. John's in St. Mary's Co.; to farm the moiety of a freehold bought of Will Lewis by Jobe Chandler and Simon Oversee;

estimate containing 1,000 acres; term of 21 years; /s/ Charles Calvert

Isaac Allerton of Northumberland Co., Virginia, Gent., assigns his rights in the preceding lease to **Edmond Lyndsy** of Portobacco; 18 Mar 1666/7; /s/ Isaack Allerton; wit. Gerard Fowke

Edmond Lyndsy of Portobacco, planter, for 10,000# of tobacco assigns his rights in above lease to **Benjamin Rozer**; 23 Feb 1668; wit. Edmond Lyndsy (mark); wit. Francis Lovelace, John Cary, James Martine
    Liber D, supplement Page 28

17 May 1667; Indenture from **Henry More** and **Elizabeth** his wife to **Thomas Hussey**; for 6,000# of tobacco; a parcel of land called *Moore's Rest*; bounded by George Gooderick and an Indian Field; containing 150 acres; /s/ Henry Moore, Eliz. Moore; wit. John Alword (mark), Francis Heydon
    Liber D, supplement Page 41

14 Jun 1670; Indenture from **Robert Robins**, planter, to **William Hensey**, planter; a parcel of land near Pekeywaxen Creek; bounded by Richard Smith and Robert Henley; /s/ Robert Robins; wit. Tho. Mathews, Samll. Cressey
    Liber D, supplement Page 53

13 Jun 1670; Indenture from **Thomas Hussey** and **Joane** his wife to **John Alward** and **Francis Heydon**; a parcel of land bounded by George Goodricke; containing 150 acres; patent for said land to Thomas Hussey called *Newport*; /s/ Thomas Hussey; Joan Hussey (mark); wit. Michaell Ashforth (mark), William Brewer (mark)
    Liber D, supplement Page 58

14 Jun 1670; Indenture from **Nathan Barton**, carpenter, to **Henry Hawkins**, planter; for 3,000# of tobacco; a parcel of land of 75 acres; bounded by plantation where Nathan Barton now lives and the Hawkings plantation which Barton bought; /s/ Nathan Barton, Henry Hawkings; wit. John Twigs (mark), Maverell Hulse
    Liber D, supplement Page 62

5 Mar 1669; Indenture from **Gerard Browne** to **Thomas King**; for 7,000# of tobacco; a tract of 75 acres, part of a larger tract sold by Richard Trew to Andrew Watson of Stafford Co., VA; Watson

sold to Browne; on east side of a run of Nangemy Creek; /s/ Gerard Browne; wit. Thomas Allanson, John Godshall

      Liber D, supplement Page 69

14 Jan 1667; Deed of Gift from **Thomas Allanson**, Gent., to **Richard Harrison**, son of Joseph Harrison; Capt. Robert Troop paid 3,000# of tobacco to Thomas Allanson for 150 acres of land called *French Lewis* which Troop devised in his will to Richard Harrison; /s/ Thomas Allanson; wit. Stephen Mountague, Jeremiah Dickenson (mark)

      Liber D, supplement Page 74

25 Nov 1670; Deed of Gift from **John Lambert** to **Ellen Lambert** his wife; in consideration of goods given his wife by her father John Nevill; a parcel of land of 150 acres which Lambert bought of Richard True; adjoining the land where Lambert now dwells; also a parcel of 100 acres of his now dwelling plantation; plus horses and cattle; /s/ John Lambert (mark); wit. Luke Greene, John Godshall

      Liber D, supplement Page 78

19 Feb 1669; Indenture from **Gerard Brown**, planter, to **George Langham**, planter; for 2,000# of tobacco; a parcel of land bounded by *Poynton Manor*, land laid out for James Lyndsey; containing 100 acres; /s/ Gerard Browne; wit. Stephen Mountague, Thomas Allanson

Circuit Court Records
1670-1674

Page numbering of these records is erratic in some cases.
Example: Left hand page has no number
Right hand page numbered, say, 50
Page 49 1/2 is used as number of left hand page

Liber E, Page 1

10 Jan 1670; Indenture from **John Chairman**, planter, to **Benjamin Rozer**, merchant; for 5,000# tobacco; a parcel of land called *St. Elizabeth's* on the east side of Piscataway River in St. Thomas Bay; bounded by *St. Joseph's*; containing 600 acres; /s/ John Chairman; wit. Philip Lines, John Douglas, Henry Bonner, Philip Gibbon

Liber E, Page 3

7 Nov 1670; Indenture from **Ignatius Causine**, Gent., to **John Hackister**; for ___ tobacco; a parcel of land called *St. Ignatius* on the west side of main fresh at head of Portobacco or St. Thomas Creek; bound by land formerly laid out for Job Chandler, Esq., and John Cain; containing 100 acres; /s/ Ignatius Causine; wit. Philip Gibbon, Thomas Stone, Mathew Stone

Liber E, Page 5

10 Jan 1670; Indenture from **Luke Greene**, planter, to **Richard Madgely** and **Rice Waineman**, planters; for 2,000# tobacco; a parcel of land called *Chosen*; bounded by land formerly laid out for Luke Greene and John Cobb called *Batchelor's Agreement*; containing 100 acres; /s/ Luke Greene; wit. John Hanson; John Payne (mark)

Liber E, Page 7 1/2

2 Jan 1670; Indenture from **George Langham**, planter, to **Thomas Maris**, planter; for 3,300# tobacco; a parcel of land bounded by Cap. Will Stone's manor called *Poynton* and land laid out for James Lindsy; containing 100 acres now occupied by George Langham; being part of a parcel purchased of Gerrard Browne called *Drury Lane* dated 10 Mar "long past"; /s/ George Langham; wit. Gerrard Browne, John Godsall

Liber E, Page 9 1/2

8 Jan 1670; Indenture from **Gerrard Browne,** planter, and **Edmond Lindsy,** planter, to **John Waters;** for 2,000# tobacco; 100 acres of land part of a greater divident of 300 acres called *Allanson Folly* on the east side of Piscataway River and south of Chingamuxon Creek; sd. divident now in possession of Thomas Allcox; /s/ Gerrard Browne, Edmond Lindsy (mark); wit. Thomas Allanson, Edward Price

Liber E, Page 12

27 Dec 1670; Indenture from **Ignatius Causine,** Gent., to **John Vaudry,** carpenter; for a certain sum of tobacco; a parcel of land called *St. Nicholas* on the west side of a fresh run of Portobacco; containing 300 acres now occupied by Causine whose patent was dated 20 Jul 1664; /s/ Ignatius Causine; wit. Mathew Stone, Francis Adames

Liber E, Page 15

8 Jan 1670; Indenture from **Thomas Stone,** Gent., to **Thomas Allanson,** Gent.; for 4,000# tobacco; a tract called *Stone's Delight* on the east side of Piscataway River; bounded by William Calvert, Esq.; laid out for 500 acres; /s/ Thomas Stone (seal); wit. Thomas Robinson, Edward Roberts

Liber E, Page 17 1/2

1 Mar 1668; Deed of Gift from **Andrew Watson,** Stafford Co., Virginia, planter, to **William Pinner,** youngest son of Richard Pinner, dec'd; grant unto Alexander White, planter, all of a parcel of land called *Watson's Addition* on the north side of Potomac River; bounded by land granted Andrew Watson and John Tomkinson and *Watson's Marsh*; containing 75 acres; granted to said Watson 6 Jun ____; to be held by White for the use of William Pinnar during his minority; /s/ Andrew Watson (mark); wit. Sam. Hayward, John Harris

Liber E, Page 19 1/2

1 Jan 1670; Indenture from **Nathan Barton,** carpenter, to **William Barton,** planter; for 8,000# tobacco; a parcel of land formerly bought of Henry Hawkings; on the north side of the Potomac and west side of the main fresh of Wicomico River; containing 225 acres; /s/ Nathan Barton; wit. John Gosling, John Walters; **Martha**

Barton, wife of Nathan Barton, acknowledged a parcel of land called *Johnson's Town* to William Barton, Jr.

Liber E, Page 22 1/2

9 Jan 1670; Indenture from **Sam Fendall**, Gent., to **William Barton**, Gent.; for 7,000# tobacco; a parcel on the west side of Wicomico River and west side of Zachia Swamp; called *Daniell Mount*; also a parcel called *Johnson's Retirement*; containing 100 acres; /s/ Samuel Fendall; wit. Josias Fendall, William Barton, Jr.

Liber E, Page 26

1 Mar 1670; Indenture from **Francis Adams**, planter, to **John Paine**; for 2,000# tobacco; a parcel of land of 100 acres called *Raley*; patent granted 30 Jan 1668; /s/ Fra. Adames (seal); wit. William Britton, Bartholomew Coates, John Luke

Liber E, Page 30

2 Jan 1670; Indenture from **Edward Knight**, planter, to **Nicholas Boade**, planter; 5,000# tobacco; a parcel of land on the east side of the easternmost branch of Avon River; bounded by Andrew Watson; now in occupation of Edward Knight; parcel taken up by and purchased from Owen Jones called *The Adventure*; containing 75 acres; /s/ Edward Knight (mark); wit. George Langham, Thomas Maris

Liber E, Page 33 1/2

10 Jan 1670 Court; Deed of Gift from **Christopher Breame**, planter, to **Richard Pinner** and **William Pinner** a heifer; wit. Richard Fowke, George Lodge; recorded by Anne Atkins

Liber E, Page 34

10 Jan 1670 Court; Deed of Gift from **Ellenor Lambert**, wife of **John Lambert** of Portobacco, to **Mary Costleton**, dau. of Robert Costleton, a heifer; /s/ John Lambert (mark), Ellenor Lambert (mark); wit. John Foord, George Langham; recorded by Robert Costleton

Liber E, Page 36

14 Feb 1670; Indenture from **James Smallwood**, planter, to **William Jenkins**, planter; for 5,000# tobacco; a parcel called *Goates Lodge*; bounded by *Zachia Manor*; laid out for 150 acres; /s/ James Smallwood (mark); wit. Henry Hawkins, John Owen, Thomas Hargas (mark)

Liber E, Page 36 1/2

14 Mar 1670; Indenture from **John Boyden**, planter, to **William Boyden** and **Mathew Sanders**, planters; for 3,000# tobacco; a tract called *St. Margaret*; on the southwest side of a branch running up St. Thomas Creek; bounded by Thomas Wentworth, Daniel Mathena and William Boyden; containing 80 acres; /s/ John Boyden; wit. Robert Robins, Richard Chapman (mark)

Liber E, Page 37

2 Mar 1670; Indenture from **William Boyden**, planter, to **Henry Moore,** planter; for a mare and other deeds; a tract called *Whitland* on the north side of the Piscataway River and south side of Mattawoman Creek; containing 450 acres; bounded by patent formerly granted to Thomas Hussey; /s/ William Boyden, Anne Boyden (mark) wit. Sa. Cressey, John Boyden

Liber E, Page 38

11 Mar 1670; Indenture from **Henry Moore**, planter, to **John Allen**, Gent.; for 15,000# tobacco; a parcel called *Moore's Lodge*; on the north side of the Potomac and on the north branch of Zachia Swamp; bounded by land laid out for Daniel Johnson and Richard Morris; laid out for 150 acres; /s/ Henry Moore, Elizabeth Moore; wit. Sa. Cressey, Philip Gibbon

Liber E, Page 45

13 Jun 1671; Indenture from **Edmond Lendsey** to **Elizabeth Emanson**, widow; land called *Glover's Point*; formerly in occupation of Giles Glover and afterwards occupied by John Lumbroso now occupied by Nicholas Emanson, late husband of Elizabeth Emanson; on the north side of the Potomac and east side of the easternmost branch of Avon River; containing 200 acres /s/ Edmond Lendsy (mark); wit. George Godfrey, Stephen Mountague

Liber E, Page 45

John Robinson and **Elizabeth** his wife acknowledged their right of 85 acres adjoining George Godfrey's land to **Thomas Jenkins**

Elizabeth Emanson acknowledged a parcel of land called *Glover's Point* in Nangemy Creek to **Francis Wine**

Stephen Mountague assigned **Edmond Lendsey**, son of Edmond Lendsey and Ellenor his wife, one red heifer

Liber E, Page 46

12 Sep 1671 Court; **John Owen**, planter, acknowledged a parcel of land called *Owen's Purchase* of 200 acres to **James Hayes** and **Philip Hoskins**

Liber E, Page 49

Declaration of Citizenship: **Ignatius Causine**, son of **Nicholas Causine**, a subject of France; born at the house of his father in St. George River of an English mother; holding lands by descent from mother

14 Nov 1671; **Sam. Cressey** acknowledges a 50 acre parcel of land to **Peter Ackilles**

Liber E, Page 52 1/2

8 Aug 1671; **John Vandreys** and **Elizabeth** his wife acknowledged their right to *St. Nicholas*; assigned to **Job Corner**

9 Jan 1671; **Thomas Ashbrooke** and **Lettise** his wife acknowledge their right to 150 acres on the east side of John Ward in Nangemy Creek; assigned to **John Boyden**

Liber E, Page 53 1/2

14 Nov 1671 Court; **Richard Midgely** and **Richard Wainman** acknowledge their right to a tract of land assigned to **Edward Knight**

Liber E, Page 58

12 Mar 1672 Court; **John Mun** acknowledged a parcel of land of 200 acres formerly laid out for David Prichard, to **William Boyden**

12 Mar 1672 Court; **Ed. Price** acknowledged a parcel of land called *Shrewsbury* of 150 acres to **John Munn**

Liber E, Page 58 1/2

2 Jun 1671; Indenture from **Gerrard Breeden** and **Elizabeth** his wife, to **Ralph Coates**, Gent.; for 909# plus 4,000# tobacco; a parcel called *River's Spring* granted Christopher Rivers; then owned by John Muns; after by John Boyden, Will Boyden and Walter Cooper; from them to James Hussey to John Hackister; then to Thomas King; from him to Gerrard Breeden; located on Nangemy Creek next to land of James Lindsey; /s/ Gerrard Breeden, Elizabeth Breeden; wit. John Wheeler, Alexander Gallant

Liber E, Page 59 1/2
8 Mar 1671; Indenture from **John Munn** to **Will Boyden**, planter; a parcel of land formerly laid out for David Prichard on the south side of Piscataway River and the east side of St. Thomas Creek; containing 200 acres; joining land laid out for David Thomas; /s/ John Munn (mark); wit. Gerrard Browne, Francis Thornton

Liber E, Page 60 1/2
8 Aug 1671; Indenture from **John Vaudry**, planter, to **Jobe Cosner**; for a certain sum; a parcel of land called *St. Nicholas*; on the west side of a fresh run of Portobacco Creek; bounded by land formerly laid out for Jobe Chandler; containing 300 acres by patent granted Ignatius Causine who sold to Vaudry 20 Jul 1664; /s/ John Vaudry (mark); wit. Thomas Corsley, Will Cocker

Liber E, Page 62
4 Jun 1672; Indenture from **George Taylor**, planter, to **Ralph Shaw**, planter; for one gray mare and colt and 1,000# tobacco; a parcel of land on the east side of Portobacco Creek; called *New Exchange*; bounded by Thomas Hussey; containing 250 acres; /s/ George Taylor, Elinor Taylor; wit. Daniell Russell, Giles Cole

Liber E, Page 62 1/2
11 Jun 1672; Indenture from **Robert Prouse** of Chingamuxon to **John Munn**; for a certain sum of tobacco; a parcel of land called *The Gift* on the north side of Piscataway River and the south side of Chingamuxon Creek; containing 150 acres; bounded by John Hatch and a parcel Robert Prouse sold Peter Achilles; /s/ John Munn; wit. Thomas Allanson, Henry Aspinoll

Liber E, Page 63 1/2
11 May 1672; Memorandum of conveyance dated 9 Jun 1671 of a parcel of 200 acres of land from **Thomas Allanson**, Gent., to **Walter Pake** of St. Mary's County; Pake sold parcel to Henry Aspinoll; boundary on Mattawoman Creek agreed on; /s/ Tho. Allanson, Henry Aspinoll; wit. Robert Prouse, Ed. Price

Liber E, Page 64
11 Jun 1672; Indenture from Joseph Harrison and Stephen Mountague, Gent., ex. of will of **Richard Randall**, to **George Godfrey**; for 12,000# of tobacco; part of a tract called *Troope's Rendevous*; located on the east side of a fresh of Avon River; bounded by

Andrew Watson, Edward Deane and Garret Synett; containing 250 acres; /s/ Joseph Harrison, Stephen Mountague; wit. Owen Jones, Geo. Langham

Liber E, Page 64 1/2

11 Jun 1672; Indenture from **Richard Chapman** and wife **Barbara** to **Thomas Craxon**; for 3,000# of tobacco a parcel of land called *Byfield Close*; sold by Giles Glover to sd. Craxon and Chapman; located on the east side of Avon River; containing 150 acres; /s/ Richard Chapman; wit. Stephen Mountague, John Godshall

Liber E, Page 65 1/2

9 Jun 1671; Indenture from **Edward Price,** planter, to **John Munn**; for 500 acres of land at the head of Piscataway Creek called *Locust Thickett*; swaps a parcel called *Shrewsbury* on the north side of Piscataway River and south side of Chingamuxon Creek; bound by land formerly laid out for Thomas Allanson now in possession of Walter Pake, near land laid out for Jeremiah Frost now in possession of John Car, and land of John Hatch; containing 150 acres; /s/ Edward Prise; wit. Thos. Allanson, Ed. Maddock

Liber E, Page 66 1/2

9 Jul 1671; Indenture from **Robert Prouse**, planter, to **Peter Achillies**, planter; for a certain sum; a parcel of land on the north side of Piscataway River and south side of Chingamuxon Creek; 50 acres formerly owned by George Thompson called *The Gift* by patent dated 20 Jul 1664; /s/ Robert Prouse, Peter Achilles; wit. Geo. Hinson, Geo. Magmillion

Liber E, Page 70

8 Aug 1672; Indenture from **Thomas Allanson** to **Gerrard Browne**; for 2,500# tobacco; a parcel called *Simpson's Supply* on the east side of the Piscataway River and south side of Mattawoman Creek; laid out for 100 acres; bounded by Cristentempell Mann; /s/ Thomas Allanson; with Rich. Boughton, Edward Roberts

Liber E, Page 71 1/2

20 Sep 1672; Indenture from **Richard Morris,** St. Mary's Co., planter, to **Alexander Smith**; for 3,000# of tobacco; a parcel of land on the west side of Wicomico fresh adjoining land of William Barton, Jr. formerly sold by Daniel Johnson, dec'd, to Richard Morris;

bounded by John Clark; laid out for 200 acres; /s/ Rich Morris; with Meverall Hulse, Jonathan Marlow (mark)

Liber E, Page 73

24 Jul 1672; Deed of Gift from **Joseph Colley** of New England to **Mary Kymborough;** a filly colt which came with mare bought of John Grubb; /s/ Joseph Colley; wit. Thomas Baker, Rich. Ambrose

11 Jan 1672; Deed of Gift from **Gerrard Sennett** and **Ann** his wife to **John Lumbrozion**; a black cow; /s/ Ger Sennett, Ann Sennett; wit. Jno. Ford, Geo. Langham

Liber E, Page 73 1/2

8 Jun 1672; Indenture from **Christopher Breams** to **Edward Muns**, planter; for 2,000# of tobacco; a parcel of 180 acres called *Antwerp* part of a tract laid out by Richard Edelin for sd. Breams for 200 acres; on the north side of a branch belonging to the land of Rich. Pinner on the north side of Piscataway River; /s/ Christopher Breams; wit. Gerrard Browne, Jon. Hill

Liber E, Page 74

7 Aug 1672; Indenture from **Edward Maddox**, physician, to **Richard Fowke**, Gent.; for 1,000# of tobacco; a parcel of land called *Lyon's Hole* located on the south side of Richard Fowke's land called *Vainall*; bounded by Zachary Wade; laid out for 100 acres; /s/ Edward Maddox, Richard Fowke; wit. Zachary Wade, Thomas Hudlestone

Liber E, Page 75 1/2

7 Sep 1672; Indenture from **John Owen**, planter, to **James Hayes** and **Philip Hoskins**, planter; for 2,350# tobacco; a parcel called *Owen's Purchase*; containing 200 acres; near a parcel taken up by Daniel Johnson called *Lyon's Denn*; /s/ John Owen; wit. Will Harris, Thomas Hargis

Liber E, Page 76 1/2

13 Jun 1671; Indenture from **John Robinson**, planter, to **Thomas Jenkins**; for a certain sum; a parcel formerly called *Troope's Rendesvous*, the other part sold to Richard Randall and now in the tenure of George Godfrey, carpenter; laid out for 85 acres; /s/ John Robinson; wit. Sa. Cressey, Nick Solby

Liber E, Page 77 1/2

16 Jun 1672; Indenture from **Elizabeth Emanson** to **Francis Wine**, cooper; for 14,000# of tobacco; a parcel of land called *Glover's Point* on the easternmost branch of Avon River; laid out for 200 acres; /s/ Eliz. Emanson; wit. Phil Lynes, Tho. Lomax

Liber E, Page 78 1/2

2 Mar 1672; Indenture from **John Godshall**, planter, to **Rich Brooke**; for 2,000# of tobacco; a tract of land on the east side of Avon River; adjoining *Poynton Manor*; laid out for 100 acres to Godsall 29 Jul 1664; /s/ Jno. Godsall; wit. Sam Cressey, Jonathan Marler

Liber E, Page 79 1/2

9 Jan 1671; Indenture from **Thomas Ashbrooke**, shoemaker, to **John Boydon**, planter; for a certain consideration; a grant of land called *Ashbrooke's Rest*; bounded by John Ward and land formerly laid out for John Delahay now in possession of John Ashbrooke; containing 150 acres now in possession of John Boyden; /s/ Thomas Ashbrooke, Lettis Ashbrooke; wit. George Langham, Ralph Coats

Liber E, Page 82

10 Oct 1670; Indenture from **Philip Coomes** of St. Mary's Co., planter, to **John Allen**; for 3,000# of tobacco; a parcel of land called *Coomes' Purchase* on the west side of Wicomico's main fresh; bounded by a swamp and John Coates; laid out for 150 acres; /s/ Philip Coomes; wit. Rich. Edlen, ____ Moore

Liber E, Page 83

11 Jun 1672; Indenture from **John Grubb**, furrier, to **George Holmes**; for a certain sum; a tract of land called *Grubb's Venture*; near Wicomico fresh; bounded by Zachia Swamp and John Ballaine; laid out for 83 acres; /s/ John Grubb; wit. Sa. Dobson, Will Baker

Liber E, Page 84

11 Jun 1672; Indenture from **John Grubb** to **George Holmes**; for a certain sum; a tract of land called *Venture Beginning*; on the west side of the Wicomico Run in the swamp; laid out for 50 acres; /s/ Jno. Grubb; wit. Samuell Dobson, Will. Baker

Liber E, Page 85

9 Oct 1672; Indenture from **Joseph Harrison**, Gent., to **Luke Greene**, planter; for endorsement of a certain parcel of land which Green

bought from Harrison called *Green's Purchase* on the east side of
the Anacostine River and southeast side of Isodores Creek;
containing 200 acres; /s/ Joseph Harrison; wit. Rich. Boughton,
Jeremiah Dobson
> Liber E, Page 86 1/2

16 Sep 1672; Indenture from **Edmond Lyndsy**, planter, to **John
Douglas**, Gent.; for 11,000# tobacco; a parcel of land called *St.
Edmonds* granted to Lyndsy by patent dated 10 Mar 1670; bound
by land laid out for William Heard; lying on the east side of the
main fresh of Portobacco Creek; containing 100 acres now in
tenure of John Douglas; /s/ Edmond Lyndsy; with Jonathan Marler,
Rich. Edelen
> Liber E, Page 88 1/2

8 Nov 1672; Indenture from **Edmond Lyndsy,** planter, to **Michaell
Minork**; for 3,500# tobacco; a parcel of land called *St. Edmond's*
granted Lyndsy by patent dated 10 Mar 1670; part of a parcel sold
John Douglas; containing 150 acres; now in tenure of Minocke; /s/
Edmond Lyndsy; wit. Rich. Edelen, Jonathan Marler
> Liber E, Page 89 1/2

12 Nov 1670; Indenture from **Thomas Brooke**, Gent., and **Ellinor** his
wife, to **Zachary Wade** and **Randolph Hanson** of St. Mary's Co.;
Gent.; for 24,000# tobacco; a parcel of land *Locust Thickett*; /s/
Tho. Brook; wit. Henry Neale, Rich. Edelen
> Liber E., Page 101

2 Oct 1672; Deed of Gift from **John Thompkinson**, carpenter, to his
wife **Jane**; all my estate; /s/ Jno. Tompkinson; wit. Edward
Maddox, Luke Green

Deed of Gift from **Ann Fowke** to her son **Richard Chandler** all the
hogs and cattle on *Goose Creek* plantation; /s/ Ann Fowke; wit.
Robt. Robins, William Chandler

11 Mar 1672; Deed of Gift from **Ann Fowke** to her 3 children,
Gerrard Fowke, Maryland Fowke, and **Eliza. Fowke**, 10 head of
cattle; /s/ Ann Fowler; wit. Robt. Robins, Rich. Chandler
> Liber E, Page 101 1/2

9 Mar 1672; Indenture from **William Hargesse** and **Thomas Hargess**
to **Henery Bedford**; for 2,500# tobacco; a parcel of land called
Hargess Hope; laid out for 100 acres; bounded by Zachia Swamp; /s/

William Hargesse, Thomas Hargesse; wit. John Twigges, John Green

Liber E, Page 102

10 Jun 1673; Indenture from **William Boyden** and **Mathew Sanders**, planters, to **Francis Thornton**, planter; for 3,800# tobacco; a parcel called St. *Margaret's*; lying on the southwest side of a branch running into St. Thomas Creek; bounded by Daniel Mathena, William Boyden and Thomas Wentworth; containing 80 acres; /s/ William Boyden, Mathew Sanders; wit. Luke Green, John Boyden

Liber E, Page 103 1/2

11 Mar 1672; Indenture from **Richard True,** boatwright, and **Anne** his wife, to **John Boyden,** planter; for 3,000# tobacco; a parcel called *Nonesuch*; lying on the west side of the main fresh of Poynton Creek; at the head of Lambert's Valley; containing 100 acres; /s/ Simond Stevens, atty. for Richard and Anne True; wit. William Nevill, William Boyden

Liber E, Page 104 1/2

8 Mar 1672; Indenture from **Thomas Allanson** to **John Lambert**; for 3.000# tobacco; a parcel of land called *Simpson's Supply*; on the east side of Piscataway Creek and south side of Mattawoman Creek; bounded by *Allanson's Manor*; containing 100 acres; /s/ Tho. Allanson; wit. Luke Green, Robert Cossellton

Liber E, Page 105

4 May 1673; Indenture from **John Cassock**, planter, to **John Lemaire**, surgeon; for 14,000# tobacco; called *Cassock's Lopp*; laid out for 100 acres; patented to John Cassock 10 Oct in the 37th year of the dominion of Cecillius; another parcel called *Lamaire's Purchase* adjoining the afsd. containing 100 acres; /s/ John Cassock; wit. Henry Bedford, Tho. Lomax, Anthony Bradbree

Liber E, Page 106 1/2

2 Jun 1673; Indenture from **William Boyden**, planter, to **Francis Furnice**, cooper; for 7,000# tobacco; a parcel of land called *Coulchester*; on the south side of Mattawoman Creek; bounded by St. *Margeret's*, *Marchantailor's Hall* and land of David Thomas; containing 200 acres; /s/ William Boyden; wit. Richard Edelen, Edward Price

Liber E, Page 107 1/2

_ Jun 1673; Indenture from **John Bissick** to **John Davis**; for 2,500# tobacco; a parcel of 100 acres called *St. John's*; located between 2 beaver dams within 2 miles of Zachery Wade on the north side of Potomac; laid out for 100 acres; /s/ John Bissick; wit. Robert Warrell, John Twigges, Henery Bedford

Liber E, Page 108

9 Jun 1673; Indenture from **Henry Bonner** to **Joseph Horton**; for a considerable sum of tobacco; a parcel of land called *Nonesuch*; laid out for 50 acres now in possession of Bonner; bounded by John Coates, Thomas Lomax and Zachia Swamp; /s/ Henery Bonner; wit. John Kimbrow, John Lambare

Liber E, Page 109

3 Jun 1673; Indenture from **Charles Woolley**, planter, to **John Ward**, planter; for 2,400# tobacco; a parcel called *Charles Towne*; on the south side of Charles Runn; containing 100 acres; /s/ Charles Woolley; wit. Richard Edelen, Edward Price

Liber E, Page 109 1/2

4 Jan 1672; Indenture from **Jobe Corner**, planter, to **William Grant**, planter; for 6,000# tobacco; a tract called *Jobe's Comfort*; bounded by William Heard; laid out for 200 acres; /s/ Jobe Corner; wit. Thomas Corke, Jeremiah Macknue

Liber E, Page 111 1/2

28 May 1673; Indenture from **Thomas Allanson** to **John Possey**, planter; for 4,000# tobacco; a parcel called *St. John's*; bounded by Jerricoe on the east side of Poynton Cr. and land of John Ward; on main fresh of Nangemy Creek; containing 200 acres; /s/ Thomas Allanson, **Mary Allanson**; wit. John Godshall, Gerrard Brown

Liber E, Page 112

10 Mar 1672; Indenture from John Hill, admn. of **Thomas Wentworth**, dec'd, to **John Wright**, merchant, for 2,000# tobacco; a parcel called *Wentworth's Rest*; on the east side of Piscataway River; bounded by land of Edward Price; containing 100 acres; /s/ John Hill; wit. George Godfrey, Wm. Britton

Liber E, Page 113

11 Mar 1672; Indenture from **John Boyden**, planter, to his brother **William Boyden**, planter; for diverse consideration; part of a tract

of land on Mattawoman Creek which William Boyden had formerly given John being part of the land William now lives on; /s/ John Boyden; wit. William Nevill, Simon Stephens
Liber E, Page 114

10 Mar 1672; Indenture from **Edmond Lyndsey**, planter, to **William Gardener,** planter; for 3,000# tobacco; a parcel of land *Lyndsey's Project*; containing 50 acres on the north side of a branch of Goose Creek; /s/ Edmond Lyndsey; wit. [blank]
Liber E, Page 115

10 Jun 1673; Indenture from **Thomas Wharton**, planter, to **Luke Green**, planter; for 2,000# tobacco; a parcel called *Wharton's Rest*; adjoining Thomas Robison; laid out for 150 acres; /s/ Thom. Wharton; wit. John Boyden, Richard Carpenter
Liber E, Page 116

10 Jun 1673; Indenture from **Henry Bedford** to **John Twiggs;** for 3,500# tobacco; a parcel of 100 acres called *Hargesse Hope*; bounded by *Zachia Manor* and Zachia Swamp; /s/ Henry Bedford; wit. John Gwen, William Hargesse
Liber E, Page 117

10 Jun 1673; Indenture from **Francis Thornton** to **Thomas Wharton**; for 6,000# tobacco; a parcel *Chrisman Milforde*; bounded by Samuell Palmer and near Burditt's Creek; containing 300 acres; /s/ Francis Thornton; wit. Luke Green, John Boyden
Liber E, Page 118 1/2

10 Mar 1672; Indenture from **Alexander Gallant**, planter, to **George Austria**, planter; for 2,000# tobacco; a parcel called *Akerden*; near John Wheeler's land called *Exeto*; on the main fresh of the Piscataway; laid out for 100 acres; /s/ Alexander Gallant; wit. Archiball Wehab, Ralph Coates
Liber E, Page 120

10 Jun 1673; Indenture from **Thomas Corker**, planter, to **Clement Theobaldes**, planter; for 3,000# tobacco; a parcel called *Corker's Hoghole*; on the west side of Portobacco Creek; bounded by land now in possession of Jacob Lee which was formerly belonging to Alexander Simpson called *Simpson's Delight*; laid out for 100 acres; /s/ Tho. Corker; wit. Henry Bonner, Phill Gibbon

Liber E, Page 122

__ __ 1673; Indenture from **John Boyden**, planter, to **Richard Carpenter**, planter; for 3,500# tobacco; a parcel called *Nonesuch*; bounded by Lambert's Valley; laid out for 100 acres; /s/ John Boyden; wit. Luke Green, Thomas Wharton

Liber E, Page 123 1/2

13 Nov 1673; Indenture from **Benjamin Rozer**, Gent., to **John Munn**, planter; for 2,000# tobacco; a parcel called *Morecraf's Friendship*; bounded by 200 acres lately taken up by James Macky; bounded by a marsh and Chingamuxon Creek and a tract formerly belonging to George Thompson now in possession of And. Hill; containing 200 acres; /s/ Benjamin Rozer; wit. Ignatius Causine, P. Gibbon

Liber E, Page 124 1/2

3 Aug 1673; Indenture from **Mathias Obrian**, planter, to **Richard Edelen** of St. Mary's Co.; for 1,900# tobacco; a tract called *Dublin*; laid out for 200 acres; /s/ Mathias Obrian; wit. John Mowld, George Godfry

Liber E, Page 126

28 May 1673; Quit Claim Deed from **George Banks** to **Humphrey Jones**; 100 acres of land; /s/ George Banks; wit. Robt. Robins, Owen Jones

Liber E, Page 127

12 Mar 1672; Indenture from **James Mackey**, planter, to **Francis Kylborne**; for 2,000# tobacco; a parcel called *Scotland Yard* on the east side of Anacostia River; laid out for 500 acres; /s/ Jacobi Mackey; wit. Tho. Hussey, Wm. Barton, Jr.

Liber E, Page 127 1/2

9 Sep 1673; Indenture from **Clement Theobalds**, planter, to **Thomas Corker**, planter; for 30,000# tobacco; a plantation called *Durham* on the west side of Portobacco Creek; containing 160 acres; bounded by land sold by Theobalds to John Paine, dec'd, on Plum Tree Point; /s/ Clement Theobalds; wit. Thomas Witter, Henry Barnes (mark)

Liber E, Page 128 1/2

9 Sep 1673; Indenture from **Thomas Corker**, to **Clement Theobalds**, planter, for 15,000# tobacco; a tract called *Planter's Delight*; on the

west side of Portobacco Creek; containing 100 acres; /s/ Tho. Corker; wit. Thomas Witter, Henry Barnes (mark)
Liber E, Page 129 1/2

1671; **Thomas Yeabsley**, merchant of Plymouth, Devon, ex. of the will of **Amos Short** who lately died "at Virginia or parts thereabout;" Robert Slye of Maryland, admn.; appoints Alexander Doniphen of Plymouth, merchant, as attorney to inventory estate with Robert Slye
Liber E, Page 133

21 Oct 1673; Quit Claim Deed from **Thomas Baker** to **Thomas Pope** for land in the easterly line of Pope's property at the mouth of Baker's Creek; /s/ Thomas Baker

3 Sep 1673; Acknowledgment from **John Jarbo** of St. Mary's Co., Gent., to **Thomas Baker**; a small parcel of land at the head of a spring being part of a patent of 300 acres, excepting assignment to John Nevill; /s/ John Jarbo; wit. Samuel Cressey, Mitholob Voyall
Liber E, Page 140

6 Nov 1673; Indenture from **Edmond Lyndsey**, Gent., to **Samuel Clarke** and **Joseph Bullott**; for 7,000# tobacco; a parcel of land called *Wellcome*; on the east side of Portobacco fresh; bounded by Job Chandler; containing 200 acres; /s/ Edmond Lyndsey (mark); wit. Michell Minox (mark), Daniel Hurly (mark)
Liber E, Page 141

18 Nov 1673; Indenture from **Thomas Galey**, planter, to **John Wright**, merchant; for 10,000# tobacco; a parcel called *Galey's Venture*; bounded by land formerly laid out for John Thompkinson called *Cheshire Thickett*; containing 200 acres; /s/ Thomas Galey (mark), Martha Galey (mark); wit. Ralph Coates, John Lewgar (mark)
Liber E, Page 147

7 Oct 1673; Indenture from **Robert Cossleton**, cooper, to **John Cassock**, planter; for 5,000# tobacco; a parcel called *Skipton*; bounded by John Cane, Garrett Sinnett, Sander Simpson, Thomas Corker and John Coffers; laid out for 200 acres; /s/ Robert Cossleton (mark); wit. Edward Abbott, John Dunshaw; acknowledged by Mary Cassleton, wife of John

Liber E, Page 148

9 Jan 1673; Indenture from **John Hill**, planter, to **Philip Lynes**, innholder; for 2,600# tobacco and a horse; a parcel called *Wheeler Palme*; on the north side of Piscataway River bounded by land formerly laid out to Robert Hudson; laid out for 150 acres; /s/ John Hill (mark); wit. Ralph Coates, Thomas Corker

Liber E, Page 149

12 Jan 1673; Indenture from **Jacob Leah**, planter, to **Clement Theobalds**, planter; for 8,000# tobacco; a parcel called *Simpson's Delight*; bounded by Indian fields; laid out for 300 acres; /s/ Jacob Leah (mark); wit. Thomas Corker, Joseph Wolfe (mark)

Liber E, Page 153

20 Jan 1673; Indenture from **George Langham,** planter, to **Philip Lines,** innholder of Portobacco; for valuable consideration; a parcel called *Thomas Street*; bounded by John Robinson's land called *Wassell*; containing 100 acres; also a parcel called *Tower Dock* adjoining afsd. land also containing 100 acres; /s/ Geo. Langham; wit. Hamon Norton, Wm. Gough, Richard Jones

Liber E, Page 154

30 Mar 1673; **John Boyden** conveys *Ashbrook's Rest* unto **Samuell Sherrell** in open court

Liber E, Page 155

8 Jun 1674; Acknowledgment from **Thomas Shuttlesworth** to the children of **Joseph Harrison**, dec'd; viz. **Catherine, Joseph, Benjamin**; cattle; /s/ Tho. Shuttleworth; wit. Geo. Lodge, Luke Green

Liber E, Page 156

12 Jun 1674; Deed of Gift from **Robert Robins** to **Elizabeth Jones**, dau. of **Owen Jones**; heifer; /s/ Robert Robins

__ Mar 1673; Acknowledgment from **Christopher Breamer**, planter, to **Philip Lynes** innholder; for consideration of considerable value; 80 acres of land called *Antwerp*; part of 200 acres laid out for Breames; adjoining Richard Pinner on the north side of, and about 1 mile from the Piscataway River; bounded by Philip Lande; /s/ Christopher Breamer (mark); wit. Gerard Browne, George Langham

Liber E, Page 157

11 Nov 1673; Indenture from **Luke Green**, planter, to **Edward Maddock**, apothecary; land called *Greene's Purchase*; for 3,000# tobacco; lying on the east side of Anacostia River and south side of a branch of St. Isodore's Creek; near an old Indian fort; containing 200 acres; /s/ Luke Green; wit. Thomas Corker, Job Corner

Liber E, Page 158

10 Mar 1673; Indenture from **Thomas Wakefield** to **Edward Solley**; for 7,500# tobacco; a parcel containing 100 acres at the head of Wicomico River lately in the occupation of John Kimbertton; near Walker's Runn and the road to Portobacco; part of a parcel of 200 acres sold by William Ward to Jonathan Marler; dec'd; /s/ Thomas Wakefield; wit. Robert Ingolsbys (mark); Thomas Hyatt (mark)

Liber E, Page 160

8 Feb 1673; Indenture from **William Thomas**, and **Susanna** his wife, to **Robert Ingolsby**, planter; for 7,000# tobacco; a tract called *Thomas His Chance*; laid out for 200 acres by Richard Edelen, depty. surveyor, dated 7 Sept 1669; /s/ William Thomas, Robert Ingolsby (mark); wit. Edw. Maddock, George Athys

Liber E, Page 161

1 Aug 1673; Indenture from **Jobe Corner**, planter, to **John Hackister**; tract called *Jobe's Comfort*; for 2,500# tobacco; containing 200 acres; bounded by William Heard's land on the east side of the main fresh of Portobacco or St. Thomas Creek; /s/ Jobe Corner; wit. John Jones

Liber E, Page 163

1674; Deed of Gift from **Thomas King** to **Owen Jones, Jr.**; a red pied heifer

Liber E, Page 163

10 Sep 1673; Indenture from **John Hackister** to **Philip Gibbon**, Gent.; for 6,500# tobacco; a tract called *St. Ignatius*; on the west side of the main fresh at the head of Portobacco Creek; bounded by land laid out for Job Chandler and John Cane; containing 100 acres; also a parcel called *Haggister's Addition* on the east side of the main fresh of Portobacco; bounded by William Heard, laid out for 50 acres; /s/ John Hackister; wit. John Jones, Sr.

Liber E, Page 164

2 Mar 1673; Indenture from **Philip Gibbon**, Gent., to **Benjamin Rozer** of Portobacco, Gent.; for 5,600# tobacco; a parcel called *St. Ignatius*; lying on the west side of the main fresh at the head of Portobacco Creek; bounded by Jobe Chandler and land formerly laid out for John Cain; containing 100 acres; /s/ Philip Gibbon; wit. John Jones

Liber E, Page 166

17 Jan 1672; Indenture from **Edward Price**, planter, to **William Ratliff**; for 4,650# tobacco; a parcel called *Price's Adventure*; lying on the north side of the Potomac; bounded by David Thomas, Richard Fowke; near the Potomac River; containing 200 acres; /s/ Edward Price; wit. Christopher Warner, Edward Minge, Richard Midgleys (mark)

Liber E, Page 171

6 Apr 1674; Indenture from **Clement Theobald**, planter, to **Thomas Witter**; for 12,000# tobacco; a parcel called *Simpson's Delight* on the west side and near the head of Portobacco Creek; laid out for 300 acres; /s/ Clement Theobald; wit. Thomas Corker, Jobe Corner

Liber E, Page 173

10 Mar 1673; Indenture from **Francis Boyden**, planter, to **John Alward**; division of undivided land held as of fee in common called *Moore's Hope*; bounded by George Goodrick, Thomas Hussey and on one of the northernmost branches of Zachia Swamp; containing 100 acres by indenture dated 8 Nov 1669 by bargain and sale from Henry Moore; another parcel called *Partnership* on the east of and about 4 miles from Portobacco fresh from bargain and sale of Henry Moore containing 300 acres; Alward to have *Moore's Hope* and 100 acres *Partnership*; /s/ John Alward and Francis Boyden; wit. John Stone, Cleborne Lomax

Liber E, Page 174

18 Mar 1673/4; Indenture from **George Gooderick**, Gent., to **Francis Gooderick**; a parcel on the north side of the Potomac and a north branch of Zachia Swamp; containing 300 acres; /s/ George Gooderick; wit. George Thompson, Humphry Jones (mark)

Liber E, Page 175

10 Mar 1673; Indenture from **John Munn**, planter, to **John Helme**; for 7,000# of tobacco; a parcel called *Shrewsbury* on the north side of Piscataway River and south side of Chingamuxon Creek; bounded by land formerly laid out for John Hatch, land formerly laid out for Thomas Allinson now possessed by Walter Pake, and land laid out for Jeremy Frost now possessed by John Cain; containing 150 acres; /s/ John Munns (mark); wit. Thomas Corker, John Boyden

Liber E, Page 182

11 Aug 1674; Indenture from **Edmund Lyndsey**, planter, to **Thomas Corker**, planter; for 12,000# of tobacco; a tract of land called *His Excellency's Gift*; bounded by Bartholomew Coates on the west side of Portobacco Creek; laid out for 150 acres; /s/ Edmund Lindsey (mark); wit. Railph Coates, Will Deane

Liber E, Page 184

9 Aug 1674; Indenture from **Ralph Coates**, planter, to **Philip Lymes**, innholder; for 8,000# of tobacco; a tract of land called *River's Spring* on the east side of a fresh of Avon River; bounded by James Lindsey; laid out for 250 acres; /s/ Ralph Coates; wit. William Chandler, William Deane

Liber E, Page 186

11 Aug 1674; Indenture from **Thomas Baker**, planter, to **Samuell Cressey**; a parcel of land called *Marsh Land* on the south side of Baker's Creek; laid out for 100 acres; /s/ Thomas Baker (mark); wit. Edmund Lindsey (mark), Thomas Allanson

Liber E, Page 187

8 Aug 1674; Indenture from **Thomas Allanson**, Gent., to **Gerrard Browne**, planter; a parcel of land on the south side of Mattawoman Creek in *Christian Temple Manor*; /s/ Thomas Allanson; wit. Samuell Cressey; Thomas Baker (mark)

Liber F #1
1674 - 1676

Liber F, Cover Page

Roger Boyden and **Susanna Clarke** was not lawfully joined in matrimony at Mr. Robert Thompson's house by Mr. Robert Barrott in ye presence of Mr. Robert Doyne and his wife, Mr. John Fanning, Mr. James Boreman on ye first day of January Anno Dom. 1675

Liber F, Page 1

8 Sep 1674; Indenture from **Benjamin Rozer**, merchant, to **Richard Becke**, planter; for 12,000# of tobacco; a tract of land called *St. Elizabeth's* on the east side of Piscataway River and St. Thomas Bay, and St. Joseph's Creek; laid out for 600 acres; /s/ Benjamin Rozer; wit. John Jones, William Boyden

Liber F, Page 2

6 Aug 1674; Indenture from **Richard Fowke**, Gent., to **Daniell Smith**, carpenter of St. Mary's Co.; for 2,500# of tobacco; a parcel of land called *Lion's Hole*; bounded by Richard Fowke's *Vaineall* and land of Zachariah Wade; containing 100 acres; /s/ Richard Fowke, Daniell Smith; wit. Zachary Wade, Ignatius Causin

Liber F, Page 4

1 Sep 1674; Deed of Gift from **Henry Bonner**, Gent., and **Elizabeth** his wife, to her natural born sons, **John Taylor** and **Thomas Taylor**; a parcel of land surveyed for **John Taylor**, father of the sons, and granted by patent to Elizabeth Taylor, relict of John, 21 Aug 1658; lying on the north side of Petit's Creek which flows into the Potomac River, Weeke's Branch, and Taylor's Bite; laid out for 450 acres; /s/ Henry Bonner, Elisabeth Bonner; wit. Robert Doyne, Matthew Stone, Joseph Bullot

Liber F, Page 14

10 Nov 1674; Indenture from **George Shenstone**, planter, to **Thomas Jenkins**, planter; a parcel called *Pinner* at Piscataway; bounded by Edward Price's *Locust Thicket*; laid out for 100 acres; /s/ George Shenstone (mark), Mary Shestone (mark); wit. Cleborne Lomax, Edward Abbot

Liber F, Page 16

10 Nov 1674; Indenture from **John Hackister**, planter, to **John Boswell**, planter; for 6,000# for tobacco; a parcel of land called *Job's Comfort* on the east side of the main run of Portobacco Creek; bound by William Heard; laid out for 200 acres; /s/ John Hackister; wit. Thomas Corker, Joseph Bullot

Liber F, Page 18

25 Oct 1673; Division of land between **Hugh Thomas** and **Thomas Lomax**; a parcel at the head of Wicomico River; south end to Hugh Thomas and the north end to Thomas Lomax; Thomas to pay Lomax 1,700# of tobacco; a parcel of Thomas' land leased to Meverell Hulse and a parcel of Lomax's part leased to Josh Posie; /s/ William Barton, John Courte, Alexander Smith (mark), John Posey (mark)

Liber F, Page 19

8 Nov 1674; Indenture from **Richard Becke**, planter, to **Robert Ware**, merchant; a parcel of land called *Hogg's Quarter* adjoining *Poynton Manor*; laid out for 100 acres; /s/ Richard Beck (mark); wit. Richard Edelen, Robert Fowke

Liber F, Page 21

30 Oct 1674; Indenture from **Edward Maddock**, apothecary, to **Henry Aspenall**, planter; for 10,000# of tobacco; a parcel of land called *Stone Hill*; laid out for 300 acres; /s/ Edward Maddock; wit. Richard Edelen, Stephen Murty

Liber F, Page 22

29 Oct 1674; Indenture from **Henry Aspenall**, planter, to **Edward Maddocke**, apothecary; for 20,000# of tobacco and 300 acres of *Stone Hill*; a tract called *Doegs Necke* on the south side of Piscataway River, bound by Chingamuxon Creek; laid out for 450 acres; also a parcel on the east side of the said neck by the sd creek containing 200 acres by patent granted Walter Hall 26 Apr 1658; /s/ Henry Aspenall; wit. Richard Edelen, Stephen Murty

Liber F, Page 25

4 Aug 1674; Indenture from Capt. **William Boreman** of St. Mary's Co., Gent., and Mary his wife, to **William Hatton** of St. Mary's Co., Gent.; for 24,000# of tobacco; a tract formerly called *Thompson's Rest* on the east side of Piscataway River and north

side of Piscataway Creek; bounded by Luke Barber, Esq.; resurvey and named *Boareman's Content*; containing 1,000 acres; /s/ William Boareman; wit. Thomas Dent, Samuel Cressey

Liber F, Page 36

10 Nov 1674; Indenture from **John Allen**, Gent., to **Lord Baltimore** for a court house and prison; for 20,000# of tobacco raised by public levy; one acre of land called *Moore's Lodge* about 4 miles from the head of Portobacco and dwelling house 25' x 22' with a porch 10' x 8' with a room over the first part and another over the porch; with a shed behind divided into two rooms; [detailed description of buildings]; /s/ John Allen; wit. Benjamin Rozer, John Jones

Liber F, Page 42

Jan 1674 Court; **Thomas Jenkins** paid Benjamin Rozer alienation money for a tract of 200 acres called *Pinner* ack. last court by **George Shenstone** and **Mary** his wife

Liber F, Page 43

11 Jan 1674; from **Jacob Leah**, planter, to **Philip Lynes**; for 1900# tobacco; a parcel called *Batchelor's Hope*; containing 100 acres; bounded by *Wheeler's Rest*; /s/ Jacob Lea; wit. Cuthbert Musgrace (mark), Thomas Witter

Liber F Page 44

28 Nov 1674; Indenture from **Matthew Harmon** to **Samuell Dobson** of St. Mary's Co.; for 3,000# tobacco; a parcel called *Lumber Street*; bounded by Mattawoman Creek; /s/ Matthew Harmon (mark); wit. Railph Coates, Philip Lines

Liber F, Page 46

11 Jan 1674; Indenture from **Clement Theobalds**, planter, to **Philip Lynes**, innholder; for 3,000# tobacco; a parcel called *Corker's Hogg Hole*; lying on the west side of Portobacco Creek; bounded by *Simpson's Delight* formerly belonging to Alexander Simpson now in possession of Jacob Leah; containing 100 acres; /s/ Clement Theobalds; wit. John Jones, Thomas Corker

Liber F, Page 47

11 Jan 1674; Indenture from **Richard Pinner** and **William Pinner**, planter, to **Philip Lynes**, innholder; for 10,000# tobacco; a parcel called *The Father's Gift*; lying on the east side of the Anacostia

River; bounded by *Rome* belonging to Francis Pope and *Layron Stone* of John Lewgar; containing 500 acres; /s/ Richard Pinner (mark), William Pinner; wit. Thomas Holgar, George Dowell (mark); James [blank]

Liber F, Page 49

11 Jan 1674; Indenture from **Francis Furnis**, cooper, and **Mary** his wife, to **Philip Lynes**; for 3,000# tobacco; a parcel of land called *Colchester*; bounded by *St. Margarett's*, *Mershantayless Hall* and David Thomas; containing 200 acres; /s/ Francis Furniss; wit. George Powell (mark) Richard Pinner (mark), James [blank]

Liber F, Page 68

9 Sep 1670; Obligation from **Edward Worrall** to **Jonathan Marler**; a house in Manchester, Lancashire, England, called *Millgeate*; /s/ Edward Worrall; wit. Richard Morris (mark), Thomas Hayes

Liber F, Page 69

9 Mar 1674; Indenture from **William Barrett**, the younger, atty. of **William Barrett**, the elder, of the city of London, merchant, to **Humphrey Warren**, planter; by letter of atty. dated 13 Jul 1674; a judgment against Humphrey Warren, the elder, for 125,000# tobacco; a parcel called *Hatton's Point* of 250 acres, value 4,000# tobacco; /s/ William Barrett, Jr.; wit. Benjamin Rozer, John Jones

Liber F, Page 71

18 Sep 1674; Indenture from **John Allen**, Gent., to **Thomas Notley** of St. Mary's Co., Gent.; for 13,000# tobacco; a parcel called *Moore's Lodge*; on the north side of the Potomac and north branch of Zachia Swamp bounded by Daniell Johnson and Richard Morris; containing 50 acres; /s/ John Allen; wit. Robert Thompson, John Jones

Liber F, Page 73

9 Mar 1674; Indenture from **Thomas Brookes**, Gent., to **John Saunders** of Bristol, England, merchant; for 10,000# tobacco; a parcel of land called *Nonesuch*; on the north side of Oxon Run; laid out for 100 acres; /s/ Thomas Brookes; wit. Luke Greene, John Asobrey

Liber F, Page 75

8 Mar 1674; Indenture from **William Russell** to **Walter Russell**; for 5,000# tobacco; 300 acres of land belonging to the plantation

where he lives; /s/ William Russell; wit. Andrew Orme, Peirsy ?Hooks

Liber F, Page 76

9 Mar 1674; Indenture from **James Keech**, planter, to **Thomas Prichard**, wheelwright; for 1,400# tobacco; containing 150 acres called *Loathbury*; bounded by land of John Belaine, *Zachia Manor* and Richard Edelen; /s/ James Keech; wit. John Courte, Jeremy Macknew

Liber F, Page 78

10 Dec 1674; Indenture from **John Holme**, planter, to **Henry Aspenall**; for 6,000# tobacco; a parcel of land called *Shrewsbury*; bounded by land of Henry Aspenall on the north side of Piscataway River and south side of Chingamuxon Creek; bounded by land laid out for John Hatch and land laid out for Thomas Allanson now possessed by Edward Maddock; laid out for 150 acres; /s/ John Holme; wit. Bennett Marshagay, Richard Edelen

Liber F, Page 79

11 Jan 1674; Indenture from **Edmund Taylor**, planter, to **Philip Lines**, innholder; for 3,000# tobacco; a parcel called *Stoke Hill*; bounded by land laid out for George Thompson called *Planter's Delight*; containing 65 acres; /s/ Edmund Taylore; wit. John Wheeler (mark), Robert Middleton, Thomas Howell (mark)

Liber F, Page 81

8 Mar 1674; Indenture from **Clement Theobald** to **George Godfrey**; for 8,000# tobacco; a parcel lying on the west side of St. Thomas Creek; containing 100 acres; /s/ Clement Theobald; wit. Thomas Fockes, John Foord

Liber F, Page 82

8 Mar 1674; Indenture from **Clement Theobald**, planter, to **John Lambert**, planter; for 9,000# tobacco; part of 150 acres formerly belonging to me and sold to Thomas Corker and by him returned to me; on the west side of Portobacco Creek a little below Plumtree Point; containing 80 acres; /s/ Clement Theobald; wit. Thomas Corker, Job Corner

Liber F, Page 95

10 Mar 1674; Indenture from **Edward Maddock**, apothecary, to **John Saunders** of Bristol, England; for 4,000# tobacco; a parcel of land

called *Greene's Purchase*; lying on the east side of Anacostia River and south east side of St. Isodore's Brooke; containing 200 acres; /s/ Edward Maddock; wit. John Faning, Luke Greene

Liber F, Page 96

1 Apr 1675; Indenture from **John Robinson**, planter, and **Elizabeth** his wife, to **Frances Wine**; for 16,000# tobacco; a parcel called *Wassell*; bounded by 300 acres taken up by Alexander Simpson and a marsh; containing 200 acres; /s/ John Robinson (mark), Elizabeth Robinson (mark); wit. Jesse Wharton, Thomas Hussey, William Tallor

Liber F, Page 102

8 Jun 1675; Indenture from **William Boyden**, planter, and **Elizabeth** his wife, to **Philip Lines**; for 6,500# tobacco; a parcel formerly laid out for David Prichard on the south side of Piscataway River and east side of Mattawoman Creek; bounded by David Thomas; containing 200 acres; /s/ William Boyden; wit. Luke Green, Gerrard Browne, Henry Barnes (mark)

Liber F, Page 103

8 Jun 1675; Indenture from **Thomas Jenkins**, planter, and **Anne** his wife, to **William Loveday**, planter; for 6,000# tobacco; a parcel on the Avon River bounded by George Godfrey; containing 85 acres; /s/ Thomas Jenkins, Anne Jenkins (mark); wit. Cliborne Lomax, Garrett Sinnett (mark)

Liber F, Page 105

9 Mar 1674; Indenture from **John Hatch**, Gent., to **Peter Achilles**, planter; for 7,000# tobacco; a parcel called *Oakington*; bounded by Potomac River, Chingamuxon Creek, and a marsh; containing 100 acres; /s/ John Hatch; wit. Sa. Cressey, Jacob Peterson

Liber F, Page 106

8 Jun 1675; Indenture from **Clement Theobald**, planter, to **Thomas Corker**, planter; for 6,000# tobacco; a parcel called *Lamaster Beginnings*; located at the head of Portobacco Creek; containing 100 acres being part of a patent of 150 acres called *Betties Delight* formerly belonging to Corker; /s/ Clement Theobald; wit. Job. Corner, Robert Ward

Liber F, Page 108
15 May 1675; Indenture from **Thomas Stone**, Gent., to **Samuell Sherrill**, planter; for 12,000# tobacco; a mill and land by virtue of an Act of Assembly; /s/ Thomas Stone, Samuel Sherrill (mark); wit. David Maddox (mark)

Liber F, Page 120
8 Mar 1673; Deed of Sale from **Thomas Witter**, planter, to **Benjamin Rozer** of Portobacco, Gent.; for 10,000# tobacco; a parcel called *Simpson's Delight* on the west side at the head of Portobacco Creek; laid out for 300 acres; /s/ Thomas Witter; wit. John Hamilton, John Jones

Liber F, Page 136
14 Sep 1675; Indenture from **Richard Pinner** to his brother **William Pinner**; for 10,000# tobacco; a parcel of land on the north side of the Potomac; containing half of the 600 acres granted John Thomkinson and Andrew Watson by patent dated 13 Jan 1654; /s/ Richard Pinner (mark) Wit. John Hamilton, Cliborne Lomax

Liber F, Page 138
13 Sep 1675; Indenture from **John Lemaire**, surgeon, to **John Cassock**; for 11,000# tobacco; a parcel called *Castock's Lop* on the east side of Portobacco Creek; bounded by Henry Hawkins; containing 100 acres; another adjoining parcel called *Lemaire's Purchase*; laid out for 100 acres; /s/ John Lemaire; wit. Thomas Lomax, Samuell Dobson

Liber F, Page 140
7 Sep 1675; Indenture from **Thomas Witter**, planter, and **Mary** his wife, to **Francis Wine**, cooper; for 11,000# tobacco; a parcel of 300 acres called *Simpson's Delight*; on the west side at the head of Portobacco Creek; /s/ Thomas Witter, Mary Witter; wit. Sa. Cressey, Philip Lines

Liber F, Page 150
8 Nov 1675; Indenture from **William Jenkinson**, planter, and **Mary** his wife, to **Henry Hawkins**, farmer; for 5,000# tobacco; a parcel of land formerly known at *Goate's Lodge*; bounded by Zachia Swamp, and Capt. Josias Fendall; containing 150 acres; /s/ William Jenkinson; wit. James Smallwood (mark), Robert Hart (mark)

Liber F, Page 151

13 Sep 1675; Indenture from **Alise Walker**, relict of **James Walker**, to **John Worland**; for 4,000 # tobacco; a tract called *Docker's Delight*; containing 150 acres; bounded by Doughties Land; /s/ Alise Walker (mark); wit. Thomas Clipsham, George Creedwell

Liber F, Page 153

9 Nov 1675; Indenture from **Job Corner**, planter, to **Philip Browne**, planter; for 2,500# tobacco; a parcel of land called *Greenah*; bounded by St. Nicholas; containing 100 acres; /s/ Job Corner; wit. Thomas Corker, Clement Theobald

Liber F, Page 155

7 Jul 1675; Deed of Gift from **Archibald Wanghob** (mark) to his daughter **Margaret Lemaire**; a mare; /s/ Archibald Wanghob; wit. Owen Jones, Peter Butler (mark); recorded by John Lemaire

Liber F, Page 163

11 Jan 1675; Indenture from **George Goodricke**, planter, to **Philip Lines**, planter; for 15,000# tobacco; a tract containing 600 acres; lying on the west side of the north branch of Zachia Swamp; /s/ George Goodricke; wit. Edward Maddock, Edmond Lindsey (mark), John Word

Liber F, Page 165

11 Jan 1675; Indenture from **Thomas Corker**, planter, to **John Hanson**, planter; for 6,000# tobacco; a parcel of land called *Lancaster*; lying at the head of Portobacco Creek near the main road; containing 100 acres; part of a patent for 150 acres called *Bettyes Delight*; /s/ Thomas Corker; wit. Job. Corner, Richard Price (mark)

Liber F, Page 173

11 Apr 1676; Indenture from **Richard Berke**, planter, to **Benjamin Rozer**, merchant; for 10,000# tobacco; a parcel called *St. Elizabeth's*; on the east side of Piscataway River in St. Thomas Bay where St. Joseph's Creek falls; laid out for 600 acres; /s/ Richard Berke (mark); wit. John Hamilton, Simon Nelson

Liber F, Page 175

10 Mar 1675; Indenture from **Samuell Fendall**, Gent., to **Robert Doyne**, Gent.; for 14,000# tobacco; a parcel called *Lyon's Denn*; on the main fresh at the head of Wicomico River; bounded by

land of Capt. Fendall, called *Fendall's Delight*, and land of Daniel Johnson; containing 150 acres; /s/ Sam. Fendall; wit. John Stone, Robert Middleton

Liber F, Page 176

14 Mar 1675; Indenture from **William Loveday**, planter, to **John Hammond**, planter; for 3,000# tobacco; half of 85 acres of land lately purchased by Loveday from Thomas Jenkins; part of a tract called *Troopes Rondesvous*; /s/ William Loveday; wit. Robert Robins, Thomas Jenkins

Liber F, Page 178

12 Apr 1676; Indenture from **George Athy**, planter, to **Edward Maddock**, apothecary; for 3,200# tobacco; a parcel called *Athey's Hopewell*; located above Piscataway; containing 100 acres; /s/ George Athy; wit. Philip Lines, Richard Brooke

Liber F, Page 180

12 Apr 1676; Indenture from **Edward Maddock**, apothecary, to **Philip Carey**; for 3,000# tobacco; a parcel called *Athey's Hopewell*; containing 100 acres; /s/ Ed. Maddock; wit. Philip Lines, Luke Greene

Liber F, Page 181

30 Dec 1669; Indenture from **Thomas Lomax**, merchant, to **Meverell Hulse**, planter; for 2,000# tobacco; a parcel of land on the west side of Wicomico River; part of a tract of 600 acres belonging to Thomas Lomax and Hugh Thomas; containing 100 acres; /s/ Thomas Lomax; wit. Cliborne Lomax, Edward Wilder, Edward

Liber F, Page 182

?3 Apr 1676; In consideration of a marriage between **John Lambert**, planter, and **Sarah Barker**; a half-part of a parcel of land called *Simpson's Supply*; /s/ John Lambert; wit. Henry Neale (mark), Cliborne Lomax

Liber F, Page 184

26 Mar 1676; Deed of Gift from **Thomas Hyatt** to **Joan Mitchell**; 23 head of hogs and working tools; to the oldest son of **Blanch Lomax**, wife of Cliborne Lomax, 50 acres of land; I was assigned by Francis Ferneley, dec'd, to look after his estate for the good of his son jointly with Thomas Breckeridge, do empower Joan Mitchell

to look after said **John Ferenley**'s estate; /s/ Thomas Hyatt; wit. Thomas Buskeridge, Thomas Wells
Liber F, Page 184

28 Mar 1676; Deed of Gift from **Joan Mitchell**, widow, to **Thomas Wells** all that belongs to me after my decease; excepting a cow to Johannah Philpott; /s/ Joan Mitchell (mark); wit. Bridgett Inglesby (mark), Elizabeth Morgan (mark)
Liber F, Page 184

[undated]; Deed from **William Marshall**, planter, to **Robert Clarke** and **John Clarke**, sons of Robert Clark; for 5,000# tobacco; a parcel of land sold to me by Walter Beane; /s/ William Marshall; wit. Daniell Johnson, John Small
Liber F, Page 200

8 Aug 1676; Indenture from **Edward Maddock**, apothecary, to **Philip Lines**; for 8,000# tobacco; a parcel called *Maddock's Folly*; on the east side of Piscataway River; containing 350 acres; /s/ Edward Maddock; wit. Henry Bonner, Joshua Guibert, John Hamilton
Liber F, Page 200

8 Aug 1676; Indenture from **Thomas Prichard**, wheelwright, to **Nicholas Gridmore**, tailor; for 2,000# tobacco; a parcel at the head of Wicomico River called *Loathbury*; containing 50 acres; /s/ Thomas Prichard; wit. John Jones, Rand. Brandt
Liber F, Page 202

24 Jan 1675; Indenture from **John Waters**, planter, to **Henry Fletsher**, planter; for 3,000# tobacco; part of *Allonson's Folly* on the east side of Piscataway River and south side of Chingamuxon; 300 acres of the said divident in possession of Thomas Allcocke; laid out for 100 acres; /s/ John Water, Esther Waters (mark); wit. John Clark (mark), Thomas Tubb
Liber F, Page 204

8 Aug 1670; Deed of Gift from **John Grubb**, to **Mary Cressey**, dau. of Samuel Cressey; heifer; /s/ John Grubb (mark); wit. Joseph Horton, John Piper (mark)
Liber F, Page 216

8 Aug 1676; Indenture from **James Tyer**, Gent., to Maj. **John Duglas**, Gent.; for 10,000# tobacco; a parcel of land given unto my uncle

John Bowles and James Tyre by our kinsman William Bowles by will 14 Feb 1662; /s/ James Tyer; wit. Robert Heroitt, Henry Hardy
Liber F, Page 221

2 Oct 1676; Deed of Gift from **Thomas Taylor** to **Margaret Graydon**; heifer; /s/ Thomas Taylor; wit. Henry Bonner, Cleborne Lomax

7 Nov 1676; Deed of Gift from **Archbald Waughob** to **Elizabeth** his wife; 6 silver spoons, a sliver tankard, a silver bowl, one Negro woman and 200 acres of land at my upper plantation; /s/ Archibald Waughob; wit. John Gray (mark), George Miller (mark)
Liber F, Page 222

23 Sep 1676; Indenture from **John Ofaine** of Portobacco, planter, to **Benjamin Rozer** of Portobacco; for 8,000# tobacco; a parcel of land called *St. Patrick's* on the west side of a fresh of St. Thomas Creek; bounding Jane Clarke, Ignatius Causine near the main branch of St. Nicholas' Runn; containing 300 acres; another parcel called *Spring Plaine* on the west side of the main fresh of Portobacco or St. Thomas Creek; bounded by James Lindsey, Garrat Sinnett; containing 50 acres; /s/ John OFaine; wit. John Lemaire, John Hamilton
Liber F, Page 223

14 Nov 1676; Indenture from **Edmund Taylor**, planter, to **Philip Lines** of Portobacco, planter; for 2,000# tobacco; a parcel called *St. Edmundsberry*; bounded by Mrs. Emenson's; containing 100 acres; /s/ Edmund Taylor; wit. John Chesson, Joseph Holton, Edward Maddock
Liber F, Page 224

6 Nov 1676; Indenture from **William Russell**, planter, to **James Neale**, Sr. of *Woolaston Manor*, Gent.; for 10,356# tobacco; a parcel of land on the west side of Wicomico River; containing 300 acres; /s/William Russell (mark), wit. John Butler, Anthony Neale
Liber F, Page 225

8 Jun 1676; Indenture from **William Russell**, planter, to **Elinor Bayne**, widow; for 3,500# tobacco; a parcel of land on the west side of Wicomico River adjoining land now in possession of Elinor; containing 75 acres; /s/ William Russell, Elinor Bayne (mark); wit. Matthew Hitt, Robert Browne (mark), George Goodwell

Liber F, Page 242

15 Jan 1676/7; Deed of Gift from **Jane Matthews**, relict of **Thomas Matthews**, Gent., to her 5 children, **Ignatius**, **William**, **Victoria**, **Jane** and **Anne**; ex. William Boarman of St. Mary's Co., Gent.; /s/ Jane Matthews; wit. Rando. Brandt

Liber F, Page 243

19 Feb 1676; Indenture from **John Allen**, Gent., to **John Saunders** of Bristol, England; for 50,000# tobacco; half part of a parcel called *Irish Damm* on the west side of Zachia Swamp; containing 50 acres; half of the Watermills, 2 grist mills on said tract; half of *Smith's Hope* of 50 acres and watermills; /s/ John Allen; wit. Richard Edelen, Tho. Russell, Cleborne Lomax

Liber G
1676-1678

Liber G, Page 1

9 Jan 1676; Indenture from **George Athy**, planter, to **Philip Lines**; for 4,000# tobacco; a parcel called *Wakefield*; bounded by Clement Hills, Richard Gardner; containing 200 acres; /s/ George Athy (mark); wit. John Hanson, Charles ?Culles

Liber G, Page 2

9 Jan 1676; Indenture from **George Athy**, planter, to **Philip Lines**; for 3,000# tobacco; a parcel called *Hutton ?Lorkrue*; above Piscataway; containing 100 acres; laid out for 100 acres; /s/ George Athy (mark); wit. John Hanson, Charles Culles (mark)

Liber G, Page 3

9 Jan 1676; Deed of Gift from **Thomas Lomax** to his brother, **Cleborne Lomax**; 100 acres being part of a tract of 600 acres called *Rich Hills*; located on the west side of the main fresh of Wicomico River; /s/ Tho. Lomax; wit. Tho. Hussey, Richard Edelen

Liber G, Page 5

6 Nov 1676; Indenture from **John Blumstead** of Stafford Co., Virginia, tailor, to **Philip Lines** of Portobacco, planter; for 3,000# tobacco; a parcel of land called *Hooke Norton*; containing 150 acres; bounded by land of Verlinda Stone; /s/ Katherine Blumsted (mark), John Blumstead (mark); wit. John Halford, William Norwood

Liber G, Page 17

13 Mar 1676; Indenture from **John Morris**, planter, to **Hugh French**, planter; for 16,000# tobacco; a parcel granted William Smoote by patent 6 May 1668; assigned by him to Richard Smoote; from him to Giles Tompkinson; from him to Morris; containing 200 acres; /s/ John Morris (mark); wit. William Rosewell, Richard Edelen

Liber G, Page 19

13 Mar 1676; Indenture from **John Barker,** planter, and **Joan** his wife, to **Alexander Standish**; for 2,000# tobacco; a parcel called *Barker's Enlargement*; lying at the head of Wicomico River; bounded by land formerly belonging to James Keech now possessed by Nicholas Serdmore; containing 50 acres; /s/ John Barker, Joan Barker (mark); wit. John Courte, Jr., Meverell Hulse

Liber G, Page 20

9 Mar 1676; Indenture from **Garrett Sennett**, planter, and **Anne** his wife, to **Matthew Saunders** and **Thomas Bryant**; for 2,000# tobacco; a parcel called *St. Peter's* lying on the west side of a fresh run of Portobacco Creek; containing 50 acres; /s/ Garrett Sennett (mark); wit. Jno. Godshall, Henry Henley

Liber G, Page 21

1 Feb 1676; Deed of Gift from **Archibald Waghope** to **John Lemaire**, physician, husband of **Margarett Lemaire**, daughter of Archibald; a tract called *Waghope Purchase* on the west side of Portobacco Creek; containing 300 acres; /s/ Archibald Waghope (mark); wit. Zachary Wade, Ignatius Causine

Liber G, Page 22

13 Mar 1676; Deed of Gift from **Benjamin Rozer**, Gent., to **Edmond Lyndsey**; a parcel of land called *Mayday*; bounded by William Chandler; containing 300 acres; /s/ Benja. Rozier; wit. James Littlepage, Frances Keene

Liber G, Page 23

6 Mar 1676; Assignment from **William Deane** to Capt. **John Allanson**; for 3,500# tobacco; 200 acres of land formerly left me by John Greene; /s/ Will. Deane; wit. Rando. Brandt, Tho. Russell

Liber G, Page 23

8 Mar 1675; Assignment from **William Stannard**, gunsmith, to **John Deane** of 100 acres of land, a mare, cow and calf left me by John Greene; /s/ Witt Deane; wit. Rando. Brandt, Tho. Russell

Liber G, Page 37

15 May 1677; Indenture from **William Lee**, Gent., to **Philip Lines**, planter; for a valuable sum of tobacco; a tract called *Lee's Purchase* lying on the east side of the Potomac adjoining land laid out for Richard Watson; containing 300 acres; /s/ Wm. Lee; wit. Rando. Brandt, Henry Hardy, Thomas Holgar

Liber G, Page 39

8 Jun 1677; Indenture from **Robert Wheeler**, and **Mary** his wife, to **David Towell**; for 4,500# tobacco; a parcel of land from the estate of Henry Fletcher, dec'd, by letter of administration; /s/ Robert Wheeler (mark), Mary Wheeler (mark); wit. John Hanson, Edward Abbott

Liber G, Page 49
9 Aug 1677; Indenture from **John Ward**, planter, to **Robert Goodrick** and **John Clement**; for 2,000# tobacco; a parcel of land called *Pomfrett*; bounded by land of Thomas Matthews, Gent.; containing 150 acres; /s/ John Ward (mark); wit. [blank]

Liber G, Page 55
5 Sep 1677; Deed of Gift from **Lawrence Younge** of St. Mary's Co., planter. to his wife **Sarah Younge**, a filly foal; /s/ Lawrence Younge (mark); wit. Richard Morris (mark), Cleborne Lomax

Liber G, Page 55
6 Jun 1677; Indenture from **George Godfrey**, planter, to **William Wells**, planter; for 10,000# tobacco; a parcel of land called *Milerne*; laid out for 200 acres; lately occupied by Daniel Johnson; also a parcel on the south side of St. Michael's Creek called *Mountaigne*; bounded by *Allanson's Folly*; containing 200 acres; /s/ George Godfrey; wit. Henry Bonner, Rando. Brandt

Liber G, Page 68
12 Feb 1676; Indenture from Capt. **John Allen** to **Henry Aspinall**; for 3,000# tobacco; a parcel of land called *Withsall* on Chingamuxon Creek; bounded by *Allanonson's Folly*; containing 200 acres; /s/ John Allen; wit. Charl. Russell, Cleborne Lomax

Liber G, Page 72
13 Nov 1677; Deed of Gift from **Thomas Hussey** and **Johannah** his wife, to **Rachell Ashford**, wife of **Michael Ashford** and natural daughter of Johannah; a parcel of land called *Moore's Ditch* lying on the west side of Zachia Swamp; containing 500 acres; /s/ Thomas Hussey, Johannah Hussey (mark); wit. Cleborne Lomax, Thomas Jenkins

Liber G, Page 86
2 Jan 1677; Indenture from **Thomas Baker**, planter, to **Richard Athman** of St. Mary's Co., planter; for 2,600# tobacco; a parcel of land called *Baker's Addition*; bounded by land called *Marsh Land*; laid out for 50 acres; /s/ Thomas Baker (mark); wit. Richard Edelen, Henry Pratt

Liber G, Page 87
13 Nov 1677; Indenture from **William Loveday**, planter, and **Joan** his wife, to **John Harmon**, planter; for 3,500# tobacco; a parcel of

land being part of *Troope's Rendezvous*; /s/ William Loveday (mark), Joan Loveday (mark); wit. Tho. Jenkins, Joseph Wolfe (mark)

Liber G, Page 88

8 Jan 1677; Indenture from **Joseph Bullott**, planter, to **John Duglas**, Gent.; Bullott and Saml. Clarke, dec'd, purchased *Welcome* from Edmond Lindsey, dec'd, by indenture dated 9 Nov 1673; for 7,000# tobacco Bullott sells to Duglas; tract lying on east side of Portobacco fresh; laid out for 200 acres; /s/ Joseph Bullott; wit. Morrise Miles, Edmond Dinnie

Liber G, Page 94

8 Jan 1677; Indenture from **Edward Rookwood** to **Thomas Allcock**, carpenter; Rookwood and Allcock, exs. and legatees of the will of **David Towell**, inherited tract called *Fletcher's Addition*; on the east side of Piscataway River at Goose Bay; sold by Henry Aspenall to Henry Fletcher by deed dated 14 Sep 1669; containing 150 acres; /s/ Edward Rookwood; wit. John Godshall, John Harrison

Liber G, Page 95

8 Jan 1677; Indenture from **Thomas Allcock**, planter, to **Edward Rookwood**, planter; a tract of land called *St. David's*; containing 200 acres; inherited by Allcock and Rookwood from will of **David Towell**; lying on the east side of Piscataway River in Goose Bay; /s/ Thomas Allcock (mark) wit. John Godshall, John Hanson

Liber G, Page 124

13 Nov 1677; Indenture from **Kellam Maglocklin** to **Thomas Jenkins**, planter; for 8,000# tobacco; part of a parcel of land called *Lyndsey* formerly belonging to Edward Deane and willed to Elizabeth Lyndsey; she willed the land to Maglocklin; bounded by William Boarman; containing 150 acres; /s/ Kenellam Maglockline, Elizabeth Maglockline; wit. William Davies, Tho. Parker (mark)

Liber G, Page 125

5 Mar 1677; Indenture from **John Duglas**, Gent, to **James Smallwood**; a parcel called *Welcome* purchased from Joseph Bullott on 8 Jan 1677; for 7,500# tobacco; containing 200 acres; /s/ John Duglas; wit. Benja. Rozer, Samuell Dobson

Liber G, Page 158

4 Jun 1678; Indenture from **William Wells**, planter, to **Henry Aspenall**, planter; for 11,000# tobacco; a parcel called *Milerne*; containing 200 acres; /s/ William Wells; wit. Francis Harrison, John Moore (mark)

Liber G, Page 160

8 Jun 1678; Indenture from **Henry Aspinall**, planter, to **Robert Wheeler**; for 8,000# tobacco; a parcel of land called *Shrewsberry*; on the north side of Piscataway River and south side of Chingamuxon Creek; bounded by land laid out for John Hatch; bounding land laid out for Thomas Allanson now in possession of Walter Peake; containing 150 acres; /s/ Henry Aspenall (mark); wit. William Wells, Richard Gibson

Liber G, Page 162

5 Mar 1677; Indenture from **Jacob Peterson**, mariner, to **Henry Hawkins**, tanner; Jacob Peterson purchased a tract from Henry Moore and Elizabeth his wife called *Moore's Branch* containing 50 acres on the west side of a branch of Zachia Swamp on 20 Sep 1665; Peterson for the sum of 5,300# tobacco sold to Hawkins; containing 100 acres; /s/ Jacob Peterson; wit. Thomas Holgar, Meverell Hulse, Edmond Dennie

Liber G, Page 164

5 Aug 1676; Bill of Sale from **Sylvanus Gilpinge** to **Margaret Wharton**; a mare; /s/ Sylvanus Gilpinge (mark); wit. Thomas Robinson, Susanna Robinson (mark)

Liber G, Page 164

1678; Deed of Gift from **John Boyden** to **Mary Boyden**, the natural born daughter of his now wife **Elinor**; to **Elizabeth**, daughter of John and Elinor; a mare

1678-1680
Liber H #1

Liber H, Page 1

13 Aug 1678; Deed of Gift from Col. **John Duglas**, Gent., to **John Hamilton**, Gent., a parcel of land called *St. Edmonds* which Duglas bought of Edmond Lyndsey, dec'd; lying on the east side of a main fresh of Portobacco Creek; bounded by land of John Heard; containing 100 acres; /s/ John Duglas; wit. Philip Lines, Henry Hawkins

Liber H, Page 3

1 Jun 1678; Indenture from **John Dent**, Gent., and **Mary** his wife, of St. Mary's Co., to **Richard Ashman**; for 7,000# tobacco; a parcel of land called *Promise*; bounded by Edward Swann and William Marshall; laid out for 100 acres; /s/ John Dent; wit. Richard Edelen, George Graves (mark)

Liber H, Page 4

11 Jun 1678; Indenture from **Bennett Marshagay**, merchant, to **William Thomas**, planter; for 5,000# tobacco; a parcel of land formerly belonging to John Geniers by patent 10 Dec 1653; assigned by him to Marshagay; on the north side of the Potomac; bounded by *Geniers' Swamp*; containing 100 acres; /s/ Bennett Marshaway; wit. Cleborne Lomax

Liber H, Page 6

10 Jun 1678; Indenture from **John Saunders**, late of the City of Bristol, Gent., to **William Wells**, Gent.; a parcel of land called *Nonesuch*; located on Oxon Runn; containing 106 acres by indentures dated 9 Mar 1674; for 9,000# tobacco; /s/ John Saunders; wit. Henry Bonner, Cleborne Lomax

Liber H, Page 8

10 June 1678; Indenture from **John Saunders**, Gent., to **William Wells**; for 4,000# tobacco; a parcel of land called *Greene's Purchase*; on the east side of the Anacostia River and St. Isodore's Creek; containing 200 acres; /s/ John Saunders; wit. Henry Bonner, Cleborne Lomax

Liber H, Page 10

6 Jun 1678; Indenture from **Francis Wine**, Gent., to **Benjamin Rozer**, Esq.; for 19,000# tobacco; a parcel called *Wassell*; bounded by 300 acres taken up by Alexander Simpson; containing 200 acres; also a parcel called *Blooksitch*; bounded by Saunder Simpson; containing 100 acres; also a parcel called *London*; bounded by George Langham's land called *Thomas Street*; containing 100 acres; /s/ Francis Wine; wit. Rando. Brandt, Edmond Dennis

Liber H, Page 12

Aug 1678; **Francis Heydon**, and **Thomasine** his wife, acknowledged indenture of 200 acres of land called *Partnership* to **Thomas Tukerell**

Liber H, Page 45

9 Sep 1678; Deed of Gift from **John Breade**, Gent., to his wife **Jane Breade** and **Ignatius, William, Victoria, Jane,** and **Anne Matthews**, sons and daughters of my wife Jane and Thomas Matthews, her late husband; for 5s paid by William Boaremen of St. Mary's Co. and Henry Adames, Gent., in behalf of my wife and her said children; all the land, buildings, servants, slaves, stock of hoggs, cattle, horses and other goods; /s/ John Breade; wit. Edmond Dennie, John Lemaire

Liber H, Page 48

17 Jan 1678; Indenture from **John Morris**, planter, to **William Smith** of Talbot Co., planter; for a certain quantity of tobacco; a parcel of land bounded by Mr. Neale's *Hungerford's Branch*; containing 200 acres; /s/ John Morris (mark); wit. John Douglas, Peter Far (mark); acknowledged by Elinor Morris, wife of John Morris

Liber H, Page 57

16 Oct 1678; Deed of Gift from **Thomas Helgar**, innholder, to his wife **Anne Helgar**; all goods, chattels, household stuff, pewter, bedding, implements, servants, cattle, etc.; /s/ Thomas Helgar; wit. Thomas Gerrard, John Bunney

Liber H, Page 58

11 Nov 1678; Deed of Gift from **Barbary Chesson** of *St. Thomas Manor*, relict of John Chesson, to **Mary Chesson**, daughter; heifers; /s/ Barbary Chesson (mark); wit. Kenelme Magloughlin (mark), John Woodard (mark), Mary Land (mark)

Liber H, Page 59

10 May 1677; Indenture from **William Lee**, Gent., to **Thomas Helgar** and **Anne** his wife; for a sum of tobacco; a tract of land called *Stump Neck* or *Doge's Necke* now called *Estep*; bounded by John Duglas; containing 75 acres; /s/ William Lee; wit. Rando. Brande, Henry Hardy

Liber H, Page 61

12 Nov 1678; Indenture from **Thomas Helgar**, innholder, and **Anne** his wife to **John Hamilton**, Gent.; for a sum of tobacco; a parcel of land called *Estep*; bounded by John Duglas; containing 75 acres; /s/ Thomas Helgar, Anne Helgar; wit. Benj. Rozer, Henry Hardy

Liber H, Page 63

10 Sep 1678; Indenture from **William Smith**, planter, to **Walter Davies**, tailor; for a certain consideration; a parcel of land bounded by Mr. Neale; called *Hungerford*; containing 100 acres; /s/ William Smith (mark); Robert Middleton, Abraham Sapwate

Liber H, Page 88

8 Jan 1677; Indenture from **Gerrard Sly** of St. Mary's Co., merchant, to **Philip Lines** in behalf of **Robert Downes**, son and heir to Robert Downes, dec'd; for 2,100# tobacco; a parcel of land called *Cow Springs* on the north side of the Potomac near the mouth of Nangemy Creek; containing 400 acres; formerly possessed by Samuel Smith, dec'd, and Robert Sly, Sr.; /s/ Gerrard Sly; wit. [blank]

Liber H, Page 91

18 Oct 1678; Indenture from **Richard Hodgson**, planter, to **Benjamin Rozer**; for love and maintenance of **Johannah** his wife and **Elizabeth** his youngest daughter-in-law [?step-dau.]; a tract of land, mill and mill house on the Avon River in Nangemy or Stone's Fresh; if Elizabeth have no heirs to my brother William Hodgson; /s/ Rich. Hodgson; wit. Humphrey Jones (mark), James Gallaway (mark), Thomas Massey, John Slater

Liber H, Page 93

3 Dec 1678; Indenture from **George Brett**, carpenter, to **Simon Stephens**, planter; for 1,400# tobacco; a parcel of land called *Brett's Beginning*; bounded by *Ashbrooke's Rest* and *Ingothorpe*;

containing 100 acres; /s/ George Brett; wit. Thomas Hussey, Stephen Mankin (mark)

Liber H, Page 94

12 Oct 1678; Indenture from **John Cassock**, planter, to **Rise Wayman** and **Joseph Wolph**, planter; for 5,000# tobacco; a parcel of land called *Skipton*; granted by patent to Robert Castleton who sold to John Cassock; containing 200 acres; /s/ John Cassock; wit. Richard Edelen, Samuel Walter

Liber H, Page 126

20 Aug 1677; Indenture from **Peter Car**, planter, to **John Gray**, carpenter; for 9,000# tobacco; a parcel of land formerly belonging to Henry Lilly; containing 250 acres; being the northwest part of land formerly granted James Lee now occupied by John Ward of Nangemy; bounded by William Stone; laid out for 500 acres; /s/ Peter Car; wit Henry Bonner, John Harvey

Liber H, Page 132

5 Sep 1678; Indenture from **Edward Maddock**, apothecary, to **John Reddick**; for 30,000# tobacco; a parcel of land called *Doges Neck*; on the south side of the Piscataway River to the mouth of Chingamuxon Creek; laid out for 200 acres; /s/ Edward Maddock; wit. Rando. Brande; Geo. Godfrey; acknowledged by Margery wife of Edward Maddock

Liber H, Page 135

25 May 1679; Indenture from **William Wells**, Gent., to **Benjamin Rozer**, Esq.; for 10,000# tobacco; a parcel of land called *Greene's Purchase*; lying on the east side of Anacostia River; bounded by an old Indian Fort; laid out for 100 acres; also a parcel called *Nonesuch*; containing 100 acres; /s/ William Wells; wit. Wm. Chandler, Tho. Hussey, Edmond Dennis

Liber H, Page 175

7 Jun 1679; Indenture from **John Clement**, tailor, to **James Browne**; for a sum of tobacco; half of a parcel of land called *Pomphrett*, adjoining land of Thomas Matthewes and John Wheeler's land called *Wheeler's Adventure*; containing 150 acres; /s/ John Clement; wit. Thomas Lomax, William Standover (mark)

Liber H, Page 185

11 Jul 1679; Deed of Gift from **Thomas Baker**, planter, to **Thomas Younge**, son of Lawrence Younge; a heifer; Tho. Baker (mark); wit. Mary Dine (mark), Cleborne Lomax

Liber H, Page 186

11 Sep 1679; Deed of Gift from **Mary Dod**, widow, relict of **Richard Dod**, to **John Baker**, son of Thomas Baker; a heifer; /s/ Mary Dod (mark); wit. Cleborne Lomax, Lawrence Younge (mark)

Liber H, Page 190

9 Sep 1679; Indenture from **George Thompson**, late of Charles Co., now of St. Mary's Co., Gent., to **Benjamin Rozer**, Esq.; for 18,000# tobacco; a parcel of land called *Poirsefield*; on the east side of St. Thomas Creek; bounded by 100 acres of land formerly laid out for Robert Clarke, Esq., and Mr. Goodwicks; laid out for 100 acres; /s/ George Thompson; wit. Henry Bonner, John Godshall, Edmund Dennis

Liber H, Page 198

30 Sep 1679; Indenture from **John Caine**, planter, to **William Wells**; a parcel of land called *The Hard Frost* on the south side of Piscataway River and south side of Mattawoman Creek; near land formerly laid out for John Halse; about a mile from land of Thomas Allanson; containing 200 acres; /s/ John Caine; wit. Cleborne Lomax, Will Theobald

Liber H, Page 242

20 Dec 1679; Indenture from **John Fanning**, Gent., to **Nathaniel Veren**; for 14,400# tobacco; a parcel called *Woodberrie*; on the north side of Potomac; containing 300 acres; /s/ John Fanning; wit. John Courte, Jr., Henry Bonner, John Harvey

Liber H, Page 245

13 Jan 1679; Indenture from **Richard Ashman**, planter, to **Jno. Bayly**, planter; for 5,000# tobacco; a parcel of land called *Promise*; bounded by Edward Swan and William Martiall; containing 100 acres; /s/ Richard Ashman; wit. Robt. Baldwin, Jno. Pope (mark)

Liber H, Page 248

12 Apr 1669; **Anne Posey**, spinster, d/o Francis Posey, to marry **Jno. Mould**, carpenter; mentions mare left her by her father; /s/ Anne Posey; Wit. Joseph Horton, Giles Willson

Liber H, Page 249
8 Mar 1678; Indenture from **Robert Wheeler** to **Cuthbert Musgrove**; for 5,000# tobacco; half of a parcel of land called *Shrewsbury* on the north side of Piscataway River and south side of Chingamuxon Creek; laid out for 150 acres; /s/ Robert Wheeler (mark), Mary Wheeler (mark); wit. Roger Fowke, Tho. Robinson

Liber H, Page 253
15 Jan 1679; Indenture from **George Thompson** of St. Mary's Co., Gent., to **John Hamilton**, Gent.; a parcel of land on Nanjemy Creek and the Potomac River between land of Thomas Burdette and William Lewis; containing 100 acres; /s/ George Thompson; wit. Robert Thompson, Roger Fowke

Liber H, Page 273
9 Mar 1679; Indenture from Capt. **Henry Aspenall**, Gent., and his wife, to **Henry Hawkins**; for 5,000# tobacco; a parcel of land called *Stone Hill*; laid out for 300 acres; /s/ Henry Aspenall (mark); wit. Cleborne Lomax, George Thompson

Liber H, Page 275
31 Jan 1679; Indenture from **Nicholas Belaine** to **John Posey**; a parcel of land called *Burlaine's Hill*; for love and affection for his brother-in-law John Posey; a parcel called *Belaine's Hill*; on the west side of Wicomico River; adjoining land of William Ward; containing 100 acres of land; /s/ Nicholas Belane; wit. John Ramos, John Coolidge, Cleborne Lomax

Liber H, Page 290
3 Apr 1680; Indenture from **Thomas Harris**, planter, to **Raiph Smith** and **Sarah** his wife, the relict of Col. John Duglas; exchange of land; a parcel of land at the head of *Petit's Creek* part of land now in possession of Thomas Harris; bound by *Pope's Hollow* and land of Thomas Petits; containing 20 acres; /s/ Thomas Haris; wit. Henry Bonner, Rando. Brandt; acknowledged by Mary Haris, wife of Thomas

Liber H, Page 291
3 Apr 1680; Indenture from **Raiph Smith** and **Sarah** his wife, relict of Col. John Duglas, to Thomas Harris, planter; exchange of land; a parcel adjoining Thomas Harris; containing 20 acres; /s/ Raiph Smith (mark), Sarah Smith

Liber H, Page 299

20 Feb 1699; Indenture from **William Langworth** of St. Mary's Co., Gent., son and heir of **James Langworth**, dec'd, to **Rando. Hanson**, Gent.; for 19,000# tobacco; a parcel of land called *St. John's* on the north side of Piscataway River; containing 800 acres; formerly surveyed for John Jarboe 18 Nov 1658; /s/ William Langworth; wit. Thomas Lomax, William Thomas

Liber H, Page 302

8 Jun 1680; Indenture from **Edward Rookerd**, planter, and **Mary** his wife, to **Thomas Hussy**, innholder; for 14,000# tobacco; lying on the east side of Piscataway River and northward of Goose Bay; containing 150 acres; also a parcel called _____ *Addition*; containing 50 acres; /s/ Edward Rooked (mark); wit. William Langworth, John Richards

Liber H, Page 304

31 Mar 1680; Indenture from Col. Benjamin Rozer, adm. of **Dominick Bodkin FitzJames** of Galway, Ireland, dec'd, by letter of attorney from Richard Foote of City of London, atty. of Peter Keewan and Francis Blake of Galway, exs. of FitzJames, to **Samuell Raspin**, merchant; a tract of land called *The Mill Land* with all equipment; lying at the head of Wicomico River; for 22,500# tobacco; also parcel called *The Mill Dam* at the head of Wicomico River and west side of Zachia Swamp; /s/ Benjamin Rozer; wit. Thomas Clipshawe, Edmund Dennie

Liber H, Page 320

13 Aug 1678; Indenture from **Francis Heydon**, planter of St. Mary's Co., and **Thomasine** his wife, to **Thomas Tiskerell**, tailor; grant to Heydon and John Allward dated 1 Sep 1670; called *Partnership*; laid out for 300 acres on the east side of Portobacco Fresh, 4 miles from the said fresh; bounded by Henry Moore; partition of land bearing date of 10 Mar 1673 between Allward and Heydon; /s/ Francis Heydon; wit. Thomas Lomax, Edmund Dennie

Liber H, Page 331

10 Aug 1680; Indenture from **Thomas Tiskerell**, tailor, and **Anne** his wife, to **Joshuah Graves**, planter; for 6,300# tobacco; a parcel of land of 200 acres being remainder of a tract containing 300 acres

called *Partnership*; /s/ Thomas Tinkerell; wit. Cleborne Lomax, Edmund Dennis

Liber H, Page 332

20 Mar 1679; Indenture from **John Mun**, planter, to **Richard Edelen** of St. Mary's Co.; for a certain sum of tobacco; a parcel called *Leverpoole*; bounded by *Tower Hills* on the east side of Potomac River, land called *Wadestone Inlargement*, and 300 acres laid out for Zachary Wade near Goose Bay; containing 250 acres; /s/ John Mun (mark); wit. Henry Aspenall (mark), Tho. Deberell (mark)

Liber H, Page 334

10 Aug 1680; Indenture from **Thomas Gerrard**, Gent., to **Richard Robinson**; for 4,000# tobacco; a tract of land called *Combe's Purchase*; on the west side of Wicomico main fresh adjoining land of John Coates; laid out for 150 acres; /s/ Tho. Gerard; wit. Tho. Lomax, Alexander Smith (mark), John Posey (mark)

Liber H, Page 336

10 Aug 1680; Indenture from **John Davis**, tailor, to **Lewis Jones**, planter; for 3,000# tobacco; a parcel called *St. John's*; within 2 miles of Zachary Wade on the north side of Potomac River; between 2 beaver dams; containing 100 acres; /s/ John Davis; wit. Daniell Mathena, Cleborne Lomax

Charles County Court
at Charles Town
commonly called Port Tobacco

Liber I
1680 - 1682

Liber I, Page 1

10 Aug 1680; **William Wells** acknowledges indenture of conveyance for a parcel called *Hard Frost* of 200 acres to **Thomas Allcock**

Liber I, Page 26

9 Aug 1679; Indenture from **Jno. Hamilton**, Gent., to **Jno. Gwyn**, planter, for 10,000# tobacco; a parcel of land surveyed by Wm. Lee, Gent., called *Es___*; containing 75 acres; /s/ Jno. Hamilton; wit. Jno. Harvey, Cleborne Lomax

Liber I, Page 33

8 Aug 1680; Indenture from **Jno. Douglas**, cooper, to **Lewis Jones**, planter; for 1,000# tobacco a parcel called *Douglas Adventure* of 100 acres; /s/ Jno. Douglas; wit. Robert Doyne, Rando. Brandt; ack. in open court by Jno. Douglas

Liber I, Page 77

1 Mar 1680; Indenture from **Jno. Lambert** to **Lewis Jones** for 500# of tobacco; 80 acres being part of 150 acres formerly belonging to Clement Theoboles on Plum Tree Point on the west side of Portobacco Creek; /s/ Jno. Lambert (mark); wit. Jno. Davis, Jno. Whitlocke, Richard Hodgson

Liber I, Page 78

1 Mar 1680; Deed of Gift from **Lewis Jones**, planter, to **Wm. Lambert**, s/o John Lambert; a tract of land on the west side of Portobacco Creek; if Wm. shd. die without heirs, to **John Lambert, Jr.**; if he shd. die without heirs, to **Elinor Lambert**, d/o John Lambert, Sr.; /s/ Lewis Jones (mark)

Liber I, Page 78

8 Mar 1680; Indenture from **Hugh French**, planter, to **Alexander Smith**, planter; for 15,000# tobacco 1/2 of a parcel of land of 800 acres called *Batchelors Harbour* on the east side of

Piscataway River about 2 miles from Piscataway Creek or Bog; /s/ Hugh French; wit. Tho. Lomax, Cleborne Lomax

Liber I, Page 80

8 Mar 1680; Indenture from **Henry Aspenall**, Gent., to **Edward Rookerd**, planter; for 15,000# tobacco a parcel of 200 acres of land called *Milersie* (?) lying on the south side of Chingamungen Creek; adjoining *Allonsons Folly*; also *Montagues Addition* containing 100 acres; also *Aspenalls Chance* of 200 acres bounded by land formerly surveyed for George Godfrey and *Montagues Addition*; /s/ Henry Aspenall (mark); wit. Thomas Witter, Cleborne Lomax; ack. in open court by Capt. Henry Aspenall and **Elizabeth** his wife

Liber I, Page 83

8 Mar 1680; Indenture from **Thomas Wharton**, planter to **Thomas Hussey**; for 2,000# tobacco a 150 acre parcel called *Woodberries Hope* on the north side of the Potomac River; located between land laid out for Jno. Delahay and 300 acres laid out for James Lee formerly known by name of the *Halfe Way Tree*; /s/ Thomas Wharton (mark); wit. Owen Newen, Jno. Richards

Liber I, Page 115

1 Apr 1681; Deed of Gift from **Jno. Faning**, Gent., to **Randll. Brandt**, Gent., for love and natural affection to my son **John Faning** and my daus. **Elizabeth Faning** and **Mary Faning**; all goods, chattels, plates and household stuff for proper use of my 3 children; /s/ Jno. Faning; wit. Tho. Burford, Jno. Gwyne; detail of items and cattle marks follows

Liber I, Page 122

1 Jun 1681; Gift from **Mary**, relict of **Jno. Payne**, dec'd, now wife of **George Godfrey**, to **William Ling**, s/o Francis and Mary Ling, one cow

1 Jun 1681; Deed of Gift from **Robert Thompson, Jr.** to **Anne Thompson** his mother-in-law, one heifer

Liber I, Page 123

13 Jun 1681; Deed of Gift from **Philip Hoskins** to **John Robins**; one sorrel mare; /s/ Philip Hoskins; wit. Jno. Cabioge (?) (mark), Thomas Hicks

Liber I, Page 125

5 Jun 1681; Indenture from **Edward Maddock**, apothecary, and **Margery** his wife, relict of **Matthew Stone**, to **William Chandler**, Gent.; a tract called *Cheshires* being part of *Poynton Manor*; inherited by Margery from the will of William Stone; containing 500 acres; for 40,000# of tobacco; /s/ Edward Maddock, Margery Maddock; wit. Tho. Hussy, John Richards

Liber I, Page 143

1 Jul 1681; Deed of Gift from Capt. **James Neale** to his son **Anthony Neale**; a horse called Trooper, a mare called Bonne with her foal; /s/ James Neale; wit. Tho. Burford, Tho. Marshall

Liber I, Page 144

9 Aug 1681; Indenture from **Joshuah Graves**, planter, to **John Paris**, presbyter; for 7,500# tobacco a parcel of 200 acres part of *Partnership* containing 300 acres; lately in joint tenure of Jno. Allward and Francis Hayden; /s/ Joshuah Graves; wit. Ho. Hussey, Cleborne Lomax

Liber I, Page 164

10 May 1681; Indenture from **Henry Bonner**, Gent., and **Elizabeth** his wife, to **James Tyer**, Gent.; for 4,000# tobacco a parcel of land called *Bonners Retirement*; bounded by *Coalchester*; laid out for 200 acres; /s/ Henry Bonner, Elizabeth Bonner; wit. Jacob Gregory, Tho. Bright (mark)

Liber I, Page 181

7 Nov 1681; Indenture from **Nicholas Skidmore**, tailor, to **John Posey**, carpenter; for 7,000# tobacco a 50 acre parcel of land at the head of Wicomico River called *Southbury*; bounded by John Courte's land called *Barnehill* and land of John Belamine; also *Aldgate* containing 41 acres; /s/ Nicholas Skidmore, Anne Skidmore; wit. Cleborne Lomax, Wm. Howell, Nicho. Belamine

Liber I, Page 184

29 Nov 1681; Indenture from Col. **William Chandler**, Gent., to **Richard Chandler**; for 40,000# tobacco a parcel called *Cheshire* on the Avon River, part of *Poynton Manor*; formerly

owned by Matthew Stone; containing 500 acres; /s/ Wm.
Chandler; wit. Ignatius Causin, Cleborne Lomax; ack. by
Mary Chandler, wife of William
Liber I, Page 186

29 Nov 1681; Indenture from **Richard Chandler**, Gent., to **Edward Maddock**, doctor; for 50,000# tobacco; a parcel of land on the Avon River called *Cheshire* of 500 acres; /s/ Richd. Chandler; wit. Ignatius Causin, Cleborne Lomax
Liber I, Page 188

23 Nov 1681; Indenture from **Tho. Dickinson** of Nanjemy, planter, and **Anne** his wife, to **James Finley**, planter; for a sum of tobacco; a parcel of land on the east side of Dickinson's land in Nanjemy Creek for 21 years; /s/ Tho. Dickinson, Anne Dickinson; wit. Tho. Burford, William Theobalds
Liber I, Page 214

30 Nov 1681; Indenture from **Josias Fendall** to **Henry Hawkins**, farmer; for 30,000# tobacco a parcel called *Fair Fountaine* on the west side of the main fresh at the head of Wicomico River; laid out for 1,000 acres; /s/ Josias Fendall, Henry Hawkins; wit. William Gwyther, Anthony Evans
Liber I, Page 225

9 Jan 1681; Indenture from **John Clarke**, Gent., to **Thomas Clarke** of St. Mary's Co., Gent.; for brotherly love and other causes, a parcel of land called *Clarke's Inheritance* containing 500 acres; /s/ John Clarke; wit. Richard Edelen, Tho. Allanson
Liber I, Page 227

10 Jan 1681; Indenture from **Thomas Clarke** of St. Mary's Co., Gent., to **John Godson**, planter; for a certain sum of tobacco a parcel called *Clarke's Inheritance*; /s/ Thos. Clarke; wit. Tho. Allanson, Richard Edelen
Liber I, Page 228

4 Jan 1681; Indenture from **William Wells** to **Thomas Allcox**; for 4,000# tobacco a parcel called *Hard Frost* on the south side of Piscataway River and Mattawoman Creek formerly laid out for Thomas Allanson; containing 200 acres; /s/ William Wells; wit. John Godshall, Tho. Allanson

Liber I, Page 259

8 Mar 1681; Indenture from **Robert Wheeler** to **Cuthbert Musgrove**; for 2,500# tobacco a parcel of land called *Shrewsberry* in Chingamuxon Creek; formerly laid out for John Hatch; bounded by land laid out for Thomas Allanson now in possession of Jno. Redish; containing 150 acres; /s/ Robert Wheeler (mark), Mary Wheeler (mark); wit. Tho. Allanson, Jno. Godshall

Liber I, Page 261

22 Feb 1681; Indenture from **John Lambert** to **Giles Collier**; for 3,800# tobacco a parcel being part of *Simpson's Supply* on the east side of Piscataway River and south side of Mattawoman Creek; bounded by Gerrard Browne; laid out for 100 acres; /s/ John Lambert (mark), Sarah Lambert (mark); wit. Tho. Allanson, Samuell Walton

Liber I, Page 294

10 Aug 1681; Indenture from **Nicholas Skidmore**, tailor, to **Elizabeth Wyne**; for 400# tobacco a parcel called *Skidmores Hope*; bounded by *Promise* now possessed by Richard Ashman; containing 12 acres; /s/ Nicholas Skidmore; wit. Geo. Groves (mark), Edw. Nibbs, William Howell

Liber I, Page 297

7 Dec 1681; Indenture from **Edward Rookwood**, planter, to **Thomas Hussy**, Gent.; for 20,000# tobacco a parcel called *Milerne* (?) containing 200 acres; also 200 acres *Mountague Mountaines* bounded by *Allansons Folly*; also 100 acres *Mountagues Addition*; also *Aspenall's Chance* of 200 acres bounded by *Milerne* (?) laid out for George Godfrey; /s/ Edward Rookwood; wit. Isaac Hall (mark), John Richards

Liber I, Page 300

7 Dec 1781; Indenture from **Thomas Hussey**, Gent., to **Edward Rookwood** for 20,000# tobacco a parcel of land on the east side of Piscataway River and north of Goose Bay of 150 acres; also *Fletcher's Addition* at Chingamungen containing 50 acres; /s/ Tho. Hussey; wit. John Clarke, John Richards

Liber I, Page 309

4 Jun 1682; Deed of Gift from **Elizabeth Wyne,** widow of *Burton* plantation, relict of **Francis Wyne**, dec'd. to her children, **Henry Wyne, Elizabeth Wyne,** and **Jno. Wyne** (not yet 21 years old), gift of cattle, goods and household stuff; /s/ Elizabeth Wyne (mark); wit. Meverell Hulse, Cleborne Lomax

Liber I, Page 318

30 Jun 1682; Indenture from **William Boyden,** planter, and **Elizabeth** his wife to **Tho. Gibson**; for 5,500# tobacco a parcel of land called *Maysemow*; bounded by Daniell Mathena, Mattawoman Creek, and land of George How___; containing 100 acres; /s/ William Boyden, Elizabeth Boyden; wit. Cleborne Lomax, William Theobalds; ack. in court by William and Elizabeth Boyden

Abstracts of Some
Miscellaneous Relationships
from
Libers C to I
1665-1688

Barton, child of William Barton, Jr., b. 25 Mar 1667 (C.251)
Barton, William, s/o William Barton Jr., b. 27 Feb 1667 (C.260)
Beade, Mary; d/o Nicholas (H.252)
Beade, Sarah; d/o Nicholas (H.252)
Belaine, Grace; orphan of John Blaiine (F.199)
Belaine, Nicholas, s/o John; chooses his bro.-in-law, John Posie, guardian (F.199)
Bonner, Henry, m. Eliz. Story, relict of Walter Story by 15 Nov 1665 (D.134)
Boyse, William; s/o John and Elenor Boyse; 1680 (H.329)
Brayne, Jane; d/o John Caine 1680 (H.292)
Brown, Gerrard m. to the relict of William Allen 1674 (F.10)
Browne, Elizabeth m. John Robinson 21 Mar 1666 (C.253)
Burdit, Elizabeth; d/o Thomas and Verlinda [reg. 1668] (C.271)
Burdit, Francis; d/o Thomas and Verlinda [reg. 1668] (C.271)
Burdit, Parthenia; d/o Thomas and Verlinda [reg. 1668] (C.271)
Burdit, Sarah; d/o Thomas and Verlinda [reg. 1668] (C.271)
Carr, Grace m. Geo. Mackmillion Jan 1669 (D.108)
Clarke, Veteres, d/o Robert, dec'd; age 5 (G.129)
Corner; child of Gilbert Corner, b. 4 Jun 1667 (C.251)
Cosleton, Marie, d/o Robert Cosleton, b. 6 Feb 1667 (C.260)
Dickason, Thomas, s/o Jeremy; chooses John Cable as guardian; Aug 1678 (H.1)
Douglas, Elizabeth; b. 6 Apr 1673; d/o John Douglas (E.126)
Farlor, William, s/o Ambrose Farlor, b. 15 Feb 1672 (E.166)
Fendall, Samuel; brother of Josias Fendall 1676 (F.194)
Godfrey, Thomas; s/o George and Mary; 1680 (H.292)
Godfrey, William; s/o George and Mary 1680 (H.292)
Harris, Richard; orphan of Richard Harris (H.330)
Harris, Susanna; orphan of Richard Harris chooses William Brown and Mary as guardians (H.330)

Harris, _____; orphan of Richard Harris; 1679 (H.330)
Hills, daughter of William Hills, b. 7 Aug 1667 (C.253)
Hunt, Alice m. Garret Synnet 21 Nov 1666 (C.253)
Hussey, Thomas m. relict of John Nevill by 15 Nov 1665 (D.134)
Izall, servant of William Marshall, bur. 31 Aug 1667 (C.251)
Kylborne, Francis, wife Eliza, court record 14 Mar 1670 (F.88)
Langhly, Mary, age 26, swore Thomas Pope father of her child (D.126)
Lindsey, Edmond, s/o Edmond, dec'd; custody of Wm. Chandler to age 21; Mar 1677/8 (G.129)
Ling, William; son-in-law of Richard Hall and natural born son of Mary his wife; 1680 (H.293)
Lomax, Katherine, d/o Cleborne and Blanche; b. 14 May 1677 (G.55)
Lumbrozo, John, s/o John Lumbrozo, dec'd, b. Jun 1666 (C266)
Mannister, Jno., dec'd; father of infant 1 1/2 yrs. old Jun 1681 (I.124)
Maris, Sarah, d/o Thomas Maris, b. 11 Nov 1667 (C266)
Mathena, Elizabeth; d/o George Mathena; 1680 (H.293)
Maycocke, Seabright, s/o Seabright Maycocke, d. 5 Sep 1674 (F.10)
Morrice, child; s/o Richard Morrice, b. 12 Sep, bur. 20 Sep 1667 (C.251)
Nevill, [Joan] m. Thomas Hussey by 15 Nov 1665 (D.134)
Obryan, Ellener, d/o Mathias Obryan, b. 5 Nov 1666 (C.222)
Payne, John; son-in-law of Geo. Godfrey; 1673/4 (E.152)
Pope, John, s/o Francis Pope, dec'd; choses Thomas Harris as guardian; 1676 (F.230)
Reason, Elizabeth; had a bastard; court of 12 Jun 1666 (C.30)
Rozer, Notley, s/o Benjamin Rozer, b. 1 Jul 1673 (D.140)
Smith, Alexander; m. _____ Belaine, widow of John Belaine; 1676 (F.199)
Smith, Richard, s/o Richard Smith, dec'd, choses William Hinsey guardian; 1676 (F.230)
Smoote, Richard; s/o Richard, dec'd; choose Richard Morris as guardian; 1679 (H.270)
Story, Elizabeth m. Henry Bonner by 15 Nov 1665 (D.134)
Turner, Anne bound apprentice to William Marshall to age 16 ; 1667-8 (C.244)
Turner, Arthur, eldest s/o Arthur Turner, chose Josias Fendall as guardian; 1667-8 (C.244)

Turner, Edward bound apprentice to James Bowling to age 21; 1667-8 (C.244)
Turner, female child of Arthur Turner, dec'd, b. ca mid-Oct 1667; to go to Susannah, wife of George Taylor as guardian (C.244)
Turner, James, second s/o Arthur Turner chose Walter Beane as guardian; 1667-8 (C.244)
Wade, child; s/o Zachery Wade, b. 22 Sep 1666 (C.222)
Warner, Christopher; wife Margaret (F.217)
Ward, John; s/o John Ward; b. 15 Mar 1674 (E.163)
Wharton, Elizabeth; d/o Thomas and Margaret Wharton (H.292)
White, Marie m. John Paine 23 Sep 1667 (C.253)
Wilkenson, William; servant of Wade, d. in Jun 1666 (C.222)
Worrell, Robert; wife Margaret; 1678 (H.55)
Wynne, Thomas; wife Elizabeth; 1670-6 (F.212)

Liber K
1682-1684

Liber K, Page 26

14 Nov 1682; Indenture from **Archibald Wahob**, planter, to **Philip Hoskyns** and Elizabeth his wife; for fatherly love and affection to his dau. **Elizabeth Hoskyns**, 1/2 of a parcel of land containing 400 acres purchased from Tho. King; bounded by land of Jno. Wheeler; /s/ Archibald Wahob (mark); wit. Cleborne Lomax, Wm. Theobalds

Liber K, Page 28

30 Aug 1682; Indenture from **Mary Mayrood**, late of Charles Co. now of Baltimore Co., widow, relict of **Seabright Mayrook**, to **Randolph Brandt**, Gent., for 1,600# tobacco a parcel of land called *Mayrooks Rest*; containing 85 acres; /s/ Mary Mayrook; wit. Henry Henly, Tho. Jones, Mith'll Judd

Liber K, Page 31

14 Nov 1682; Indenture from **David Thomas** of Stafford Co., Colony of Virginia, planter, to **Richard Jones**, planter; for good and diverse causes, a parcel called *Want Water*; bounded by Francis Adames' land called *Batchelors Hope*; containing 100 acres; /s/ David Thomas (mark); wit. Tho. Hussey, Francis Adams

Liber K, Page 32

Orphan **Henry Franckum**, s/o **Henry Franckum**, dec'd, remain and be with his father-in-law (?step-father) **Edward Maddock**

Liber K, Page 33

30 Nov 1682; Indenture from **Tho. Wakefeild**, planter, to **Paul Burrowes**, planter; for good causes, part of a tract of land formerly surveyed by Jonathan Maslee (?) now in possession of Wakefeild; containing 50 acres; /s/ Tho. Wakefeild (mark); wit. Rand. Brandt, Francis Sheifeild

Liber K, Page 44

4 Dec 1682; Indenture from **Daniell Mathena**, late of Charles Co., now of Stafford Co., Colony of Virginia, to **Nathan Barton** of Stafford Co., Virginia; for 12,000# tobacco, a 300 acre parcel of land called *Wentworths Woodhouse* on the north

side of Piscattaway River and south side of St. Thomas Creek; also a parcel called *Cow Land* of 28 acres; /s/ Daniell Mathena (mark), Sarah Mathena (mark); wit. Martin Scarlett, Ma_. Robinson

Liber K, Page 46

4 Dec 1682; Indenture from **James Ashbrook** to **Rich. Hodgson**, planter; for 2,500# tobacco 150 acres of land called *Layhay* on the Potomac River; /s/ James Ashbrooke (mark); wit. George Miller, Geo. Athy (mark), Jno. Gray (mark)

Liber K, Page 83

Edward Rookwood gave **Elizabeth Deberell**, d/o **Thomas** and **Anne Deberell** a cow and mare

9 Jun 1682; Gift from **Richard Chandler** to **Anne Chandler**, d/o **Wm. Chandler** a mulatto girl named Susanna

Liber K, Page 85

10 Oct 1682; Indenture from **John Pope**, planter to **Thomas Burford**, Gent.; for 10,000# tobacco; half the plantation where John Pope now dwells on the Potomac River; containing 200 acres; /s/ John Pope (mark); wit. Elinor Bayne (mark), Francis Mason, Wm. Dent

Liber K, Page 113

14 Jun 1682; Gift from **James Ashton** of Stafford Co., Virginia, to his godson, **James Makey**, s/o **James Makey**, ca Oct 1674 a yearling heifer

Liber K, Page 128

13 Mar 1682/3; Deed of gift from **John Courte, Sr.**, to **John Courte, Jr.**; a parcel of land called *Barnehill*; containing 150 acres; /s/ John Courte; wit. Robert Henley, Rando. Brandt, Jno. Francis (mark)

Liber K, Page 130

13 Mar 1682; Indenture from **Richard Wakelin** and **Mary** his wife to **Tho. Mitshell**, planter; for 2,500# tobacco a parcel called *Green Chase* at Nanjemy containing 200 acres; /s/ Richd. Wakelin (mark), Mary Wakelin (mark); wit. Jno. Faning, Hen. Hardy, Robt. Thompson

Liber K, Page 132

10 Oct 1681; Marriage agreement between **James Neale**, Gent. and **Wm. Rosewell** of St. Mary's Co.; intended marriage of Anthony Neale, s/o James Neale, and **Elizabeth Rosewell**, d/o William Rosewell; one month after the ceremony James Neale to convey one equal half of all his manor lands called *Wolleston Manor* patented for 2,000 acres; also 300 acres adjoining said manor; also 200 acres patented by Neale adjoining *Gills Land*; for the use of Anthony Neale for life; after that to his intended wife Elizabeth for her natural life after that for the use of the heirs of the body of the said Elizabeth; also 3 Negroes, two white hand, 20 head of cattle, ten ewes, a ram; Neale to be paid 5,000# of tobacco and 10 barrels of corn yearly for the term of his life and that of his wife; Rosewell to deliver to Anthony Neale one Negro man and his wife with his said daughter on or before Christmas day next and will pay Anthony 20,000# of tobacco on 10 Oct 1682 and 20,000# tobacco on 10 Oct 1683; /s/ James Neale, Wm. Rosewell; wit. Josh. Pile, Tho. Grunwin

Liber K, Page 170

28 Apr 1683; Indenture from **Josias Fendall**, Gent., and **Mary** his wife to **William Digges** of St. Mary's Co.; for 60,000# tobacco 14,000 acres on Wicomico River; two tracts both in possession of Walter Bayne and conveyed from Walter Bayne to Henry Fendall; also 50 acres granted John Franson, planter, with landing and liberty to build boats upon 40 acres; /s/ Josias Fendall, Mary Fendall; wit. William Dent, Richard Beaumont

Liber K, Page 173

17 Aug 1682; Indenture from **James Neale, Sr.**, Gent., and **Anne** his wife to **Anthony Neale**, s/o **James Neale**, and **Elizabeth** his wife, d/o **William Rosewell**; mentions Joseph Pile and William Boarman; 5 pages of a document relating to the marriage settlement between the Neale and Roswell families; /s/ James Neale, Ann Neale, Anthony Neale, Elizabeth Neale, William Rosewell, Joseph Pile, Wm. Boarman, Jr.; wit. Tho. Burford, Rando. Brandt, Tho. Grunwin

Liber K, Page 179

8 Jun 1683; Indenture from **John Godson**, planter, to **Philip Lynes**; for 20,000# tobacco a parcel called *Clarkes Inheritance* at the head of Mattawoman Creek; containing 500 acres; /s/ John Godshall, Sarah Godshall (mark); wit. Rot. Thompson, Jno. Faning, Mathew Sander (mark)

Liber K, Page 180

17 May 1683; Indenture from **Wm. Smoote**, planter, to **Thomas Smoote** his brother; for 10,000# tobacco a parcel of land formerly granted John Goldsmith of St. Mary's Co., lately deceased; lying on the west side of the Wicomico River; containing 150 acres; /s/ Wm. Smoote; wit. Hum. Warren, Francis Mason

Liber K, Page 181

25 May 1683; Indenture from **George Athee**, planter, and **Ann** his wife, to **James Martine**, planter; for 1800# tobacco and other considerations; *Hopewell* at the great Beaver Dan about 3 miles from Zachariah Wade; survey dated 17 Apr 1680 for 80 acres; /s/ George Athee (mark), Ann Athee (mark); wit. Tho. Wharton (mark), Wm. Dent

Liber K, Page 183

8 Jun 1683; Indenture from **Phillip Lynes** to **Mathew Sander**; for 10,000# tobacco a parcel of land formerly laid out for David Prishard on the south side of Piscataway River; adjoining land of David Thomas; containing 200 acres; /s/ Philip Lynes; wit. Robt. Thompson, Jno. Godshall, John Faning

12 Jun 1683; Gift from **Eliz. Marlow**, widow, to **Bur & Susanna Marlow**; a black heifer; /s/ Eliza. Marlow (mark)

Liber K, Page 185

5 Apr 1683; Bill of sale from **William Taylor** to **Thomas Ashbrook**, shoemaker, a bay mare; /s/ Wm. Taylor (mark); wit. Francis Adames, Wm. Newman

25 Jan 1682; More documentation regarding marriage settlement between s/o **James Neale** and d/o **William Rosewell**

Liber K, Page 219

14 7br 1682; Indenture from **Jno. Thompson** from London and Scotland, age 18, to **Robt. Henly** of London, merchant, service

for 5 years; for passage on *The Mary*, Capt. Jno. Harris, /s/ Robt. Hely; wit. Jno. Ingham. The ship *Mary and Ann* to any anchorage within the Capes of Virginia.

Liber K, Page 241

23 Oct 1684; **Jno. Wilkeson** sold a young heifer on behalf of **Garrett Synett, Jr.** to **Thomas Jenkins**; /s/ Jno. Wilkerson (mark); wit. Mary West (mark), Lewis Jones (mark)

11 Sept 1683; Indenture from **Thomas Shuttleworth**, planter, to **Thomas Hussey**, Gent.; for 7,000# tobacco a parcel called *Dourasler* (?) containing 200 acres; /s/ Thomas Shuttleworth; wit. Wm. Hulse, Jno. Richards

Liber K, Page 242

4 Aug 1683; Indenture from **Michaell Ashford**, carpenter, and **Rachell** his wife to **Jno. Butcher**; for 4,500# tobacco a parcel called *Tatshall* (?); bounded by land surveyed for Edmond Lynsey now in possession of James Smallwood; laid out for 40 acres; /s/ Michaell Ashford (mark), Rachell Ashford; wit. Rando. Brandt, Thomas Robinson

Liber K, Page 244

30 Aug 1683; Indenture from **Edward Mings**, planter, to **Wm. Pinner**; for 1,600# tobacco; a parcel of land on the Potomac River and the west side of *Watson's Marsh*; bounded by Ann Pinner; containing 30 acres; /s/ Edw. Mings, Wm. Pinner; wit. Michaell Webb (mark), Geo. Delahay (mark); ack. by Jeane Mings, wife of Edward

Liber K, Page 246

12 Nov 1683; Indenture from **Jno. Cane**, planter, and **Jno. Godshall**, planter, for 10,000# tobacco; a parcel called *St. Bridgetts* on the west side of Portobacco Creek; containing 200 acres; /s/ John Cane (thumb mark); wit. Rando. Brandt, _____ Thompson

Liber K, Page 249

21 Nov 1683; Indenture from **Wm. Barton**, Gent., and **Wm. Hungerford** to **Wm. Smoote**, planter; for indentures containing a parcel of land called *Johnsons* of 150 acres and land called *Smoots* of 250 acres; land on the west side of the Wicomico River at the head of Forked Creek bounded by

Humphery Attwicks and Tho. Mitchelll; containing 240 acres; /s/ Wm. Barton, Wm. Hungarford; wit. Jno. Barker, Cleb. Lomax, Jno. Godshall

Liber K, Page 251

21 Nov 1683; Quit Claim Deed from **Wm. Hungerford** to **Wm. Smoote** for tract called *Wicomico Fields;* bounded by Humphery Warren and Tho. Hatton on Forked Creek; laid out for 500 acres; /s/ Wm. Hungerford; wit. Humphrey Warren, Tho. Humfray, Tho. Warren

Liber K, Page 252

8 Oct 1683; Indenture from **Wm. Smoote**, planter, and **Humphery Warren**; for 7,000# tobacco a parcel called *The Hills* on the west side of the Wicomico River; bounded by Humphrey Attwicks; containing 240 acres; /s/ Wm. Smoote; wit. Tho. Smoote, Wm. Herbert (mark), Tho. Humfray

Liber K, Page 253

4 Jun 1683; Indenture from **Thomas Clipsham**, Gent., and **Susannah** his wife, to **Thomas Burford**, Gent.; for 4,000# tobacco; a parcel of land called *Mount Clipsham;* bounded by the Potomac River; containing 68 acres; /s/ Tho. Clipsham, Susannah Clipsham (mark); wit. Hum. Warren, Hen. Bonner

Liber K, Page 255

21 Nov 1683; Indenture from **Wm. Smoote**, planter, to **Wm. Hungerford**, planter, for **Wm. Barton**, Gent; an indenture for 240 acres to Wm. Smoote; to Hungerford a parcel called *Johnsons* adjoining 700 acres of land laid out for him and Richard Morris near Zachia Swamp; bounded by land laid out for Daniell Johnson called *Johnsons Choice* now in possession of Smoote; containing 250 acres; /s/ Wm. Smoote 2; wit. Hum. Warren, Tho. Humfray, Tho. Warren

Liber K, Page 271

5 Jan 1685; Indenture from **John Hamilton**, Gent., to **Philip Lynes**; for 2,000# tobacco a parcel of land on Nanjemy Creek in Potomac River between land of Tho. Burditt and Wm. Lewis; containing 100 acres; /s/ Jno. Hamilton; wit. Tho. Brown (mark), Edw. Greenhalgh

Liber K, Page 273
9 Sep 1682; Deed of Gift from **Wm. Nevill** to **Lydia Shuttleworth** a parcel of land in Nanjemy Creek called *Hornefaire* (?); contingent legatee Edw. Shuttleworth; children of Thomas Shuttleworth; /s/ Wm. Nevill; wit. Mathew Harmon (mark), Robert Castleton, Rich Hodgson

Liber K, Page 273
8 Jan 1683; Indenture from **Hugh Frensh**, planter, to **Philip Lynes**; for 8,000# tobacco; a parcel of land called *Barthelo_ Harbor*; located on the east side of Piscattaway River about two miles from Piscattaway Creek; containing 800 acres; /s/ Hugh Resnsh; wit. Daniell Murphy, Jno. Cossack (mark)
[*The remaining pages in this Liber appear to be water damaged which adds to the difficulty of reading the very tiny writing.*]

Liber K, Page 317
11 Mar 1683; Indenture from **Wm. Smith** to **Rando. Brandt**; land called *Thomas Town* on Piscattaway Creek and the south side of Mattawoman Creek; containing 200 acres; (barely able to read); /s/ Wm. Smith; wit. Nicholas Swinburne, Henry Hardy

Liber K, Page 318
8 Mar 1683; Indenture from ?**Roger Dickeson** to **John Munn**, planter; for 10,000# tobacco a parcel of land called *Little ?Crayner* (?) on the south side of Mattawoman Creek; bounded by 200 acres of land laid out for Walter ?Ball; laid out for ?200 acres; also 50 acres called *Hardshift*; /s/ Roger Dickeson (mark); wit. John Hoskins, Wm. Dent

Liber K, Page 336
22 May 1684; From **Parthema Burditt** and **Sara Burditt** to ?**Rich. Boughton** for 12,000# tobacco; cattle, hogs, household goods; /s/ Parthema Burditt (mark), Sara Burditt (mark); wit. Rich. Chandler, _____ Cooper

Liber K, Page 369
22 May 1684; Indenture from **Nicholas Skidmore**, tailor, to **Rich. Mason,** cooper; for 2,600# tobacco a parcel of land called *Low Land* adjoining Jno. Grubb, Charles Garrett; laid out for 100 acres; /s/ Nicholas Skidmore; wit. Wm. Smoote, Jno. Faning

Liber K, Page 370

28 Apr 1684; Indenture from **John Cane** to **Susannah Cane**, his daughter; mentions Potomac River, Portobacco Creek; appears to be part of a tract call *Blewplaines* by virtue of a grant to George Thompson transferred to Jno. Cane; /s/ Jno. Cane (mark); wit. Jno. Butterfield (mark), Giles Blizard

Liber K, Page 421

11 Mar 1683; Indenture from **James Neale**, Gent., and **Elizabeth** his wife, to **Giles Blizard** of the City of London; for £32.4 a parcel of land formerly surveyed by Capt. James Neale by a deed of gift from Wm. Calvert, Esqr., dec'd, and Elizabeth his wife and Capt. James Neale and Anne his wife, assigned James Neale, Jr. and Elizabeth his wife by deed of gift dated 4 Dec 1681; a tract of land on Piscattaway Creek called *St. James*; containing 700 acres; /s/ James Neale, Elizabeth Neale; wit. Jos. Doyne, Wm. Dove, Edw. Pye

Liber K, Page 424

30 Jul 1684; Indenture from **Robt. Goodrick**, planter, to **Geo. Henson**; for 4,000# tobacco a parcel of land called *Pomfrees*; adjoining land of John Wheeler called *Wheelers Adventure* and land formerly laid out for Thomas Matthews, Gent, being 1,000 acres; containing 150 acres; /s/ Robt. Goodrich; wit. Wm. Hall, Wm. Howell; Elizabeth Goodrick, wife of Robert, ack. deed

Liber L # 1
1684-1685

Liber L, Page 1

4 Aug 1684; Indenture from **John Caine**, Gent., to **Giles Blizard** of City of London; whereas marriage is intended between Giles Blizard and Susanna Cane, d/o John Cane; in consideration of this marriage, a parcel called *Blew Plane* formerly granted to Geo. Thompson; containing 1,000 acres; /s/ Jno. Cane; wit. Wm. Wells, Rich. Dodson Tho. Rigg

Liber L, Page 3

12 Aug 1684; Indenture from **Wm. Smoote**, planter, to **Sam'll Luckett** for 2,000# tobacco a parcel of land called *Johnsons Choyse*; bounded by land formerly laid out for Geo. Goodrick; containing 150 acres; /s/ Wm. Smoote; Wm. Theobalds; Jno. Richards

Liber L, Page 17

Peter Evans, age 25, of Derby, Woolcombey, contracts to serve **Richard Batts**; [unable to read]

Liber L, Page 48

30 Jan 1684; Deed of Gift from **George Graves**, planter, to **Philip Cole**, s/o Philip Cole, a cow

Liber L, Page 49

30 Nov 1684; Indenture from **Geo. Thompson** of St. Mary's Co. to **Richard Boughton**, Gent.; [can't read]; a parcel called *Square Adventure* of 100 acres; formerly surveyed for Geo. Goodrich; mentions Philip Lynes; /s/ Geo. Thompson; wit. Joshuah Graves, Ralph ___, Wm. Dent

Liber L, Page 51

26 Dec 1684; Indenture from **Jno Butcher** and **Mary** his wife to **Cornelius Maddocks**; for 5,000# tobacco a parcel called *?Talshell*; bounded by *Moredick*; mentions Ralph Shawe, Edmd. Lindsey, James Smallwood; containing 60 acres; /s/ Jno. Butcher (mark), Mary Butcher (mark); wit. Tho. Wheeler, Philip Hoskins

Liber L, Page 52

30 Feb 1684; Indenture from **Jno. Wheeler**, Gent., to **Robt. Middleton** and **Mary** his wife; for fatherly love and affection to his dau. Mary, wife of Robert Middleton, and her bodily heirs; a tract called *Wheeler's Hope* on Piscattaway Creek; laid out for 300 acres; /s/ Jno. Wheeler; wit. Phill. Hoskins, Cleborne Lomax

Liber L, Page 53

10 Nov 1684; Indenture from **Hugh Thomas** to **Jno. Harrison** of St. Mary's Co.; for 13,000# tobacco; a tract called *Rich Hill* containing _00 acres; also a parcel called *Thomases Additions* containing 83 acres; bounded by *Rich Hall*; /s/ Hugh Thomas, Jno. Harrison; wit. Wm. Barton, Henry Hawkins

Liber L, Page 56

7 Nov 1684; Indenture from **Edw. Smoote**, carpenter, to **Humphrey Warren**; for 4,000# tobacco a parcel of land called *Smootes Purchase* of 100 acres; /s/ Edw. Smoote (mark); wit. Wm. Harcutt, Tho. Warren

Liber L, Page 81

13 Mar 1683; Indenture from **Wm. Davis**, Gent., to **Edward Frawver**; for diverse good causes and considerations; a parcel of land called *Prises Adventure*; bounded by land of David Thomas on the north side of the Potomac River; containing 200 acres; /s/ Wm. Davis; wit. Jno. Bayne, Sam'll Fendall

Liber L, Page 132

1 Mar 1684; Indenture from **Humphery Aspinall** of London, England, to **Eliz. Swinborne**; for 3,000# tobacco; a parcel of land called *Allansons Folly*; granted Tho. Allenson "doth appear 300 acres of the divident being in possession of Tho. Alcock"; also land called *Wicksall* on the south side of Chingamoxon Creek of 100 acres; /s/ Humphery Aspinall; wit. Tho. Husse, Jno. Hoskins

Liber L, Page 134

9 Mar 1684; Indenture from **Jno. Lemaire**, surgeon, to **Jno. Cassock**; for 900# tobacco a parcel of land called *Hispanola*; bounded by Nathaniel Barbour, *Rich Hills*; containing 100

acres; /s/ Jno. Lemaire, Margaret Lemaire; wit. Cornelius Maddock, Tho. ____

Liber L, Page 136

25 Dec 1685; Indenture from **Thomas Gaven** of Portobacco to **Richard Boughton** of Nanjemy; [can't read]; mentions Portobacco Creek, Indian Cabbin; containing 400 acres; /s/ Richard Boughton, Tho. Gavin; wit. John Land, Josias Hawkins

Liber L, Page 137

25 Dec 168_; Indenture from **Richard Boughton**, Gent., to **Ralph Bartlett;** a certain parcel of land "lying in St. Thomas his manor" containing 400 acres lately in occupation of Hugh Moungurrah, dec'd now left Richard Boughton; /s/ Ralph Bartlett, Richard Boughton; wit. Sam'll Boughton, Ja. Lee (mark)

Liber L, Page 139

25 Dec 1685; Indenture from **Henry Moore**, planter, to **Jno. Boyer**, planter; 100 acres of a tract of land of 200 acres called Ma_____ left by will of "my dec'd father Henry Moore" to be equally divided between Henry Moore and **Elizabeth Moore**; /s/ Henry Moore (mark); Wm. Theobalds, Chriso. Farmer (mark)

Liber L, Page 140

19 Feb 1684; Indenture from **Edward Maddock** of Stafford Co., Virginia, surgeon, and **Margery Maddock** his wife, to **Gerard Fowke**, Gent.; for 440 acres of land in Stafford Co., a tract in Nangemy of 500 acres where Edward and Margery Maddock lately dwelled; willed by Capt. Wm. Stone to Mathew Stone; from Mathew to Margery [his wife]; /s/ Edw. Maddock, Margery Maddock; wit. Ralph Elkins, Wm. Dent

Liber L, Page 175

10 Jul 1684; Indenture from **Thomas Hussey**, Gent., to **Richard Harrison**; for 1400# tobacco a parcel of land called *Woodberry's Hope*; lying between 300 acres laid out for Jno. Dellahay and land of James Lee called *Half Way Tree*; containing 150 acres; /s/ Tho. Hussey; wit. Jno. H____, Joshuah Graves

Liber L, Page 176

1 Feb 1682; Indenture between **Jno. Lawrence** and **Michell Ashford**; Ashford to be apprenticed for 5 years; /s/ Jno. Lawrence; wit. Tho. Hussey, Jno. Richards

Liber L, Page 177

27 May 1684; Indenture from **Jno. Delahay**, planter, to **Richd. Harrison**; for 1,500# tobacco; a tract called *Delahay Chance* on the north side of the Potomac; bounded by ____ Watson; laid out for 300 acres; /s/ Jno. Delahay (mark); wit. Edw. Mings, Geo. Delahay (mark)

Liber L, Page 178

11 Aug 1685; Indenture from **Jno. Wheeler**, Gent., to **Jno. Speaks** and **Winifred** his wife, d/o Jno. Wheeler; a parcel of land called *Plimoth* on a fresh of the Piscattaway River; containing 350 acres; /s/ Jno. Wheeler (mark); wit. Ignatius Causcene, Wm. Barton

Liber L, Page 179

10 Jul 1685; Indenture from **Eliz. Young**, widow, to **Joseph Corvell**; for 9,000# tobacco; a parcel of land called *Dover*; bounded by Wm. Worrell and the Potomac River; containing 200 acres; /s/ Eliz. Young; wit. Edmd. Dennis; Richd. Edline

Liber L, Page 182

9 Jul 1685; From **Elizabeth Young** of St. Mary's Co., widow, for 20s, to **Wm. Worrell** a tract of land being part of a parcel called *Dover* on the Potomac containing 100 acres; /s/ Eliza. Young; wit. Edmd. Dennis, Richard Edelen

Liber L, Page 183

8 Sep 1685; Indenture from **Nicholas Skidmore**, tailor, and **Ann** his wife, to **Robt. Hagar** of St. Mary's Co.; for 6,000# tobacco; a parcel of land called *Skidmore Rest*; bounded by land of Jno. Beloyne called *Burloyne Hill*; containing 80 acres; /s/ Nicholas Skidmore, Ann Skidmore; wit. Jno. Hawkins, Cleb. Lomax

Liber L, Page 185

8 Sep 1684; Indenture from **Robt. Hagar** of St. Mary's Co. to **Geo. Gover**; for 6,000# tobacco; a parcel of land called

Skidmore Rest; laid out for 80 acres; /s/ Robt. Hagar, Mary Hagar (mark); wit. Jno. Hawkins, Cleborne Lomax

Liber L, Page 187

10 Apr 1685; Indenture from **Jno. Barker**, planter, and **Joane** his wife; to **Wm. Dent**; for 5,500# tobacco; a plantation where sd. Barker now dwells called *Barker's Rest*; 150 acres by patent dated 1 Jun 1673 recorded at St. Mary's; /s/ Jno. Barker, Joane Barker; wit. Geo. Graves (mark); Jno. ?Carney

[At the end of of the court records of Liber L there is a summary of Proprietary Acts such as punishment for counterfeiting the Great Seal of Lord Baltimore and regulations for various activities. Following this is a volume also titled Liber L [no number] dated 1677 titled *Perpetual Laws of Maryland*. This contains acts relating to goods, indentures, pagans, religion, Indian lands, war, cattle and hog marks, adultery, deserted plantations, setting up a mint, purchasing, etc. - Microfilm CR35,691]

Acts of Naturalization

Jno. Garbor & others	1666
James Neal	1666
Dymossa and others	1673
Mathias Decosta	1671
Hans Hanson & others	1671
John Johnson & Henry Greane	1674
John Long of London, merchant	1674
Jacob Dulsstatway & others	1674

CATTLE MARKS, Libers C - L (1665-1685)

Abbot, Thomas	1667		Bonner, Henry	1679
Adames, John [Indian]	1680		Booth, John	1680
Addames, Francis	1666		Boswell, John	1667
Addames, Henry	1666		Boswell, John	1672
Alcock, Thom.	1669		Boswell, Mathew [s/o Jno]	1672
Allcock, Mary	1682		Boyden, John	1667
Allcock, Tho., Jr.	1682		Boyden, Mary	1682
Allen, John	1671		Boyden, Mary [d/o Jno]	1673
Allonson, Thomas	1667		Boyse, Elizabeth	1682
Allward, John	1672		Boyse, William	1680
Ashbrooke, James	1677/8		Bracener ?, Henry	1682
Ashbrowke, Tho.	1669		Brandt, Randolph	1676
Ashman, Elizabeth	1677/8		Brasher, John	1680
Ashman, Richard	1677/8		Brayner, Henry	1683
Aspenall, Capt. Henry	1680		Browne, Gerrard	1667
Aspinoll, Henry, Jr.	1669		Bulloit, Joseph	1672
Athy, Geo.	1672		Burford, Thomas	1682
Bailies, Tho.	1672		Burnam, William	1675
Baker, Thomas	1678		Burnham, Jno.	1682
Barbous, Wm.	1683		Burnham, Sam	1682
Barker, Will, Jr.	1672		Burnham, Wm.	1682
Barker, William	1669		Bushere, John	1673
Barnes, Henry	1667		Cable, John	1678
Bartlett, Ralph	1677/8		Caine, John	1680
Barton, George	1680		Caldwell, George	1672
Barton, Nathan	1668		Carpenter, Richard	1676
Barton, Wm [s/o Nath.]	1668		Carr, Peter	1675
Barton, Wm. Jr.	1667/8		Carson, Sarah	1672
Bayly, Thomas	1673		Cassock, John	1675
Beade, Nicholas	1679		Chaireman, John	1669
Benson, Robert	1673/4		Chandler, Richard	1675
Bezick, John	1669		Chandler, Richard	1676/7
Bissell, Mary	1672/3		Chandler, Will	1672
Blumstead, John	1673		Chandler, William	1680
Bond, John	1667		Chandler, Wm. [s/o Jobe]	1680

Clarke, John	1681
Clarke, Thomas	1676
Clarke, Vet____ (d/o Robt.)	1681/2
Clements, John	1678
Coates, Thomas	1676/7
Colliar, Gyles	1678
Coomes, Eliza. (d/o Philip)	1682
Cooper, Edward	1667/8
Cooper, Joseph	1668
Cooper, Mary [d/o Jos.]	1668
Cooper, Nicholas	1683
Cooper, Walter	1668
Corner, Gilbert	1667
Cornish, John	1679
Coslinton, Jno.	1683
Cox, James	1681
Craxon, Sarah	1672
Credwell, George	1672
Cressey, Samuell	1669
Crouch, Edward	1681
Cullis, Charles	1678
Cunney, John	1685
Cunnoy, John	1678
Cutler, Elizabeth	1667
Cutler, Samuel	1667
Cuttler, Margaret	1667/8
Davies, Walter	1677/8
Davis, John	1678
Degregor, Jno.	1684
Dent, John	1666
Deverell, Elizabeth	1682
Dixon, Thomas	1678
Douglas, Charles	1680
Douglas, Elizabeth	1680
Douglas, John	1673
Douglas, Joseph	1680
Douglas, Robert	1680
Douglas, Sarah	1680
Douglas, Sarah [d/o Jno]	1673
Dunstan, John	1669
Elsey, Thomas	1667
Everite, Francis	1673
Faelor, Ambrous	1672
Fanning, John	1675
Fanning, John	1677
Farloe, Amborus	1672
Faulkner, Jno.	1680
Fendall, Samuel	1669
Fendall, Tho.	1672
Fernandos, Peter	1682
Fernandos, Wenefrett	1682
Fernson, John	1672
Fershing, Jno.	1672
Fletcher, Henry	1669
Fox, James	1675
Frawners, Henry	1683
Furnase, Elizabeth	1682
Gardiner, Hugh	1682/3
Gardner, Jno. (mulatto)	1681
Glyn, Francis	1667
Godfrey, George	1680
Godfrey, George, Jr.	1681
Godfrey, William	1680
Godson, John	1667
Goodge, John	1666
Goomes, John	1679
Gramboe, Domingoe	1678
Graves, Joshuah	1680
Graves, Sam'll	1683
Gray, John	1678
Green, Luke	1669
Greene, Francis	1675
Greene, Robert	1673
Groves, George	1677/8

Name	Date
Grub, John	1673/4
Gwirlye, Jno.	1672/3
Hall, Mary (relict of Richard)	1680
Hall, Richard	1678
Hall, Richard	1682/3
Hamer, Susannah	1676
Hamman, John	1676/7
Hanson, John	1673
Hanson, John	1675
Harguess, Tho.	1685
Harmon, Mathew	1667
Harrington, John	1667/8
Harris, Samuel	1667
Hatton, Thomas	1676
Haughton, Joseph	1667
Hawkins, Elizabeth	1682
Hawkins, Henry	1669
Hay, James	1674
Helgar, Thomas	1676
Helm, John	1669
Henley, Henry	1677
Henley, Henry	1679
Henshall, Thomas	1667
Henson, Thomas	1667
Hereman, John	1669
Heydon, Francis	1672
Hinson, Geo.	1672
Holmes, John	1667
How, Richard	1681
Hulse, James (s/o Meverell)	1682
Hunter, William	1682/3
Hussey, Johannah	1673
Hussey, Thomas	1673
Hussy, Johannah (w/o Thos.)	1681
Hutchinson, John	1668
Jackson, William	1678
Jenkins, Eliz. [d/o Tho]	1673/4
Jenkins, Mary [d/o Tho]	1673/4
Jenkins, Thomas	1671
Jenkins, Thomas	1673/4
Jenkins, William	1668
Johnstone, Anne	1682
Johnstone, Henry	1682
Jones, Eliz. [d/o Owen]	1673/4
Jones, Joanna	1667
Jones, Owen	1667
Jones, Owen, Jr.	1673/4
Jones, Richard	1667
Jones, Richard	1672
Jones, Thomas	1676
Jones, Walter	1676
Kennedie, Jeremie	1668
Kersey, Thomas	1677/8
King, Thomas	1673
Kirkley, Christopher	1682
Knight, Edward	1681
Lambert, Elisa.	1672
Lambert, Ellinor	1672
Lambert, John	1672
Lambert, Josias	1672
Lambert, Richard	1672
Lambeth, Edmund	1667
Lambton, Marke	1676/7
Lee, John	1667
Lemaire, John	1675
Leman, Jno.	1683
Lewger, John	1666
Lindsey, Edmond	1666
Ling, Francis	1680
Ling, Michaell	1680
Ling, Wm. [s/o Francis]	1671
Lomax, Cleborne	1676/7
Lomax, Thomas	1674
Long, Jemima	1667

Long, Robert [1660 error]	1667	Neale, James	1682/3
Love, William	1668	Newby, Jno.	1681
Love, William	1669	Newton, Jo., Jr.	1669
Lyndsey, Edmund	1667	Norton, Hamond	1667
Lynes, Philip	1673	Norton, Hamond	1676
Maddox, Edward	1672	Norton, Hamond	1679
Madgely, Rich.	1672	Parke, John	1679
Maglouglin, Kelham	1672	Parker, Jo.	1668
Maris, Sarah [d/oThos.]	1668	Parker, Jos.	1677/8
Marloe, John [s/o Wm.]	1678	Parker, Thomas	1669
Marsh, Gilbard	1682	Parker, Wm. [s/o Jo.]	1668
Marshiguay, Benj.	1669	Payne, John	1673/4
Maryes, Thomas	1673/4	Pen, William	1680
Maston, Richard	1680	Perkins, Robert	1667
Maston, Robert [s/o Rich.]	1680	Peterson, Jacob	1667
Mathena, Daniel	1680	Pinnar, Amos	1670
Mathena, Daniell	1672/3	Pinnar, Ann	1670/1
Mathena, Daniell	1676	Pinnar, Richard	1670
Mathena, Elizabeth	1680	Pinnar, William	1670
Mathena, Sarah [d/o Dan.]	1672	Pinner, Richard	1666
Maud, Isaac	1680	Plea, Jacob	1669
Middleton, Robert	1675	Polter, Matthew	1678
Midgely, Rich.	1672	Posey, John	1674
Millar, John	1667	Potts, Robert	1680
Miller, Francis	1683	Powell, George	1675
Miller, John	1678	Price, Edward	1667
Minocke, Michaell	1674	Price, John	1669
Moore, Henry	1667	Prodday, Nicholas	1675
Moore, Henry	1669	Randall, Richard	1667
Morrise, John	1669	Raspin, Samuel	1680
Mould, Barbara (d/o John)	1676	Roberts, John	1667/8
Mould, John	1676	Robinson, Jno. Jr.	1672
Munkister, James	1673/4	Robinson, John	1667
Munkister, James	1676	Robinson, Richard	1678
Muns, John	1666	Rozer, Benjamin	1672
Musgrave, Cuthbert	1678	Saunder, John	1676/7
Neale, Anthony	1682	Saunders, Matthew	1677

Selby, Nicholas	1672		Ward, William	1674
Sherwood, Francis	1672		Warner, Elizabeth	1672
Shuttleworth, Thomas	1672		Warner, Tho., Jr.	1672
Simson, Geo.	1672		Warren, Capt. Humph.	1678
Sinnett, Catherine	1681/2		Warren, Eliza.	1672
Sinnett, Mary	1681/2		Warren, Ellinor	1671
Sinnett, Robert	1681/2		Warren, Hump., Jr.	1666
Smith, George Geer	1679		Warren, Humphry	1671
Smith, John	1669		Warren, Humphry	1673
Smith, John	1682		Waye, Richard	1678
Smith, John	1683		Wayneman, Rice	1672
Smoote, Thomas	1682		Webber, Thomas	1674
Snow, Christopher	1669		Wells, Henry	1668
Soute ?, Wm.	1682		Wells, William	1678
Standish, Alexander	1678		Welsh, Jason	1678
Steed, Thomas	1666		Wentworth, d/o Francis	1672
Stephens, Simon	1677/8		Wharton, Elizabeth	1680
Stephens, Symon	1680		Wharton, Margaret	1672
Tanshall, Edward	1676		Wharton, Margaret	1680
Tanshall, Edward	1679		Wharton, Thomas	1673
Tanshall, Jno. (s/o Edward)	1681		Wharton, Thomas	1680
Tanshall, Thos. (s/o Edward)	1681		Wheeler, James	1680
Taylor, Edmond	1672		Wheeler, Robert	1678
Taylor, William	1679		Wheeler, Thomas	1680
Theobalds, William	1682		Wilkinson, Jno.	1681/2
Thomas, David	1673		Wilkinson, Lancellott	1680
Thomas, William	1676		Williams, John	1685
Thompson, Robert	1675		Willson, Thomas	1681
Tiskerell, Thomas	1677		Wine, Francis's dau.	1672
Towell, David	1676		Witter, Thomas	1673/4
Trew, Priscilla	1681		Wolph, Mary (d/o Joseph)	1682
Twiggs, John	1673/4		Wood, John	1676
Tylly, James	1679		Wood, Mary (d/o John)	1676
Vassall, Leny	1680		Woodard, John	1666
Vos, Richard	1677		Woodard, John	1669
Wakelin ?, Richard	1682		Worland, John	1672/3
Walters, John	1669		Wright, John	1676

Servants and Masters
Libers C - L (1665-1685)

Servant	Age	Master	Date
Abbott, Susanne	20	Philip (& Margaret) Simes	1680
Abis, Matthew	18	William Smith	1678
Acres, John,	13	Jeremiah Dickeson	1673
Adames, Edwd.	17	Jacob Morris	1682
Ailer, Elizabeth	20	Francis Wyne	1679/0
Alden, Mary	21	John Dent	1677/8
Aldis, William	10	Owen Jones	1675
Allinson, Annabella	17	Philip Lines	1677
Anderson, Lawrence	20	William Boreman	1671
Anderson, Railph	20	Railph Shaw	1674
Anglish, John	16	Arthur Turner	1676/7
Armstrong, Richard	19	Wm. Barton	1669
Attchison, George	16	John Paine	1668
Attkins, William	17	Robert Henley	1674/5
Aunley, James	13	Tho. Speeke [St. M. Co.]	1678
Aushish, William	13	James Tyre	1676
Bacoke, John	15	Anne Fowke	1674/5
Bailey, Grace	20	Henry Towne	1678
Baily, William	14	Robert Middleton	1676
Baiteman, Patrick	17	Wm. Chandler	1679
Ball, Margaret	18	Mr. Young	1673
Ball, Thomas	17	Ignatius Causine	1668
Bard, Peter	18	Robert Henley	1672
Barker, John	15	Jeremiah Dickinson	1670
Barker, Robert	21-22	Daniell Johnson	1669
Barlow, Joel	12	James Neale, Jr.	1671
Barnes, Edward	[serve 4 yrs.]	William Chandler	1673/4
Baron, Richard	15	Humphrey Warren, Jr.	1666
Barrett, John	14	Michael Minork	1678
Barrett, John	15	William Smith	1676/7
Barrett, Wm.	20	Ignatius Causin	1681/2

Barrow, John	15	William Hatch	1679
Barton, George	21-22	Zachary Wade	1673/4
Barton, Robert	21	Wm. Boareman	1682
Batherton, John	12	Edward Prise	1673
Battle, Anthony	16	John Okeane	1669
Bawlding, Mary		Wm. Marshall	1668
Bawlding, Robert	21	Robert Henly	1668
Bayly, Nicholas	16	Ignatius Causine	1673
Bell, Bridgett	16	Maj. Jno. Wheeler	1679
Bell, Elizabeth	21	Robert Henley	1678
Bellingham, Alise	16	Robert Henley	1674/5
Bene ?, Thomas	17	Tho. Gerrard	1680
Bennett, John	20	Hugh French	1674/5
Bennett, Mary	20-21	Edward Price	1673/4
Bennett, Mary	22	Henry Hardy	1679
Benson, John	11	Mr. Prouce	1669
Berry, Elizabeth	14	Thomas Baker	1681/2
Berry, John	17	Ralph Shaw	1685
Binningham, Mary	12	Matthew Hill	1674/5
Bishop, Will	15	James Walker	1671
Bonner, Mary	20-12	Edward Prise	1673
Booker, John	18	Alexander White	1673/4
Bourd, Jane	17	John Wood	1678
Bowing, William	26	Archiball Wahob	1667
Bradshaw, Thomas	20	John Paine	1669
Bridgets, Elizabeth [to age 18]	9	mother Michle	1669
Bright, Edward	12	James Smallwood	1678
Bright, Thomas	21	Mr. Young	1669
Broadhead, Anne		John Thompkinson	1671
Brooke, Thomas	11	John Lambert	1673/4
Brookes, Hen.	19	Mr. Beane	1673
Broonely, Thomas	21	Edmond Lindsey	1669
Browne, Tho.	16	Peter Car	1681/2
Browne, Thomas	18	John Fanning	1675
Bruxbanke, Abraham	15	William Hatch	1679
Bull, William	18	John Goosh	1679
Burkhaine, John	15	Jeremiah Dickinson	1670

Busklow, Benjamin	9	Tho. Mitchell	1681/2
Campton, Christopher	16	Philip Lines	1681
Canland, John	16	Capt. John Wheeler	1678
Capshaw, Francis	15	Alexander Smith	1674
Carey, Hugh	14	Edward Prise	1678
Carpenter, Christopher	12	James Smallwood	1681/2
Carpenter, Henry	16	William Porfit	1676
Carreddale, Thomas	16-17	Capt. Boareman	1669
Cartie, Demud Mack	13-14	Rice Jones	1667
Caryl ?, Richard	17	Richard Wade	1685
Cathew, Christopher	14	Philip Lines	1682
Cayne, James	12	Richard Beck	1673/4
Chaplin, Thomas	11	Garratt Sinnett	1675/6
Chapman, George	22	Benjamin Rozer	1671
Chew, Edith	14	Garrett Synet	1667
Chomley, Francis	16	Henry Adams	1669
Clarke, Anne [d/o Robt. & Mary; to age 16]		Mathew Stonehill	1675/6
Clarke, Beteres [d/o Robt. & Mary; to age 16]		Richard Midgeley	1675/6
Clarke, James	13	Richard Edelen	1671
Clarke, Mary [d/o Robt. & Mary; to age 16]		Henry Hawkins	1675/6
Clarke, Robert [s/o Robert & Mary; to age 21]		John Allward	1675/6
Clarke, Susannah [d/o Robt. & Mary; to 16]		Robt. Thompson	1675/6
Clary, Morris	18	Owen Newen	1681/2
Cobb, Sam.	15	Tho. King	1669
Collingwood, Robert	21	Robert Clarke	1671
Collins, Alise	21-22	Robert Robins	1673
Cooper, John	15	Capt. William Barton	1678
Cooper, Roger	16	Wm. Hinsey	1678
Cooper, Thomas	15	Richard Randall	1667
Cornute, Hendrick	20	John Okeane	1669
Cornwall, Francis (f)	20	Thomas Jenkins	1681/2
Cottwell, James	16	Thomas Gerrard	1676/7
Court, Cleat.	17	Daniell Johnson	1668
Crips, Nicholas	[serve ? yrs.]	Richard Fowkes	1673/4
Cumpton, William	17	John Hatch	1675/6
Cunningham, George	16	Alexander Smith	1671
Curtis, John	16	Francis Wine	1674

Dallyson, Mary		Thomas Mason of VA	1680
Damer, Tho.	17	John Cage	1668
Damer, Thomas	[for 4 yrs. to1668]	Thomas Tolson	1672
Daverill, Thomas	20	Thomas Dent	1669
Davies, Alise	19	Thomas Howell	1675
Davies, Griffith	17	Nicholas Prodday	1675
Davies, James	16	John Ward	1669
Davies, William	6	John Stone	1672
Davis, Jno.	13	Humphry Warren	1673/4
de Creyger, John	[bound Holland 1663; freed]	James Neal	1671
Deakons, Tho.	11	Henry Bonard	1668
Dickeson, Thomas	18-19	Thomas Harrison	1676/7
Dickson, Elizabeth	20	Cleborne Lomax	1679
Dike, Mathew	20	Mathew Stone	1671
Divell, James	14	Thomas Stone	1670
Dods, Thomas	12	Robert Henley	1674/5
Dolton, Richard	18	Richard Chandler	1678
Donohau, Cornelius	19	Tho. Hussey	1685
Donohau, Fincene		Tho. Hussey	1685
Dosett, Edward	21	Humphrey Warren	1676
Doughty, Robert	15	John Ward	1669
Dover, Christopher	20	Thomas Mathews	1673/4
Downes, Elizabeth [d/o Robt.]	10	John Wright	1678
Dunn, Isaac	14	John Hatch	1673/4
Duppe, Thomas	15	Alexander Smyth	1667
Eason, John	11	Humphrey Warren	1678
Eaton, Thomas	18	Thomas Clipsham	1679
Edge, Thomas	17-18	Zachary Wade	1673/4
Edwards, John	12	Margarett Mark Cormack	1676/7
Ellis, Hugh	13	Francis Goodricke	1674/5
Ellis, Thom.		William Barton	1668
Ellison, John	16	Samuell Cressey	1675/6
Enibruson, Drick	14	Capt. James Neale	1668
Eniburson, Christopher	16	Capt. James Neale	1668
Ennis, David	16	Tho. Hussey	1685
Eure, Christopher	19	William Marshall	1668
Evans, Joan		Josias Fendall	1682/3

Farmer, Rice	16	John Allen	1673
Farrow, James	15	John Ward	1673/4
Farrows, James	15	Richard Book	1674
Fenner, Thom.	19	Samuel Eaten	1669
Fernandez, Pedro	17	Capt. James Neale	1668
Field, Charles	20	Maj. Wm. Boareman	1680
Fire, Ralph	20	Thomas Taylor	1678
Fish, Elinor [bound to age 21]	3	Seabright Maycocke	1674
Fisher, Elisabeth	16	James Smallwood	1677
Fletsher, Catherine		Philip Lines	1681/2
Fortas, Margrett	19	Richard Fowke	1674
Fowler, William	14	William Boarman	1677/8
Fowtrell, George	22-23	Richard Edelen	1676
Francisson, Francis	10	Benj. Rozer	1668
Franckum, Francis	16	William Barton	1676
Galey, Edward	[return to work]	Thomas Matthews	1674
Galey, Loranso	14	Capt. James Neale	1675
Garett, James [s/o James]	7	Thomas Chysham	1680
Gaskoyne, Sam.	17	John Wheeler	1669
Gateley, Edward	13	Thomas Harris	1678
German, Geo.	21	Wm. Barton	1669
Ghogh, Jane	20	Jom. Harguess	1678
Gibbs, John	19	Peter Carr	1668
Gibson?, Dorothy	22	Benjamin Rozer	1673
Gilbard, James	21	Philip Lines	1679
Ginney, John	14	John Ward	1671/2
Gloover, George	21	Capt. James Neale	1680
Glover, Mary	20	Thomas Hussy	1679
Goddard, George		Tho. Gibson	1682
Golbard, James		Philip Lines	1681/2
Gosh, Richard	15	Joseph Bullott	1677/8
Graves, Thomas	16	Jno. Vaudry [St. M. Co.]	1678
Gray, Ruth	21	Richard Edelen	1676
Gray, Ruth		Henry Bonner	1678
Green, John	14	Benjamin Rozer	1668
Green, Richard	17	John Allen	1673
Greene, James	15	Benjamin Rozer	1673/4

Greyden, Margaret	22	Henry Bonner	1671
Griffin, Robert	17	Henry Goodrich	1681/2
Grosser, Mary	18-20	Peter Carr	1673/4
Groube ?, Richard	13	Joseph Manninge	1680
Gryer, John	20	Rise Williams	1682
Gutridge, James	15	Philip Lines	1681/2
Hagar, Wm.	14	Tho. Baker	1668
Hall, Charles	22	Edward Ming	1682
Hall, Isack	13	Henry Bonard	1668
Hall, John	18	William Hensly	1673/4
Hall, Margrett	18	Mrs. Young	1673
Hall, William	17	Thomas Speeke	1675/6
Hammonds, John	15	Jeremiah Dickenson	1667
Hanns ?, Jno.	21	Alexander Smith	1681
Harris, Jane	20	Richard Jones	1676
Harrison, Anne	20	William Barton, Jr.	1674
Harrison, Robert	13	Alexander Smith	1674
Haselton, Elizabeth		Nicholas Emerson	1666
Hatherton, John	12	Edward Price	1673/4
Hawkins, John		Philip Lines	1681/2
Hayles, Mary	20	Mr. Wade	1670
Hayward, John [s/o Phillis; for 21 yrs.]		William Barton	1668
Haywood, Mary	12	Thomas Jenkins	1681/2
Hendall, Francis	14	John Newton	1676
Hensely, Edward	17	John Bowles	1673/4
Herbert, John	18	Humphrey Warren	1676/7
Herbert, William	17	Robert Rowland	1676
Hey, Charles	16	Benjamin Rozer	1668
Hicks, Thomas	15	Robert Robins	1680
Hill, Thomas	16	Mr. Rozer	1669
Hill, Walt	12	William Hinsey	1672
Hinch, Mathew	21	Mr. Rozer	1669
Hincks, Dorothy	19	John Wheeler	1668
Hinde, William	12	Thomas Clarke	1677/8
Hindle, Joshua	20	Francis Gooderick	1678
Hinton?, Zachary	14	Josias Fendall	1676
Hodgly, John	21	Joseph Harrison	1669

Hogdin, Johnathan	18	John Redish	1680
Hoggin, Henry	21	Philip Lines	1675/6
Holmes, Grace	22	Philip Lines	1681
Holton, Joseph	22	Mr. Rozer	1669
Hosking, Thomas	12	Robert Thompson	1678
Hoskins, Jeremi	21	John Bowles	1668
Hoskins, Lauran	17	John Bowles	1668
Houghton, James	14	Henry Aspenall	1682
Howard, John	[see Mackmere; s/o Jeremiah Mackmere and Phillis]		
Hubberton, Mary	18	Bartholomew Coates	1670
Howell, Alexander	[craves disch.]	Elizabeth Weeks	1666
Howes, Thomas	16	Capt. Josias Fendall	1677/8
Hoyle, Samuell	21-22	Edmond Lindsey	1669
Hudson, Robert	13	Richard Midgeley	1676
Humble, Barbary	20	Philip Lines	1675/6
Humerton, Mary	18	Bartholomew Coates	1670
Hunt, John	16	Wm. Barton	1668
Hunter, Richard	21	Benjamin Rozer	1671
Hunter, William	14	Thomas Hussey	1675/6
Huntsman, Samuell	14	Thomas Allanson	1678
Hutchins, Elianor	13	Henery Hawkins	1673/4
Hu___, Elianor	16	Henry Hawkins	1674
Ivarson, Alise	[petitions for freedom]		1676/7
Jackson, James	19	John Wright	1674
Jackson, Mary	21	Robert Henley	1670
Jeffrey, Tho.	18	Joseph Manninge	1680
Jeffs, John	13	John Courts	1669
Johnson, Cornelius		Antho. Bridges	1669
Johnson, Jemimima	13	Benjamin Rozer	1679/0
Johnson, John	18	Humphrey Warren	1677/8
Johnson, Thomas	17	Henry Adams	1676
Jones, Edward	14	John Lambert	1673/4
Jones, Elizabeth	[had bastard]	John Munn	1680
Jones, Mary	18	John Stone	1682
Jones, Moses	17	Zachary Wade	1675
Jones, Moses	[petitions freedom]	Zachery Wade [estate]	1679
Jones, Philip	21	Robert Henly	1676/7

Jones, Richard	19	William Chandler	1677/8
Jones, Robert	21	Tho. Hussey	1682
Kanedagh, Jeremy	[servant in 1667]	Daniel Johnson	1671
Keelby, John	16	Peter Carr	1673/4
Kekley, William	10	Richard Morris	1671
Kent, Robert	12	John Dent	1668
Kingstone, Thomas	14	Tyre, James	1676
Kirby, Paul	16	William Barton	1675
Kirten?, Zachary	14	Josias Fendall	1676
Knight, Hannah	20	Thomas Taylor	1681
Korkbey, William	10	Richard Morris	1672
Lakemore, James	[4 yrs to serve; sold by Wm. Barrett]	Peter Carr	1676/7
Lans, William	14	William Perfect	1667
Lawrence, Thomas	12	Henry Bonner	1671/2
Lee, Margaret	[had bastard child]	John Newton	1681/2
Lee, Margaret	[had bastard child]	John Newton	1680
Leesh, James	11	Edmund Taylor	1675
Lenham, John	19	Henry Hardy	1679
Lloyd, Headrick		Alexander Smith	1673
Loodgham?, Charles	14	Archebald Walhop	1673
Lues?, Thomas	20	Richard Edelen	1671
Lybscome, Dorothy	22	Benjamin Rozer	1673
Mackenhine, John	18	James Mackey	1668
Mackmere, John Howard	[to age 21]	Robert Littlepage	1670
Manhew, John	16	Philip Lines	1675/6
Mannexley, Margaret	9	Joshuah Doyne	1678
Manwarren, Walter	20	Richard Smoot	1668
Marchall, Richard	14	Benjamin Rozer	1676
Marden, John	13	Alexander Sympson	1668
Maris, Sarah	[d/o Thomas Maris, dec'd]	Johannah Hodgson	1680
Marken, John	20	Maj. Jno. Wheeler	1679
Markeneard, Elinor	[had bastard child]	Robert Doyne	1680
Marlow, Anthony	17	Sam. Fendall	1671
Marsh, William	18	Thomas Gerrard	1673/4
Mason, Jno.	21	John Redish	1680
Mason, William	13	Philip Lines	1676/7
Massey, John	[bound for 5 yrs.]	Benjamin Rozer	1671

Maybanck, Elizabeth	13	John Wood	1673/4
Miles, Elizabeth	17	William Wells	1678
Miles, Nathaniel	14	Archibald Wahob	1679/0
Milshaw, John	15	John Ward	1678
Milstead, Edward	19	William Chandler	1674/5
Mirandy, Andrew	21	John Douglas	1670
Mires, Christopher	21	Thomas Craystone	1682
Mitchell, Anthony	17	Thomas Gerrard	1677/8
Morgan, Frances	[had bastard child]	Madam Rozer	1681
Morrell, Christopher	20	Richard Chandler	1673
Morris, Annas	18	Richard Morris	1676
Morris, Ellis	19	James Neale	1682
Morris, John	16	Peter Carr	1673/4
Moulton, Margaret	[had bastard child]	Hamon Norton	1680
Moulton, Margrett	14	Robert Greene	1673/4
Mouraster, James	[to serve to age 21]	Rish. Way	1685
Mouraster, Wm.	[to serve to age 21]	Rish. Way	1685
Move, Peter	7	Christopher Brimins	1669
Murphy, Daniell	[tailor, freed]	James Neale	1670
Murraine, Nicholas	17	Ann Fowke	1677/8
Nash, Samuell	20	Philip Lines	1681/2
Neale, Henrie	16	John Courts	1668
Neeves, Mary	17	Thomas Mudd	1677/8
Newman, Ann	17	Wm. Barton	1669
Newton, Jno.	20	Henry Hawkins	1681
Nichols, Rachell	17	James Neale	1681/2
Nicholson, Esther	7	Henry Hawkins	1680
Nicholson, John	10	Henry Hawkins	1680
Nicholson, William	6	John Stone	1680
Nicolls, Christobell	20	Thomas King	1674/5
Nolinn, Patrick	20	Mr. Dickinson	1668
Norman, Tho.	21	Henry Adames	1668
Norton, Amy	15	Thomas Mitchell	1680
Oard, Peter	18	Robert Henley	1671
Orson, Bearer	13	Robert Clarke	1668
Oulson?, John	21	Robert Rowland	1671
Owen, John	[tailor, freed]	Samuel Fendall	1669/70

Parker, Ann	19	John Cage	1669
Parker, James	15	John Courtes	1675
Parker, John	18	Jeremiah Dickison	1669
Parkes, Robert	18	Thomas Dent	1675/6
Pattison, John	13	Benjamin Rozer	1673
Pauding, Wm.	16	Henry Adames	1668
Peacocke, Wm.	14	Philip Lines	1676/7
Pearson, John	17	Ralph Shaw	1675/6
Pearson, Nathaniell	16	Dennis Husoula	1676
Peeso, Comape	13	William Marshall	1668
Pembrooke, Mary	20	Robert Rowland	1678
Persivall, Charles	12	Mr. Coates	1673
Phillips, Edward	17	Thomas Dent	1675/6
Phillips, John	16	John Fearson	1677/8
Phillips, Thomas	17	James Bowling	1676/7
Phogg, Charles	14	Tho. Gerrard	1681/2
Phyllips, Hugh	21	Gerrard Fowke	1668
Picherd, Robert	17	John Lambert	1678
Piper, James	11	Richard Morris	1671/2
Poore, Peter	21	Wm. Smith	1682
Potts, Thomas	20	William Wells	1679
Powell, Robt.	16	Mr. Adams	1669
Prince, Abigall	23	Thomas Dent	1669
Prise, Edward	[bound to age 21]	Domindego Agambra	1685
Ranford, William	13	John Clark	1673
Ranford, William	13	Richard Chandler	1673
Ray, Edward	14	James Bowling	1676/7
Raylor, Richard	16	John Posie	1675/6
Read, John [to age 21]	5	Robert Rowland	1669
Redding, Isable	[had bastard child]	Thomas Hussy	1680
Reeding, Isabell	19	Thomas Hussey	1674
Rennicke, Anne	16	Mrs. Elinor Beane	1674
Richardson, Bernard	17	Col. John Duglas	1676/7
Richardson, Joseph	21	John Clark	1674/5
Ring, Ralph	22	Sam. Cressey	1670
Roberts, Anne	[had bastard child]	James Neale	1681/2
Roberts, Anne	[had bastard child]	James Neale	1680

Roberts, William	[runaway]	Edward Saunders	1681
Robertson, Marie	17	John Coates	1667
Robins, Henry	17	Benjamin Rozer	1676
Robinson, Ann	23	John Clark	1674/5
Robinson, Mary	[bound]	Jno. Harrison	1685
Robinson, Samuell	21	Capt. Humph. Warren	1678
Robods, Richard	22	Wm. Boareman	1682
Rogers, Mary	21	Philip Lines	1681/2
Rose, John	15	Mr. Adams	1669
Rouze, Anne	19	William Smith	1678
Salt, Mary	20	Tho. Speeke [St. M. Co.]	1678
Scarry___?, Richard	12	Archibald Wahob	1671
Seawell, Rebeckah	20	Thomas King	1676/7
Seer, Thomas	13	Col. Gerrard Fowke	1667
Seney, Daniell	14-15	Henry Moore	1667
Serewitt ?, Tho.	[bound]	Jno. Harrison	1685
Shaw, John	17	Railph Smith	1682
Shelton, Mary	17	John Piles	1681/2
Shoreman, Jno.	[to serve to age 21]	Rish. Way	1685
Short, George	17-18	Clement Theobals	1670
Sigeloy, Samuell	16	Jno. Mun	1680
Simpson, Samuel	15	John Goodge	1673
Simpson, Samuell	15	Capt. Josias Fendall	1673
Singleton, Richard	13	Richard Beck	1673/4
Sinnett, Alise	[had bastard child]	Philip Lines	1681
Skinner, Thomas	15	Robert Hunly	1667
Slater, John	16	Thomas King	1676/7
Smith, Elizabeth	12	Thomas Clarke	1677/8
Smith, Robert	15	John Munn	1673/4
Smoot, William [s/o Richard]	9	William Hatton	1680
Snell, Margaret	20	Ann Fowkes	1671/2
Snowden, Wm.	10	Jno. Vaudry [St. M. Co.]	1678
Spicer, Absolon	[serve to age 21]	Zachary Wade	1673/4
Steede, Thomas [to age 21]	13	Richard Waye	1678
Stephens, Mary	19	John Lambert	1673/4
Stephens, Mary	19	Thomas Stonestreet	1682
Stephens, Richard	10	Thomas Gerrard	1678

Stidman, Edward	14	Capt. Ignatius Causine	1677
Stone, Mathias	14	Archebald Wahob	1673/4
Stonehouse, Thomas	13	Richard Pinner	1675
Stringer, George	15	Henry Hawkins	1677/8
Sudberie, Gregorie	16	Robert Hunley	1668
Swaine, George	14	Josias Fendall	1676
Sween, Sarah	20	Francis Goodwick	1677/8
Taylor, Elizabeth	19-20	Alexander Smyth	1667
Taylor, George	14	William Porfit	1676
Taylor, Thomas	13	George Godfrey	1677
Thatryer, Mary	19	John Clarke	1678
Thomas, Anne	22	John Buttler	1675/6
Thomas, Edward	12	Capt. Igna. Causene	1685
Thompson, Henry	16	Thomas Clipsham	1678
Thompson, John	15	Robert Greene	1678
Thorneton, Jermett ?		Tho. Hussey	1682
Tibbett, John	17	James Bowling	1673
Tiblee, Thomas	20	Nathaniel Barton	1668
Tigner, Richard	6	John Cage	1673
Tillsey, Mabella	18	Thomas Harrison	1676/7
Tipton, Edward	18	Humphrey Warren, Jr.	1668
Tod, Thomas	18	William Love	1670
Trench, Ann	21	Mr. Rozer	1669
Tubb, Tho.	21	Zachery Wade	1668
Turner, William	22	Humph. Warren	1669
Tymothie, Will	15	John Bowles	1667
Typton, Edward	[requesting freedom]	Humphry Warren	1673
Vaine, Henrie	14	George Newman	1667
Verritt, John	17	John Hatch	1676
Wallwort, Isaac	22	William Marshall	1667
Ward, Henry	15	Richard Smoote	1675
Ward, Richard	12	Humphrey Warren	1676
Warner, Christopher	20	Robert Downes	1668
Waterworth, Catherine	14	John Munn	1682
Waterworth, John	12	John Bayne	1682
Watridge, Anne	[had bastard child]	William Hatch	1680
Wheeler, David	18	Tho. Mitchell	1681/2

Name	Age	Master	Year
Whilden, John	24	Edward Swanne	1667
Whitehorne, Jno.	16	Thomas Mudd	1681/2
Whitt, Samuell	11-12	Benjamin Rozer	1676
Wiggs, David	13	Robert Downes	1668
Wilder, Robert	16-17	John Bowles	1670
Wilfray, Lusi	18	Bennett Marshagay	1675
Wilkinson, John	18	John Taylor	1673/4
Willbee, Mishael	12	George Godfrey	1678
William, Peter	13	Thom. Hussy	1668
Williams, Edward	20	Henry Hawkins	1678
Williams, Hugh		Robert Henly	1681/2
Williams, Jane	14	Philip Lines	1676/7
Williams, Jno.	10	Jno. Allward	1681/2
Williams, John	21	Thomas Gerrard	1676/7
Williams, Katherin	17-18	Josias Fendall	1676
Williams, William	22	Capt. Ignatius Causine	1678
Williamson, Lancelot	18	Humphrey Warren	1671
Willman, Henry	12	William Smith	1678
Wilson, Lawrence	20	William Boreman	1671
Wilson, Robert	16-17	John Bowles	1671
Winter, John	15	Capt. Ignatius Causine	1678
Worthington, Joseph	14	Edward Rockard	1685
Wright, George	18-19	Benjamin Rozer	1676
Wyott, John	16	Mr. Beane	1673
W____, Margaret	20	Mr. Rozer	1669
Young, Charles	6	Samuel Fendall	1673
Young, Jane	20	Elinor Bayne	1678
____, Ruth	14	John Stone	1669
____, Edward	17	John Bowles	1674
____, Robert	15	John Munn	1674
_____	13	John Breade	1680

[Note: Other servants names can be found in court cases relating to misbehavior by both servants and masters which have not been included in this list.]

Liber M
1685-1686

Liber M, Page 8

12 Oct 1685; Deed of Gift from **Rando. Brandt** and **Mary** his wife, to their son-in-law **Joseph Bullett** and their dau. **Elizabeth** his wife; a tract called *Thomas Town* on the south side of St. Thomas Creek adjoining land formerly laid out for Thomas Simpson; containing 200 acres; /s/ Rando. Brandt, Mary Brandt (mark); wit. Henry Bonner, Jos. Meriton

Liber M, Page 9

__ Jul ____; Indenture between **Thomas Wyck**, merchant, and **Rebecca?** Hall age 18 years; service for 5 years from her arrival in Virginia; /s/ Thomas Wyck; wit. Phillip Holland Saml. Hibert

Liber M, Page 9

20 Nov 1684; Indenture from **Mary Power**, spinster, and **Richard Reeves** of Waterford, merchant; service for 5 years from her arrival in Maryland; /s/ Robert Reeves; wit. Terlaugh? Byers, John Smolare

Liber M, Page 10

Cattle Marks: **John Francis, Jno. Booker, Francis Meeke**
Birth: **John Worland**, s/o Jno. Worland, b. 2 Jan 1685
Gift: From **Richard Pinnar** to **Richard Woodgard**, s/o Henry Woodgard; a heifer

Liber M, Page 27

16 Mar 1685/6; Deed of gift from **James Smallwood** to his dau. **Mary Maddocks**; a cow and mare; /s/ James Smallwood; wit. Elizabeth Singleton, Wm. Theobalds

Liber M, Page 31

7 Dec 1685; Indenture from **James Barrett** and **Elizabeth** his wife, and **Henry Moore**, to **Joseph Cornall**, planter; for 4,000# tobacco a tract called *Moore's Fishing Place*; bounded by Howland, Hopewell and Obrian's tract; on south side of Mattawoman Creek; containing 234 acres; /s/ James Barrett (mark), Elizabeth Barrett, Henry Moor (mark); wit. Cleborne Lomax, Thos. Whickaley, Rando. Brandt

Liber M, Page 32

10 Nov 1685; Indenture from **John Wheeler**, Gent., to **John Speake**; for a quantity of tobacco and love of his natural dau. **Winnifred**; a parcel of land called *Plymouth*; containing 350 acres; near fresh of the Piscattaway; /s/ John Wheeler (mark); wit. Wm. Thompson, Sam'll Cooksey, Tho. Sympson, Jr.

Liber M, Page 33

20 Apr 1686; Deed of gift from **Richard Boughton** to **Sarah Pigott**, d/o Bartholomew Pigott, physician, dec'd; a heifer; /s/ Ri. Boughton; wit. Edw. Potter

Liber M, Page 45

Cattle Marks: **Ignatius Wheeler, Tho. Riggs, Mary Morrise, Richard Morrise, Penelope Morrise, Christopher Morrise, Mary Morrise**

Liber M, Page 67

Portobacco Court; 12 Jan 1685; servants presented to the court:
Jno. Killcart, serv't to William Hatch, judged age 15
James Browne, serv't to Domindigo Agambrah, judged age 15
Hannah Newman, serv't to Henry Hawkins, judged age 11
George Kingsbury, serv't to Henry Hawkins, judged age 19
John Brooke, serv't to Henry Hawkins, judged age 21
Elizabeth Coddington, serv't to Henry Hawkins, judg. age 14
Edw. Sackimore, serv't to Henry Hawkins, judged age 14
Jno. Thompson, serv't to Henry Hawkins, judged age 17
Jeremiah Spurling, serv't to Henry Hawkins, judged age 18
Rog'r Yappe, serv't to Henry Hawkins, judged age 21
Geo. Graves, serv't to Edw. Evans, judged age 11
Francis Hambye, serv't to Giles Blizard, judged age 19
Francis Dunnington, serv't to Mary Chandler, judged age 20
Jno. Purnie, serv't to Mary Chandler, judged age 18

(p. 68-87 missing)

Liber M, Page 88

Francis Simmes, serv't to Wm. Barton, judged age 17

Liber M, Page 89

James Leech, serv't to Elinor Boise; runaway
Tho. Gibbens, serv't to William Barton, Jr., judged age 14
James Smith, serv't to Sam'll Luckett, judged age 21

Jno. Archiball, serv't to Alex. Smith, judged age 22
Tho. Powcher, serv't to Jno. Court, judged age 20
Anne Crouch, serv't to Jno. Coll, judged age 18
Jno. Cooke, serv't to Rich'd Newman, judged age 14
Robt. Neale, serv't to Tho. Gerrard, judged age 20
Wm. Maddock, serv't to Tho. Gerrard, judged age 20
   Liber M, Page 90
Jane Gilbert, serv't to Wm. Hatch, judged age 20
Tho. Normansell, serv't to Tho. Clarke, judged age 19
Tho. Sees, serv't to Jno. Court, Jr., judged age 22
Theophen Bridges, serv't to Jno. Court, judged age 25
   Liber M, Page 92
Runaway: **Mary Gubbins**
Cattle Mark: **Wm. Burnham**; 26 May 1686
   Liber M, Page 98
5 Mar 1685; Indenture from **Gerrard Fowke**, Gent., to **Thomas Mudd** of St. Mary's Co., Gent.; for 17,000# tobacco; a parcel of land called *Beyerwood*; lying on the main fresh of Mattawoman Creek; bounded by Thomas Mathews, land laid out for Richard William and John Wheeler; containing 650 acres; /s/ Gerrard Fowke; wit. John Clemens, James Browne (mark), William Hall (mark)
   Liber M, Page 100
Cattle Marks; 14 Jun 1686 **Mary Rigg**, d/o Thomas Rigg;
26 Jun 1686 **Richard Simscon**
3 May 1686; Deed of Gift from **Wm. Thomas** to **John Marlow**; a heifer
   Liber M, Page 115
12 Jun 1585; Deed of Gift from **Eleanor Boyce** to **John Boyce**, s/o John Boyce, dec'd, a sorrel mare, cow and calf, featherbed and furniture; to **William Boyce**, s/o John Boyce, dec'd, a heifer; featherbed and furniture; to **James Boyce**, a mare filly and black heifer and calf; to **William Boyden**, s/o John Boyden, dec'd, heifer; to **Mary Boyden** 2 cows and calves
John Lemaire, surgeon, gives **Jno. Beamont**, s/o Thomas Beamont a young sorrel mare

Elizabeth Maglockery gives Esther Macoy a black heifer; gives James Macoy a black heifer

William Smith gives William Maglockery, s/o William Maglockery, dec'd, a red heifer

Liber M, Page 122

28 Sep 1686; Cattle Mark; James Rigon

Liber M, Page 131

John Lemaire gives John Beamont, s/o Thomas Beamont a sorrel mare

John Lemaire gives Edward Saunders, s/o Edward Sanders a yearling sorrel mare

Liber M, Page 154

14 May 1686; Indenture from John Harrison, Gent., to Robert Surling of London, mariner; for 10,000# tobacco; a parcel of land on the Wicomico River called *Rich Hill* containing 600 acres; and a parcel called *Thomas's Addition* containing 83 acres; /s/ Jno. Harrison, Robt. Surling; wit. Henry Adames, Ignatius Cuasine; ack. by Martha Harrison, wife of John

Liber M, Page 164

20 May 1685; Indenture from William Dent, attorney at law, and Elizabeth his wife, to John Barker; for 2 tracts of land by indenture dated 10 Apr last; 200 acre part of a tract of 900 acres now in possession of Dent; /s/ William Dent, Elizabeth Dent; wit. George Graves, John Cunney

Liber M, Page 165

9 Mar 1685; Indenture from Gilbert Clarke of St. Mary's Co., Gent., to Joshua Doyne of St. Mary's Co.; for 6,000# tobacco; a parcel of land on the north side of the Potomac; bounded by land of John Thomkinson near a bluff point, called Maryland Point, and the river; containing 400 acres laid out for Philip Land 19 Aug 1658; sold to John Askins of St. Mary's Co. 9 Jul in the 44th year of the reign of Cecillius; conveyed to Rebekah Askins his wife; conveyed to Clarke 1 Jun 1685 after death of Rebekah; /s/ Gilbert Clark; wit. William Dent, Robt. Doyne

Liber M, Page 166

25 Jun 1685; Indenture from Christopher Breams, planter, to Francis Meeke; for one gray gelding; a parcel of land called

Mings his Chance on the Potomac; containing 30 acres; /s/ Christopher Breams (mark); wit. Richard Harrison, Edward Ming

Liber M, Page 190

16 Dec 1685; Indenture between **John Cage**, planter, son and heir of John Cage, dec'd, and **Susannah Clipsham**, widow, former wife of John Cage, the father; Susannah now seized for her lifetime by virtue of a devise made to her by her former husband a parcel of land on the west side of Wicomico River; bounded by Michaell Marsh; for 4,000# tobacco Susannah gives up her rights to John Cage, the son; /s/ Susannah Clepsham, widow; wit. Edward Middleton, Wm. Harbut

Liber M, Page 192

14 Sep 1686; Indenture from **Richard Wade**, planter, to **Thomas Hussey**, Gent.; for 14,000# tobacco; a parcel of land formerly laid out for Zachary Wade called *Wade's Land* on the north side of Piscataway River about 1/2 mile east of Goose Bay; containing 300 acres; also another tract laid out for Zachary Wade called *Wadestones* containing 100 acres; /s/ Rich Wade; wit. Samuell Luckett, Cleborne Lomax

Liber M, Page 194

24 Sep 1686; Gift from **Henry Branner**, planter, to **Elizabeth Farnandis**, d/o Peter Farnandis, cooper, a cow

14 Sep 1686; Gift from **Peter Farnandis**, cooper, to **Edward Branner**, s/o Henry Branner, a mare

Cattle Mark: **William Elliot, Sr., Wm. Elliot, Jr.**

Liber M, Page 212

9 Nov 1685; Quit Claim from **William Pryor**, planter, and **Marie** his wife, d/o Nicholas and Elizabeth Emerson, dec'd to **Henry Hawkins** and **Elizabeth** his wife, relict of Francis Wine; for 1,200# tobacco; a parcel of land called *Glovers Point* on the north side of the Potomac on Nanjemy Creek; formerly sold by Elizabeth Emerson to Francis Wine 16 Jun 1671; /s/ William Pryor (mark), Mary Pryor (mark); wit. Clebo. Lomax, Wm. Hacorte, Jno. Hawkins

Liber M, Page 220

Portobacco Court, 8 Jun 1686; Servants presented to Court

Francis Oakes, serv't to Henry Hawkins, judged age 19
John Potts, serv't to Capt. Bowling, judged age 24
Thomas Hill, serv't to Giles Blizard, judged age 13
Richd. Guesse, serv't to Henry Adams, judged age 15
James Hickson, age 8; orphan of Henry Hickson, bound to
  James Finley
Richd. Fowke, age 18, orphan of Ri. Fowke to return to Henry
  Hardye; bound to age 21
Hallilujah Fowke, age 15, bound to Henry Hardye to age 21
Tho. Warner, serv't to Tho. Baker (dec'd) return to his present
  master Jno. Harrison and serve to 10 Nov next
Nicholas Cole, Geo. Gleine?, Mathew Perrie, Ellice Morris,
  Charles Grey; servants to James Neale absent for 14 days
Gilbert Clarke ordered to keep ordinary at Charles Towne
  for horse and mare
Cornelius Butwell and Tho. Bouge serve Col. Pye according
  to their indentures to Col. Rozer

Liber M, Page 221

Ordered that James Smallwood deliver Eliz. Rowles to her
  mother Eleanor Lees; security to be paid Smallwood
Ordered that Mrs. Witters children be returned to her; Tho.
  Wheeler and Tho. Jenkins to be paid 1,000# tobacco
  each; Mrs. Witter to be ready to go to Barbadoes and
  children to remain with Wheeler and Jenkins
John Bradshaw, serv't to Phillip Lynes, judged age 17-18
Katherine Jones, serv't to Phillip Lynes, judged age 16
John Kue, serv't to Phillip Lynes, judged age 19
Joseph Vanse, serv't to Phillip Lyne, judged age 19

Liber M, Page 222

7 Aug 1686; Indenture from William Smoot, planter, and Anne
  his wife, to Humphery Warren, Gent.; for one servant boy and
  6,000# tobacco; part of a tract called *The Hills* formerly in
  occupation of Richard Smoot, dec'd; containing 50 acres; and a
  parcel called *Wicomico Fields* of 100 acres; /s/ William
  Smoot, Anne Smoot; wit. Edw. Smoot (mark), Ri. Smoot
  (mark), Tho. Smoot, Tho. Warren

Liber M, Page 230

10 Dec 1686; Indenture from **George Athey,** planter, to **Thomas Shuttleworth,** planter; for 1,600# tobacco a parcel of land called *Southrisk*; bounded by Edward Knight; containing 20 acres; /s/ George Athey (mark); wit. Joseph Harrison, Fran. Harrison

Liber N
1686-1688

Liber N, Page 8

Court of 15 Dec 1686; Cattle Mark: **Wm. Halton**

Liber N, Page 9

Cattle Marks: **Richard Wheeler**, s/o Tho. Wheeler; **Tho. Wheeler**, s/o Tho. Wheeler; **Benjamin Wheeler**, s/o Tho. Wheeler

Liber N, Page 10

Cattle Mark: **William Sergant**

Liber N, Page 10

1 Dec 1686; Agreement between **William Hatch**, Gent., and **William Hawton**; to maintain Hatch for his natural life, pay his debts, and care for his dau. Sarah Hatch to age 18; for all goods, chattel, slaves, stock, etc.; at age 18 Sarah to receive featherbed, furniture, cattle, etc.; /s/ Will Hatch; wit. John Barron, Abraham Brookesbanck, Cleborne Lomax

Liber N, Page 20

Cattle Mark: **John Lanham**

Liber N, Page 27

16 Oct 1686; Gift from **William Watkins** to friend **Jane Pembrooke**, wife of **Jno. Pembrooke**; a cow; /s/ William Watkins (mark); wit. William Howell, John Bracher

Liber N, Page 28

10 May 1686; Indenture from **Edward Evans** of St. Mary's Co., planter, to **William Keech** of St. Mary's Co.; for 5,000# tobacco; a parcel of land called *Lower Poole*; bounded by Tower Hill on the east side of the Potomac River and a 300 acre tract laid out for Zachariah Wade near Goose Bay; containing 250 acres; /s/ Edward Evans; wit Richard Edlen, Edw. Rookwood (mark); ack. by **Elizabeth Evans**, wife of Edward

Liber N, Page 29

17 Dec 1686; Indenture from **William Keett**, planter of St. Mary's Co., to **William Simpson** of St. Mary's Co., planter; for _,000# tobacco; a tract called *Lower Poole*; bounding *Tower Hill*, the

east side of the Potomac, land of Morgan Jones, land called *Wadestons Enlargement*, and land laid out for Zachariah Wade; containing 250 acres; /s/ Wm. Keett (mark); wit. Rob't Goat?, James Ellis; ack. by his wife Elizabeth Keett
Liber N, Page 32

Cattle Marks: **Thomas Dixon, John Gwin**
Liber N, Page 137

1 May 1686; Deed of Gift from **Marie Boswel**, widow of John Boswell to her 6 children, **Mathew Boswel, Michael Boswel, William Boswel, John Boswel, Marie Boswel** and **Martha Boswel**; goods and cattle; /s/ Mary Boswel (mark); wit. Meverel Hulse, Cleborne Lomax
Liber N, Page 151

8 Mar 1686; **Joan Tomkins**, age 20, servant to Rando. Hanson
Liber N, Page 202

9 Dec 1687; Cattle Mark: **Tho. Lindsey**
Liber N, Page 204

Cattle Marks: **Robt. Powell; Benjamin Cassock**, s/o John Casock; **Emmanuell Ratcliffe, Mullenex Ratcliffe**
Liber N, Page 206

6 Apr 1687; Deeds of Gifts of household goods and cattle from **George Pouncy** to the children of his wife **Mary Pouncy** to be rec'd immediately after her death: to **Mathew Boswell, John Boswell, Mary Boswell, Martha Boswell, Michell Boswell, William Boswell**; /s/ George Pouncy (mark); wit. Thomas Mitchell, William Hall
Liber N, Page 209

2 Jun 1687; Indenture from **Joseph Cornall** and **Margaret** his wife, to **William Griffin** and **Thomas Phillips**, planters; for 4,000# tobacco; a parcel called *Moore's Fishing Place*; bound by *Howland* on the south side of Mattawoman Creek, OBrian's land, *Hopewell*; containing 234 acres; /s/ Joseph Cornall; wit. Wm. Theobalds, Joshua Graves
Liber N, Page 210

20 Apr 1687; Indenture from **Edmond Lindsey** to **James Smallwood**; for 2,100# tobacco; a parcel of land called

Mayday; containing 300 acres; /s/ Edmond Lindsey (mark); wit. Edw. Fr__ner, Wm. Theobalds
Liber N, Page 212

__ Jun 1687; Indenture from **William Hutchison**, dept. surveyor, to **Phillip Mason**, planter; for 3,000# tobacco; a parcel of land called *Leads*; containing 100 acres; /s/ Wm. Hutchison; wit. William Howell, William Clarkson
Liber N, Page 213

5 Aug 1684; Indenture from **William Smoote**, planter, and **Anne** his wife, to **William Newman**, planter; for 8,000# tobacco; a parcel of land which was reserved by Capt. Randolph Brandt 6 Sep 1683 on the west side of Wicomico River; being part of a tract granted William Smoote by patent 1 Nov 1671 called *Wicomico Fields*; containing 105 acres; /s/ William Smoote, Anne Smoote; wit. Hum. Warren, Thomas Clipsham, John Wilder
Liber N, Page 216

7 Sep 1685; Indenture from **James Barrett** and **Elizabeth** his wife, and **Henry Moore** to **Joseph Cornall**, planter; for 4,000# tobacco; a parcel called *Moore's Fishing Place* [see N.209 for description]; /s/ James Barrett (mark), Elizabeth Barrett, Henry Moore (mark); wit: Catharine Lenox?, Tho. Whichalley, Rand. Brandt.
Liber N, Page 217

Gift from **Jane Waye**, wife of Richard Waye, to **Ruth Martin**, d/o John Martin; heifer
Liber N, Page 265

Cattle Marks: **Richard Gambara, William Thomas, Jr., James Pencott, John Dickson, Richard Conner, Moses Jones**
Liber N, Page 267

Cattle Marks: **John Davis, Sarah Pigot, Richard Conner**
Liber N, Page 288

Cattle Marks: **Thomas Liwes, George Leet, Henry Franklings**
Liber N, Page 297

27 Feb 1687; Gift from **Henry Bransoner**, planter, to **John Miller**, s/o John Miller, a cow; /s/ Henry Bransoner (mark); wit. Edw. Potter

Liber N, Page 302

5 Nov 1687; Indenture from **Edward Mings**, planter, to **William Pryor**; a parcel granted 10 May 1671 to Edward Mings called St. Edward on the north side of the Potomac; bounded by St. Barbara of John Lewger; laid out for 100 acres; /s/ Edward Ming; wit. Francis Chummey, Edw. Potter; ack. by **Jane Mings**, wife of Edward

Liber N, Page 308

9 May 1683; **John Watson**, joiner, from Yorkshire, left from London, age 28, bound to **William Haneland**, merchant of London, for 4 years from the time of his arrival in Maryland; /s/ Wm. Haneland; wit. Jno. Ingham, Jn. Earle
Memo: The ship Elizabeth and Mary of London, John Bowman, Commander; anchored at Wicomico River 18 Oct 1683

Liber N, Page 310

10 Jan 1687; Indenture from **Henry Moore**, planter, to **Henry Hawkins**, Gent.; for 4,800# tobacco; a parcel called Moore's Folly; bounded by Oversee's Swamp, land of Capt. Wm. Lowe's; containing 50 acres; /s/ Henry Moore (mark); wit. Wm. Smith, Cleborne Lomax, Edw. Potter

Liber N, Page 318

2 Mar 1687; Indenture from **John Godshall**, planter, to **Edward Hill**, sawyer; for 3,000# of tobacco; a parcel of land called Ipswich on the south side of Mattawoman Creek; laid out for 100 acres; /s/ John Godshall; wit. Will Forster, Moses Jones (mark)

Liber N, Page 320

1 Mar 1687; Indenture from **William Pryor** to **Henry Branner**, planter; for 2,000# tobacco; a tract called Hopewell on the south side of Mattawoman Creek; bound by George Howland's land called Howland; laid out for 100 acres; /s/ William Pryor (mark), **Mary Pryor** (mark); wit. Tho. Lewger (mark), Thos. Plynkes, Phill. Hoskins

Liber N, Page 329

Cattle Mark: **Charles Bell**, s/o Maj. Ninian Bell [Beall]

Liber O # 1
1687

Court cases only; no land records

Liber P # 1
1688-1689/90

Liber P, Page 1

27 May 1688; Indenture from **Cornelius Maddock**, merchant, and **Mary** his wife, to **James Smallwood**; for 3,000# tobacco; a tract of land called *Nuthall*; bounded by *Merdilla?*, the land of Ralph Shaw called _____, land formerly surveyed for Edmond Lindsey now in possession of James Smallwood; containing 60 acres; /s/ Cornelius Maddock; wit. Wm. Theobalds, John Robey (mark), Thomas Gannett (mark)

Liber P, Page 4

28 Jun 1688; Cattle Marks; **Thomas Burford, Walter Evans, Peter Dent**

7 Jul 1688; Cattle Marks; **Wm. Hutchison, Wm. Tannyhill, Gaven Hamilton, John Barefoot**

Liber P, Page 5

2 Jun 168_; Indenture from **Joseph Cornall** and **Margaret** his wife to **William Griffin** and **Thomas Phillips**; for 4,500# tobacco; a parcel of land called *Moore's Fishing Place*; bounded by *Howland* and land of Mathias Obryan; containing 234 acres; /s/ Joseph Cornall; wit. Wm. Theobals, Joshua Graves

Liber P, Page 5

12 Jun 1688; Indenture from **Thomas Lewgar** to **John Wright**; for 6,000# tobacco; a parcel of land called *St. Barbarie Manor*; /s/ Thomas Lewgar (mark), John Wright

Liber P, Page 6

13 Jun 1688; Indenture from **Wm. Barton**, Gent., to **Thomas Warren**, planter, and **Mary** his wife; for natural love for his dau. **Mary Warren**; a parcel of land called ____; bounded by land taken up by Daniel Johnson; containing 140 acres; /s/ Wm. Barton, Mary Barton (mark); wit. Randolph Hinson, John Addison

Liber P, Page 26

17 Mar 1688; Indenture from **John Gooch**, planter, to **Humphrey Warren**; for a sum of money, Warren to take care of Gooch for his natural life and provide for his niece **Brigett Fendall** to age 16 or day of marriage; Gooch gives a parcel of land on the west side of Wicomico River formerly in possession of Briget Legate, now in possession of John Gooch; patent dated 1 May 1676; containing 400 acres; /s/ John Gooch; wit. Thomas Whichaley, Michael Webb, Jeffery Cole (mark)

Liber P, Page 30

12 Sep 1688; Indenture from **Robert Clark**, planter, to **Philip Lyne**; 2,000# tobacco; a parcel called *Small Hopes* on the main fresh of the Wicomico River; containing 100 acres; also a parcel called *Purchase* adjoining a parcel laid out for Henry Mor called *Small Hopes*; also 50 acres formerly surveyed by Richard Edelen for Robert Clark; joining 600 acres formerly laid out for George Goodrich; /s/ Robert Clark (mark); wit. Cleborne Lomax, Ralph Shaw, Peter Dent

Liber P, Page 30

16 May 1688; Indenture from **Thomas Warner**, planter, to **Wm. Dent**; for a certain plantation of William Dent at Nanjemy where John Baker now lives with 200 acres of adjoining land conveyed to Thomas Warner; a parcel of land on the north side of the Potomac next above and joining Thomas Baker where John Harrison, Gent., now dwells; adjoining land of James Ballis, land of Thomas Baker, land laid out for John Jarbo, Gent., dec'd, assigned to John Nevill then conveyed Thomas Bennett then to Thomas Warner then to Thomas Warner the son; likewise all that land called *Witten* containing 150 acres; /s/ Thomas Warner; wit. John Barker (mark), Eliza. Warren (mark)

Liber P, Page 32

13 Nov 1688; Indenture from **Richard Fowks**, planter, to **Richard Hes** and **Philip Mason**; for 10,000# tobacco a parcel of land called *Bartonzee* on the north side of the Anacostia River; containing 500 acres; /s/ Richard Fowke; wit. John Knowlwater (mark), Richard Gambra, Cleborne Lomax

Liber P, Page 34

Cattle Marks; 31 Dec 1688; At *Grisbrough*, *Barnabis*, *Mount Nabo*, *Ashen Swamp*, *Swan Harbor* and a general brand.
James Thompson, Arther Eathyes, Nathaniel Eathyes, Daniell Carrill, Wm. Bishop, Josias Jenkins, John Wilkinson, Richard Comer, Henry and Katherine Ward

Liber P, Page 35

26 Sep 1688; From **Charles Calvert** of St. Mary's Co., son and heir of William Calvert, dec'd, and **Elizabeth**, widow and relict of William, to **Joshua Doyne** of St. Mary's Co.; 600 acres of land at Nangemy part of 5,000 acres taken up by William Stone, dec'd, father of Elizabeth; for £5; /s/ Charles Calvert; wit. James Cullin, Thomas Collier, Phillip Lynes, Tho. Grurwin

Liber P, Page 36

Cattle Marks; **George Delehay, Edw. Philpott, Richard Eglin, Roger Harris, James Martin, Thomas Delahay, Joseph Bridges, Christopher Mayers**

Liber P, Page 61

Cattle Mark: **Oliver Harrison**

Liber P, Page 62

1 Feb 1687; Indenture from **Thomas Lugar**, planter, to **Thomas Linzy**; for 1,200# tobacco; a parcel of land called *Galleys Discovery*; bounded by *Wheeler's Palm* and *St. Thomas* belonging to John Lugar; laid out for 100 acres; /s/ **Thomas Lugar** (mark); wit. Francis Meeker, Robert Pery (mark)

Liber P, Page 63

8 Jan 1688; Indenture from **Edward Ming**, planter, to **Phillip Lynes** of St. Mary's Co., merchant; for 2,500# tobacco; a parcel of land of 120 acres called *Antwerp*; /s/ Edward Ming, Jane Ming (mark); wit. Edward Potter, Henry Hardy, Cleborne Lomax

Liber P, Page 65

8 Jan 1688; Indenture from **Thomas Lee**, planter, to **Phillip Lynes** of St. Mary's Co., merchant; for 4,000# tobacco; a parcel of land called *Hall Spring* on the north side of the Potomac;

containing 150 acres; /s/ Thomas Lee; wit. Edward Potter, Hen. Hardy, Cleborne Lomax

Liber P, Page 67

10 May 1688; Indenture from **Richard Smith**, planter, and **Anne** his wife, to **Daniell Jenkins**; for 4,200# tobacco; part of a parcel of 80 acres lying near Pickawaxon Creek; mentions William Burnband, Robert Douglas; containing 40 acres

Liber P, Page 89

Regarding division of land from will of **Thomas Dent**, late of St. George's Hundred, St. Mary's Co., to his sons **Peter Dent** now age 21, and his brother **George Dent**, now 14 yrs.; a tract of land called *Gisbrough* to be equally divided; mentions his mother **Rebecca Addison** as ex. of will of Thomas Dent; /s/ Peter Dent; wit. Will. Hatton; John Lowe, Rob't Hopkins

Liber P, Page 90

8 Jan 1688; Indenture from **Thomas Green**, planter, to **Henry Deakes**; for £23; 200 acres of land called *Cuckold's Delight*; mentions James Mullikin; [document faded] /s/ Thomas Green; wit. Benjamin Haddock, Rob't Middleton, James Thornton

Liber P, Page 91

12 Mar 1688; Indenture from **Richard Maston**, planter, to **Phillip Lynes** of St. Mary's Co., merchant; for 2,500# tobacco a parcel called *Low Land* on the west side of a main fresh of Wicomico River; adjoining John Grubb and Nicholas Belaine; containing 100 acres; /s/ Richard Maston (mark), **Mary Maston** (mark); wit. Ham. Warren, John Court, Cleborne Lomax

Liber P, Page 92

8 Jan 1688; Indenture from **John Wheeler**, Gent., and **Mary** his wife, to **Joshua Doyne** of St. Mary's Co., Gent.; for 7,000# tobacco; a parcel of land called *Exiler* laid out for Wheeler 18 Jan 1687; on the south side of a main fresh of Piscataway Creek; mentions an Indian field; containing 316 acres; /s/ John Wheeler (mark), Mary Wheeler (mark)

Liber P, Page 93

19 Nov 1688; Indenture from **Thomas Hussey**, Gent., to **William Smith**; for 6,000# of tobacco; a parcel of land on the north side of the Potomac called *Prises Adventure*; bounded by David Thomas; containing 200 acres; /s/ Tho. Hussey; wit. Ralph Shaw, James Miller

Liber P, Page 95

20 Mar 1688; Indenture from **John Fearnley**, planter, to **John Bracher**; for 3,600# tobacco; a parcel of land called *Fernleys Rest* on the west side of the Wicomico; containing 50 acres; /s/ John Fearnley (mark); wit. Philip Lynes, Cleborne Lomax

Liber P, Page 97

13 Mar 1688; Indenture from **Robert Middleton**, tailor, to **Philip Lynes** of St. Mary's Co.; for 2,250# tobacco; a parcel of land called *Hardshift*; bounded by Morgan Jones; laid out for 160 acres; /s/ Rob. Middleton, **Mary Middleton** (mark); wit. Hum. Warren, John Courts, Claiborne Lomax

Liber P, Page 99

12 Mar 1688; Indenture from **Robert Middleton** to **Robert Doyne**; for 10,000# tobacco; a parcel called *Saturday's Work*; laid out for 400 acres; /s/ Robert Middleton, Mary Middleton (mark); wit. Hum. Warren, John Courts, Cleborne Lomax

Liber P, Page 174

11 Jun 1688; Indenture from **Henry Frankam**, planter, to **John William**, planter; a grant to James Lindsey called ____ located 4 leagues above Nangemy; containing 250 acres; from Lindsey to Henry Frankam, father of Henry Francam; for 10,000# tobacco; /s/ Henry Frankam (mark); wit. ____ Wheeler, Tho. Whichaley, Edward Potter

Liber P, Page 177

23 Apr 1689; Indenture from **Richard Hes**, tailor, to **William Thompson**, planter; for 5,000# tobacco; a parcel called *Batterzee* which Hes and Phillip Mason lately purchased from Richard Fowke; containing 500 acres; /s/ Richard Hes; wit. Will. Dent, Tho. Burford

Liber P, Page 178

5 Oct 1688; 4th year of the reign of James II; **Henry Wine**, now of Pitchley, Northamptonshire, exchanges a parcel of land left him by his father, Francis Wine, in Wicomico called *Burton* of 90 acres with his mother, **Elizabeth Hawkins**, /s/ Henry Wine; wit. Nicholas Colborne, Siscillya Bradley

Liber P, Page 179

11 Jun 1689; Indenture from **John Wheeler**, Gent., to **Robert Doyne**, Gent.; for 8,000# tobacco; lots no. 10 and 11 in Chandler Town at the head of Portobacco Creek; /s/ John Wheeler (mark); wit. Wm. Barton, Henry Hawkins, Cleborne Lomax

Liber P, Page 180

16 Jul 1689; Deed of Gift of cattle from **John Dansy** to his wife **Jane Dansy** and her children by her former husbands, Rich'd Flower and Edw. Knight: **Elizabeth Flower, Elinor Knight, John Knight, Rebecca Knight**; /s/ John Dansy; wit. Roger Kemp, Edward Potter

Liber P, Page 181

23 Feb 1666; Indenture from **Francis Pennington** of *St. Inigoes Manor*, St. Mary's Co., Gent., to **Emanuell Ratchliff** of St. Mary's Co.; for diverse causes; a parcel of land on the south side of Portobacco Creek at a swamp just above the old dwelling house; containing 500 acres; formerly in possession of James Lindsey, Gent.; /s/ Francis Pennington; wit. Wm. Lourey, Tho. Hithersall

Liber P, Page 183

25 Apr 1689; Indenture from **William Smoote**, planter, to **Edward Smoote**, planter; for 2,400# tobacco; a parcel called *Wicomico Fields*; bounded by Wm. Newman, Humphrey Warren, and Wicomico River; laid out for 100 acres; /s/ William Smoote; wit. Rando. Brandt, Thomas Gibson (mark), Eliza. Butler

Liber P, Page 184

10 Sep 1689; Gift from **Joseph Gray** and **Richard Newton**, planters, to **John Jones**, s/o Moses Jones; cattle; /s/ Joseph Gray (mark), Richard Newton

14 Jan 1689; Gift from **Joan Waye** wife of **Richard Waye** to her God-dau. **Ruth Martin**; d/o John Martin and Mary his wife; cattle

14 Jan 1689; Gift from **Richard Hobart** to **Elizabeth Mankin**, d/o Stephen and Mary Mankin of Portobacco; mare

Cattle Marks: **Henry Thompson; Philip Lynes; Walter Hope; John Bayne**, mark given him by William Cage; **Mary Howling**, d/o William and Mary Howling; **Ignatius Wheeler; Elizabeth Dike**, d/o Matthew and Mary Dike

Liber P, Page 191

Cattle Marks: **William Nichols, Benjamin Haddock, Francis Huytinge, Jeffrey Cole**

Liber P, Page 196

10 Jun 1689; Indenture from **Richard Fowke**, planter, to **Thomas Warren**; for 5s and a sum of tobacco; Warren to take care of Fawke for his natural life; to give a cow and calf to **Hallaleujah Fowke** at age 21; a parcel of land called *Haggetts Priory* on the north side of Piscataway River bounded by David Thomas, also *Little Marsh*; containing 150 acres; also *Little Ease* of 200 acres and *God's Gift* of 280 acres; /s/ Richard Fowke; wit. Wm. Hutchinson, Cleborne Lomax, Edward Typton

Liber P, Page 198

11 Mar 1689; Indenture from **George Athey**, planter, and **Sarah** his wife, to **Edward Williams**; for _,600# tobacco; a parcel called *Yorkshire* of 91 acres in *Zachia Manor*; /s/ George Athy (mark), Sarah Athy (mark); wit. Willm. Hutchison, Joshia Graves

Liber P, Page 199

18 Jan 1674; Bill of Sale from **James Walker** to **John Worland**; for valuable consideration; a parcel of land called *Dorkers Delight*; /s/ James Walker (mark); wit. John Gooch, Samll Clarke; **Alise Walker**, relict of Robert Walker and ex. of James Walker, ack. deed in court 9 Nov 1675

4 Jul 1689; Indenture from **George Thompson** of St. Mary's Co., Gent., to **Susanna**, relict of **John Posey**; for 5,000# tobacco; a parcel of land called *Johnson's Choise*; containing 250 acres in

Zachia Manor; bounded by Smootes Choise; /s/ George
Thompson; wit. John Eastwood (mark), Cleborne Lomax
Liber P, Page 200

Cattle Marks: **John Raines; Elizabeth Raines,** d/o John; **Lucy Raines,** d/o John
Liber P, Page 201

Elizabeth Raines, d/o John; **Ann Harguesse,** d/o William; **John Lannum,** s/o John; **William Sunley**
Liber P, Page 202

19 Jul 1690; Gift from **Charles Barrow** to **George Potter,** s/o Robert Potter; cattle; /s/ Charles Barrow (mark); wit. Francis Harrison, Margaret Harrison (mark)

Cattle Marks: **George Potter; William Cable, Charles Cartee**

Gift from **Michaell Ashford** to **Anne Rought,** d/o William and Sarah Rought; bay mare

Gift from **John Smith** to his dau.-in-law **Elizabeth Symons;** cow and calf
Liber P, Page 203

Cattle Marks: **John Smith,** carpenter; **Francis Marberry; Morris Loyd; Peter Ord; John Jones; Hugh Teares**

Gift from **John Allward** to **William Langham;** a mare; 10 Feb 1690; /s/ John Allward; wit. John Thomas (mark)

Gift from **Mary Pounsey** to her children: **Michael Boswell, William Boswell** and **Martha Boswell;** cattle; 12 Feb 1690; /s/ Mary Pounsey (mark); wit. Blanch Lomax (mark), Margaret Cassock, Cleborne Lomax

Cattle Marks: **John Saunders,** s/o Matthew Saunders; **Wm. Browne,** s/o William Browne; **Elizabeth Browne,** d/o Wm. Browne; **Ambros Palmer; Hugh Gardiner; Edward Gardiner,** s/o Hugh Gardiner; **Nicholas Wise**
Liber P, Page 204

Register of Births, Burials and Marriages from
books of record until the year 1687

Grace Barton, d/o William Barton, b. 26 Aug 1659
Mary Wade; d/o Zachary Wade, b. 21 Apr 1661
Richard Harrison, s/o Joseph Harrison, b. 12 Oct 1659
Mary Harrison, d/o Joseph Harrison, b. 21 Dec 1661

Sarah Wade, d/o Zachary Wade, b. 7 Jul 1662
William Barton, s/o Wm. Barton, Jr., b. 29 Jun 1662
Richard Dod, s/o Richard Dod, b. 4 Jan 1662
Mary Dod, d/o Richard Dod, b. 25 Feb 1666
Elinor Obry, d/o Mathias Obry [Obrian; C.222}, b. 5 Nov 1666
Wm. Emerson, s/o Nicholas Emerson, b. 17 Nov 1666
John Ashbrooke m. 1687 [1667; C.222]
Anne Ward, d/o John Ward, b. 5 Feb 1663
Mary Ward, d/o John Ward, b. 5 Jul 1665
Anne Ward, d/o John Ward, b. 10 Apr 1667
Elizabeth Harrison, d/o Joseph Harrison, b. 11 Mar 1663
Catherine Harrison, d/o Joseph Harrison, b. 4 Jan 1666
Ambros Clark, s/o John Clark, b. 13 Sep 1666; bur 18 Feb 1666/7
Elizabeth Marshall, d/o Wm. Marshall, b. 15 Apr 1667
Charles Philpot, s/o Edward Philpot, b. 19 Feb 1667
William Barton, s/o Nathan Barton, b. 19 Feb 1667
John Smyth, m. Margaret Barker 14 Feb 1666
Grace Smoot, wife of Wm. Smoote, d. 14 Jan 1666 [1665; C.251]
Thomas Peircy, d. 5 Nov 1666
John Rouse, servant to John Cage, d. 25 Jan 1666
Richard Baron, servant to Humphrey Warren, d. 27 Jul 1666
Elizabeth Smoote, d/o Richard Smoote, b. 15 Dec 1666
John Browne, s/o Elizabeth Browne, b. 5 Jul 1666
James Lindsey, s/o James Lindsey, b. 10 Feb 1666 [18 Feb; C.253]
Mary Hunt, d-i-l of Garrett Sinnett, b. 2 days before Easter 1665
Thomas Coffer, s/o John Coffer, b. 25 Nov 1667 [15 Aug; C.253]
John Robinson, m. Elizabeth Browne 21 Mar 1666
Wm. Hills, m. Edith Headlow __ Jun 1667 [at Mr. Montague's; C.253]
John Paine, m. Marie White 23 Sep 1667
Garret Synnet, m. Alice Hunt 21 Nov 1666
John Browne, d. 7 Nov 1666
Richard R_____, d. 7 Sep 1667 [Richard Randall, d. 7 Nov 1667 (C.253)]

Liber P, Page 205

Thomas Asborough, serv't of Alexander Sympson, d. 10 Aug 1667
Dennie Murfrey, d. 23 Sep 1667 at James Lindsey's
John Wheeler, s/o John Wheeler, b. in year of 1654

James Wheeler, s/o John Wheeler, b. 9 days before Christmas 1656
Mary Wheeler, d/o John Wheeler, b. 22 Mar 1658
Thomas Wheeler, d/o John Wheeler, b. 18 Mar 1660
Winnifrett Wheeler, d/o John Wheeler, b. in Mar 1663
Ignatius Wheeler, s/o John Wheeler, b. in May 1665
Margarett Sinnett, d/o Garrett Sinnett, b. 24 Oct 1667
Jemima Long, d/o Robert Long, b. 5 Jan 1667
Elizabeth Lane, d/o Wm. Lane, b. last day of May 1668
John Court, s/o John Court, b. 19 Feb 1655
Elizabeth Court, d/o John Court, b. 16 May 1663
Margarett Court, d/o John Court b. 15 Jan 1665
Elizabeth Obryan, wife of Mathias Obryan, d. 6 May 1670
Geo. Mackmillion m. Grace Carre, Jan 1669
Peter Mackmillion, s/o Geo. and Grace, b. Apr 1670
Edward Wade, s/o Zachary Wade, b. 2 Nov 1670
Elizabeth Barton, d/o Wm. Barton, Jr., b. 27 Feb 1671
John Lambert, s/o John Lambert, b. 5 Feb 1664; [age 8 on 4 Feb 1672 (E.72)]
Elizabeth Lambert, d/o John Lambert, b. Jan 1667; [Elinor Lambert age 5 in Jan 1672 (E.72)]
William Lambert, s/o John Lambert, b. 27 Feb 1669; [age 3 in 1672 (E.72)]
Samuel Lambert, s/o John Lambert, b. 10 Mar 1671; [age 1 on 10 Mar 1672 (E.72)]
Edward Wade, s/o Zachary Wade, b. 22 Aug 1672
Elizabeth Moore, d/o Henry Moore, b. 13 Mar 1664 [30 Mar; E.87]
Henry Moore, s/o Henry Moore, b. 3 Oct 1665
Thomas Moore, s/o Henry Moore, b. 9 Oct 1667
John Moore, s/o Henry Moore, b. 13 Mar 1669; [b. 15 Mar 1674 (D.163)]
Elizabeth Douglas, d/o John Douglas, b. 26 Apr 1673
Notley Rozer, s/o Benjamin Rozer, b. 1 Jul 1673
John Ward, s/o John Ward, b. 16 Mar 1671
John Smallwood, s/o James Smallwood, b. Jan 1666
James Smallwood, s/o James Smallwood, b. Oct 1668
Mary Smallwood, d/o James Smallwood, b. Jan 1670

Mathew Smallwood, s/o James Smallwood, b. Apr 1673
Mary Goodrick, d/o Robert Goodrick, b. 13 Mar 1673
William Farlowe, s/o Ambros Farlowe, b. 15 Feb 1671; [15 Feb 1672 (E.166)]
William Wade, s/o Zachary Wade, b. 3 Nov 1673; [3 Dec 1673 (E.170)]
Martha Baker, d/o Thomas and Martha Baker, b. last of Mar 1675
Ralph Lomax, s/o Cleborne & Blanch, b. last day of Jul 1673

Liber P, Page 206

Susanna Lomax, d/o Cleborne & Blanch, b. 3 Apr 1675
Katherine Lomax, d/o Cleborne & Blanch, b. 16 May 1677
Onsley Hill, s/o Thomas and Mary Hill, servants to Benj. Rozer, b. 5 May 1677 [bapt. 3 Jun 1677; F.244]
Mary Rozer; d/o Benjamin & Mary, b. 6 Apr 1675
Elizabeth Beck, d/o Richard & Elizabeth, b. 2 Oct 1669
Mary Beck, d/o Richard & Elizabeth, b. 15 Nov 1673 [1672; G.166]
Margarett Becke, d/o Richard & Elizabeth, b. 1 May 1674
William Chandler, s/o William & Jane of Portobacco, b. 13 Oct 1678
Cleborne Lomax, s/o Cleborne & Blanch, b. 22 Jan 1678
Margarett Jones, d/o Richard & Elizabeth of Mattawoman, b. 6 May 1673
____ Jones, d/o Richard & Elizabeth, b. 27 May 1677
Elizabeth Jones, d/o Richard & Elizabeth, b. 27 Apr 1679
William Obryan, s/o Matthias & Magdalen of Mattawoman, b. 6 Mar 1672
Mary Allward, d/o John & Mary of the head of Portobacco Creek, b. 20 Dec 1676
John Allward, s/o John & Mary, b. 18 Dec 1678
Andrew Baker, s/o Thomas & Martha of Potomac River, b. 29 Mar 1679
John Young, s/o Lawrence & Sarah of the head of Baker's Creek, b. 4 Dec 1673
Thomas Young, s/o Lawrence & Sarah, b. 18 May 1678
John Dod, s/o Richard & Mary, b. 2 Jun 1666
Richard Dod, s/o Richard & Mary, b. 13 Jan 1670

Marke Lampton, s/o Marke & Elizabeth of the head of
    Portobacco Creek, b. 6 Oct 1680
Mary Lampton. d/o Marke & Elizabeth, b. 4 Jan 1674
Thomas Vassall, s/o Lewis & Elizabeth, b. 8 Sep 1680
John Cole, s/o Phillip & Mary of the head of Wicomico River, b.
    10 Jan 1678
Phillip Cole, s/o Phillip & Mary, b. 4 Dec 1680
Thomas Lomax, s/o Cleborne & Blanch of head of Wicomico
    River, b. 4 Jul 1681

Liber P, Page 207

Margarett Allward, d/o John & Mary of head of Portobacco
    Creek, b. 4 Mar 1680
William Ling, s/o Francis & Mary, b. 11 Mar 1669
Michaell Ling, s/o Francis & Mary, b. 2 Jan 1671
Mary Ling, d/o Francis & Mary, b. 27 Mar 1673
Francis Ling, s/o Francis & Mary, b. 9 Oct 1676
Richard Hall, s/o Richard & Mary of Portobacco, b. 28 Jul 1679
Katherine Martin, d/o Joseph & Mary of Portobacco, b. 3 Dec
    1681
Thomas Witter, s/o Thomas & Mary, b. 9 Feb 1672
Bulkeley Witter, s/o Thomas & Mary, b. 26 Jul 1675
William Witter, s/o Thomas & Mary, b. 26 Sep 1678
Robert Downes, s/o Robert Downes, b. 4 Feb 1670
Ellino. Right, d/o George Rights, b. 7 Oct 1683
John Lomax, s/o Cleborne & Blanch, b. 20 Nov 1683
William Lampton, s/o Marke & Elizabeth of the head of
    Portobacco Creek, b. 29 Apr 1682
Samuel Luckett, s/o Samuel & Elizabeth, b. 10 Oct 1685
Elizabeth Deverell, d/o Thomas & Anne, b. 1 Jan 1679
Elizabeth Mankin, d/o Stephen & Mary, b. 22 Jun 1682
Stephen Mankin, s/o Stephen & Mary, b. 4 Jul 1685
John Mankin, s/o Stephen & Mary, b. 16 Jan 1686
John Bayly, s/o John & Mary, b. 20 Jan 1680
James Bayly, s/o John & Mary, b. 17 Jan 1683
Elizabeth Mason, d/o Philip, b. 6 Oct 16__
Samuell Mason, s/o Philip, b. 18 Apr ____

Liber P, Page 208

8 Feb 1684 Mrs. Anne Fowke at Portobacco joined together Wm. Dent & Elizabeth Fowke, d/o Anne, in the holy estate of matrimony; wit. Mrs. Anne Fowke, Col. Wm. Chandler, Madm. Mary Chandler, Mr. Gerard Fowke, Mrs. Mary Fowke, Owen Newen & diverse others; license from Hon. Wm. Diggs, Esq.

19 Dec 1685; baptized Thomas Dent, s/o William & Elizabeth
25 Dec 1687; baptized William Dent, s/o William & Elizabeth
3 Feb 1688; baptized Gerard Dent, s/o William & Elizabeth; these 3 children bapt. at their home at Portobacco by John Turlinge; document dated 25 May 1689

Thomas Luckett, s/o Samuel & Elizabeth b. 12 Aug 1688
John Cooper, s/o Nicholas & Penellopy, b. __ __ 16__
Anne Cooper, d/o Nicholas & Penellopy, b. 15 Mar 1688
William Milstead, s/o Edward & Susanna, b. 20 Jul 1685
Richard Jones, s/o Richard & Jane, b. 4 Apr 1680
Anne Jones, d/o Richard & Jane, b. Christmas 1684
Charles Charleson, m. Dorothy Mulgraves, widow, 14 Nov 1689
Mary Mankin, d/o Stephen & Mary, b. 20 Mar 1688
Susannah Robinson, d/o Richard & Joyse of head of Portobacco Creek, b. 20 Oct 1677
Mary Robinson, d/o Richard & Joyse, b. 17 Dec 1679
Charles Garrett, s/o Charles & Joyse of head of Wicomico River, b. 7 May 1684
Elizabeth Sapercote, d/o Abram & Rachel of ye river side, b. 12 Nov 1677
William Williams, s/o John & Sarah of ye river side, b. 2 Oct 1685
John Williams, s/o John & Sarah, b. 2 Aug 1688
Mary Hawking, d/o William & Mary, b. 20 Jun 1687
Henry Hawking, s/o Henry, Jr. & Sarah of Zachia Hundred, b. 5 Jan 1689
William Hawking, s/o William & Mary of Portobacco, b. 18 Mar 1689
William Herbert, s/o John & Elizabeth of Zachia Hundred, b. 6 Jul 1688

Liber P, Page 209

Lewis Mingoe, s/o Lewis & Elizabeth of Nanjemy, b. 12 Mar 1681
Charles Mingoe, s/o Lewis & Elizabeth, b. 14 Mar 1685
Elizabeth Mingoe, d/o Lewis & Elizabeth, b. 11 May 1689
Elizabeth Raines, d/o John & Elizabeth of Mattawoman, b. 26 June 1684
Henry Raines, s/o John & Elizabeth, b. 3 Sep 1686
Lucy Raines, d/o John & Elizabeth, b. 7 Dec 1688
Mary Goos, d/o George & Anne of head of Wicomico River, b. 12 Jun 1683
Sarah Goos, d/o George & Anne, b. 1 May 1686
George Goos, s/o George & Anne, b. 13 Jul 1689
Henry Karnes, s/o Robert & Mary of Portobacco, b. 3 Sep 1688
Philip Mason, s/o Philip & Mary of Piscataway, b. 2 Jun 1689
Elizabeth Cornish, d/o John & Martha of Mattawoman, b. 18 Aug 1678
Richard Cornish, s/o John & Martha, b. 11 Dec 1679
Edward Cornish, s/o John & Martha, b. 10 Oct 1682
Martha Cornish, d/o John & Martha, b. 14 May 1687
Mary Ord, d/o Peter & Anne of Wicomico, b. 24 Mar 1683
Thomas Ord, s/o Peter & Anne, b. 19 Nov 1686
James Ord, s/o Peter & Anne, b. 21 Aug 1690
George Dent, s/o William & Elizabeth of Nanjemy, b. 27 Sep 1690; bapt. Christ Church 16 Apr 1691
Margarett Cornish, d/o John & Martha of Mattawoman, b. 8 Nov 1690
Elizabeth Ashman, d/o Richard & Anne of Wicomico, b. 29 Jun 1680
Richard Ashman, s/o Richard & Anne, b. 4 Feb 1682
Mary Ashman, d/o Richard & Anne, b. 3 Aug 1685
Standidge Ashman, s/o Richard & Anne, b. 1 Oct 1687
Allward Hardy Ashman, s/o Richard & Anne, b. 12 Jun 1691
John Miller, s/o John & Grase, b. 5 Nov 1673
Peter Miller, s/o John & Grase, b. 7 Jul 1682

Liber P, Page 210

William Mason, s/o Philip & Mary of Piscataway, b. 3 Jan 1690
George Witter, s/o Thomas & Mary, b. 9 Oct 1683

John Duglas, s/o John Duglas, cooper, & Mary of Pickawaxen, b. 29 Oct 1686

William Karnes, s/o Robert Karnes, tailor, and Mary of Portobacco, b. 3 Apr 1691

Notley Warren, s/o Humphrey & Elizabeth of Wicomico, b. 16 Dec 1675

Dinah Roolants, d/o Robert and Margery of Wicomico, b. 2 May 1677

Benjamin Warren, s/o Humphrey & Margery of Wicomico, b. 23 Jan 1682

Charles Warren, s/o Humphrey & Margery, b. 10 Nov 1684

John Warren, s/o Humphrey & Margery, b. 18 Jun 1687

Humphrey Warren, s/o Humphrey & Margery, b. 15 Nov 1691

Ignatius Luckett, s/o Samuell & Elizabeth, b. 30 Jan 1689

Penelope Martin, d/o John Martin, carpenter, & Demaris of Wicomico, b. 13 Nov 1690

Josiah Mankin, s/o Stephen & Mary of Portobacco, b. 18 Jan 1690

Charity Courts, d/o John & Charity of Pickawaxen, b. 4 Oct 1680

John Courts, s/o John & Charity, b. 3 Mar 1691

Thomas Browne, planter, m. Alise Horton, 26 Jul 1692

Edward Wilder, s/o John & Ever Elday Wilder, of Wicomico, b. 27 Nov 1689; bapt. 4 Dec afsd.

John Wilder, s/o John & Ever Elday Wilder, b. 30 Sep 1692; bapt. 2 Oct afsd.

Thomas Dixon, s/o Thomas Dixon of Pickawaxen, b. 8 Jun 1692

Edward Philpott, s/o Edward & Susanna of Wicomico, b. 14 Jan 1687

Susanna Philpott, d/o Edward & Susanna, b. 9 Jun 1690

John Philpott, s/o Edward & Susanna, b. 13 Oct 1692

William Marshall, s/o William & Elizabeth of Wicomico, b. 12 Sep 1690

Barbary Marshall, d/o William & Elizabeth, b. 30 Oct 1692

Anne Dod, d/o Richard & Jane of the head of Baker's Creek, b. 24 Sep 1692

Anne Gwynn, d/o Christopher & Susanna, b. 27 Jul 1692

John Dawson & Elizabeth Thirst, m. 16 Sep 1690

Mary Dawson, d/o John & Elizabeth, b. 22 Sep 1692

Liber P, Page 211

Robert Yates, s/o Robert & Rebeckah of Pickawaxen, b. 10 Apr 1690

Charles Yates, s/o Robert & Rebeckah, b. 29 Apr 1692

Catherine Herbert, d/o William & Mary of Pickawaxen, b. 6 Dec 1692

Elizabeth Snoggin, d/o George & Susanna of Pickawaxen, b. 14 May 1686

John Snoggin, s/o George & Susanna, b. 27 Dec 1687

Mary Snoggin, d/o George & Susanna, b. 16 Mar 1688

George Snoggin, s/o George & Susanna, b. 13 Nov 1692

John Hall, s/o William & Mary of Portobacco, b. 4 Nov 1692

Mary Prise, d/o Robert & Anne of Portobacco, b. 12 Nov 1692

John Barker, s/o John & _____ of Nangemy, b. 3 Apr and bapt. 17 Apr 1691

Giles Thompkins, s/o Giles & Sarah of Pickawaxen, b. 23 Nov 1692

George Bateman, s/o George & Elizabeth of Pickawaxen, b. 7 Dec 1692

Robert Powell, s/o Robert & _____ of Pickawaxen, b. 17 Nov and bapt. 10 Jan 1692

Henry Lewis, s/o David & Jane of Pickawaxen, b. 16 Oct 1687

Isable Lewis, d/o David & Jane, b. 4 Aug 1690

Mary Lewis, d/o David & Jane, b. 28 Nov 1692

Marke Penn, s/o William & Mary of Wicomico, b. 24 Nov 1692

Edward Rookewood, s/o Edward & Mary of Pickawaxen, b. 25 Dec 1692

Richard Ratelife, s/o John & Bathsheba of Wicomico, b. 16 Dec 1692

Jane Jones, d/o Moses & _____ of Portobacco, b. 4 Jan 1692

Susanna Kirkley, d/o Christopher & Catherine of the head of Wicomico, b. 17 Mar 1681

Christopher Kirley, s/o Christopher & Catherine, b. 23 Feb 1684

Matthew Dutton, s/o Thomas & Elizabeth of Wicomico, b. 28 Sep 1692

John Taylor, s/o Thomas & Anne of Pickawaxen, b. 8 Jan 1692

Elizabeth Groves, d/o George & Alise of head of Wicomico River, b. 1 Nov 1692

Humphrey Posey, s/o John & Susanna of head of Wicomico River, b. 1 Feb 1683

John Posey, s/o John & Susanna, b. 30 Jul 1685

Jemima Belayne, d/o Nicholas & Mary of head of Wicomico River, b. 21 Mar 1686

Elizabeth Belayne, d/o Nicholas & Mary, b. 25 Feb 1688

Liber P, Page 212

Mary Harris, d/o Thomas & Mary of Pickawaxen, b. 16 Nov 1680

Thomas Harris, s/o Thomas & Mary, b. 26 Feb 1682

John Harris, s/o Thomas & Mary, b. 5 Mar 1684

Mary Morris, d/o Richard & Penelope of Cedar Point, b. 22 Dec 1680

Penelope Morris, d/o Richard & Penelope, b. 13 Nov 1684

Richard Land, s/o Richard & Penelope of Pickawaxen, b. 8 Oct 1687

John Land, s/o Richard & Penelope, b. 12 Jan 1689

Elizabeth Land, d/o Richard & Penelope, b. 4 Apr 1691

Elizabeth Cherrybub, d/o John & Mary of Pickawaxen, b. 28 Mar 1687

John Cherrybub, s/o John & Mary, b. 20 Mar 1690

Mary Francklin, d/o Henry & Mary of Wicomico, b. 12 Oct 1689

Jane Francklin, d/o Henry & Mary, b. 31 Jan 1692

Susanna Posey, d/o Benjamin & Mary of Wicomico, b. 1 Jun 1691

Anne Hanson, d/o John & Mary of Wicomico, b. 18 Jan 1692

James Coghill, s/o William & Christian of Portobacco, b. 10 Jan 1692

Anne Dent, d/o William & Elizabeth of Nanjemy, b. __ Mar 1692

Godshall Barnes, s/o Matthew & Elizabeth, b. 20 Dec 1692

Mary Mankin, d/o Stephen & Mary of Portobacco, b. 9 Feb 1692

Anne Moody, d/o William & Jane of head of Wicomico, b. 2 Mar 1692

Mary Saunders, d/o John & Sarah of Portobacco, b. 19 Apr 1692

John Goureleg, s/o John & Barbary of Cedar Point, b. 23 Apr 1693

Richard Newton, s/o Richard & Jane of Wicomico, b. ___ and
   bapt. 13 May 1693
Joseph Bullett, s/o Joseph & Elizabeth of Mattawoman, b. 8 Feb
   1688
Benjamin Bullett, s/o Joseph & Elizabeth, b. 28 Apr 1693

Liber R # 1
1690-1692

Liber R, facing Page 1

26 Aug 1690; Deed of Gift from **Sarah Banckes**, relict of Richard Banckes, dec'd merchant, to her 4 children, **Mary Banckes, Richard Banckes, Samuel Banckes** and **Sarah Banckes**; slaves, household goods, cattle, etc.; /s/ Sarah Banckes; wit. Cleborne Lomax, Mary Whittaker (mark), Thomas Tofle, Robert Barrett

Liber R, Page 3

16 May 1690; **Henry Moore** had acknowledged moiety of *Maismore* sold by **William Boyden** & **Elizabeth Boyden** alias **Moore**, relict of Henry Moore, dec'd, to Thomas Gibson; /s/ **Philip Lynes**; wit. Ignatius Wheeler, James Barrett (mark)

Liber R, Page 4

1_ Feb 1689; From **John Breeden** of Stafford in Colony of Virginia, planter, to **Joshua Graves**, planter; for 2,500# tobacco; called *Howland* alias *Breedens Neck*; bounded by *Howland* and land of Matthias OBryan; /s/ John Breeden (mark); wit. Robt Brant, Robt. Thompson, Rich Nelson (mark)

Liber R, Page 5

10 Jun 1690; Indenture from **William Smoote**, planter, to **Philip Lynes** of St. Mary's Co., merchant; for 5,000# tobacco; a parcel on Chesapeake Bay and the north side of Patapsco River containing 1,100 acres; /s/ Wm. Smoote; wit. Robert Barrett, William Herbart

Liber R, Page 7

11 Jun 1690; From **Richard Boughton**, Gent., to **George Thompson** of St. Mary's Co., Gent.; for diverse causes and considerations a tract of land called *Square Adventure* of 100 acres; formerly conveyed by George Thompson by indenture dated 13 Nov 1684; /s/ Ric. Boughton; wit. Robert Yates, Cleborne Lomax

Liber R, Page 30

16 May 1690; Indenture from **Thomas Lewgar**, planter, to **Philip Lynes** of St. Mary's Co.; for 1,000# tobacco; a parcel called *Hardshift* on the west side of Avon River; bounded by land

formerly laid out for Andrew Watson; containing 300 acres; /s/ Thomas Lewgar; wit. John Wright, Ignatius Wheeler
 Liber R, Page 31

12 Aug 1690; Indenture from **Nicholas Skidmore**, tailor, and Anne his wife, to **Henry Trenn**; for 2,000# tobacco; a parcel called *Hill Port*; /s/ Nicholas Skidmore, Anne Skidmore; wit. Thos. Burford, Wm. Penn (mark), Hugh Owen (mark);
 Liber R, Page 32

13 Aug 1688; From **Nicholas Proddy**, late of *Barnabye* now of *Gisbrough*, County of York, Kingdom of England, heir of Nicholas Proddy late of Nanjemy, and **Jane** his wife; two tracts, one called *Barnabye* of 545 acres and the other called *Batchelor's Horne* containing 250 acres; for £35; to **Thomas Hobb** of St. George's in St. Mary's Co.; /s/ Thomas Proddy, Jane Proddy; wit. Thomas Pearson, Robert Hope, Jo. Parrett
 Liber R, Page 48

14 Feb 1689/90; From **Charles Allison**, for 40,000# tobacco, to **Edward Ford**; a tract known as *Christian Temple Manor* containing 1,000 acres in Mattawoman; /s/ Charles Allison (mark); wit. Rich Hobart. Francis Hammersley, Robert Brant
 Liber R, Page 97

18 Sep 1690; From **Thomas Hobb** and his wife **Isable**; £36.12.0; to **John Addison**; land purchased from Nicholas Proddy [Liber R, page 32]; /s/ Thomas Hobb, Isable Hobb (mark); wit. John Maskey (mark), Wm. Fowler (mark), James Maskey (mark)
 Liber R, Page 104

11 Nov 1690; Indenture from William Hutchison to **John Thompson, James Greene** and **Thomas Hardwick**, planters; for 12,000# tobacco; a tract called *Aix* on the south side of Mattawoman Run; for 522 acres in *Zachia Manor*; /s/ Will. Hutchison; wit. Ignatius Wheeler, Ignatius Matthews
 Liber R, Page 105

1 Oct 1690; Indenture from **Job Corner** of Talbot Co. to **John James** of sd. co.; for 6,000# tobacco; a parcel called *Chestnut Point*; bounded by William Marshall; containing 200 acres; /s/ Job Corner (mark); wit. Thos. Whichaley, Jon. Godshall, Francis Meeke

Liber R, Page 131
28 Nov 1690; Indenture from **Edward Scutt**, planter, and **Mary** his wife, to **Francis Marbury** and **Morris Loyde**; for 8,000# tobacco; a parcel called *Thomas his Chance* on Piscataway Creek; laid out for 200 acres; /s/ Edward Scutt (mark), Mary Scutt (mark)

Liber R, Page 132
9 Dec 1690; Indenture from **John Attwood**, carpenter of Ann Arundel Co. to **Gowan Hamilton**; for 5,000# tobacco; a parcel of land called *Attwood Purchase* on the east side of the Eastern Branch of the Potomac River a little above Anacostian Fort; containing 400 acres; /s/ John Attwood; wit. James Thomson, Will. Hutchison

Liber R, Page 134
14 Jan 1689; Indenture from **Charles Calvert** of St. Mary's Co., Esq., son and heir of William Calvert, Esq., to **Charles Edgerton** of St. Mary's Co.; granted by the late Right Honorable Cecilius 11 Feb 1662 to William Calvert; a tract on the east side of Piscataway River and south side of Piscataway Creek; bounded by Randolph Hanson; containing 3,000 acres; further William Calvert upon marriage of his daughter Elizabeth with James Neale, Gent., did grant sd. Neale and his wife 600 acres part of afsd. 3,000 acres; for 30,000# tobacco Charles Calvert conveys afsd. to Charles Edgerton excepting 600 acres; /s/ Charles Calvert; wit. Elizabeth Baker (mark), J. Mackewen, Daniell Magniell?, Tho. Grunion?

Liber R, Page 142
12 Jan 1690; Indenture from **Thomas Warren**, planter, to **William Herbert**, planter; for 6,000# tobacco; a tract called *Little Ease*, bounded by *Thomas his Choice*, Edward Prise's land called *Locust Thickett*, and Piscataway Creek; containing 200 acres; also a parcel called *God's Gift* of 285 acres; /s/ Thomas Warren; wit. Robert Middleton, Thos. Whichaley

Liber R, Page 144
31 Dec 1690; Indenture from **Daniell Smith** of St. Mary's Co., carpenter, to Henry Goodridge; for 6,000# tobacco; a tract

called *Lyons Hole*; bounded by Richard Fowkes' *Vaineall*; containing 100 acres; formerly granted to Edward Maddocks by patent; /s/ Daniell Smith (mark); wit. John Wilder, Cleborne Lomax; ack. by **Elizabeth Smith**, wife of Daniel
      Liber R, Page 158

4 Dec 1690; Indenture from **John Sheereman**, planter, to **Richard Waye**, planter; for 1,200# tobacco; a half part of 300 acres at the mouth of Avon River or Nanjemy Creek; adjoining land where Richard Waye now lives; /s/ John Sheereman; wit. Cleborne Lomax, Philip Dyzer, Richard Loman
      Liber R, Page 185

3 Aug 1686; Petition to His Lordship's Council regarding an order for patent confirming a tract of land for **Nicholas Proddy** to be granted **Thomas Proddy**; within *His Lordship's Manor*; annexed certificate of Ninian Beale who laid out this manor; 9 Oct 1686; Ninian Beale confirms land lies in *His Lordship's Manor*
      Liber R, Page 186

27 Mar 1687; rent of *Barnaby* of 445 acres rec'd from **Col. Rozers** receipt Feb 1677 being 1310# tobacco of **John Addison** 27 Mar 1687
      Liber R, Page 186

27 Mar 1691; Indenture from **Richard Evans**, carpenter, to **George Miller**; for 4,500# tobacco; a parcel called *Barbadoes*; formerly an assignment of Col. Henry Darnall to Richard Evans; part of a warrant for 5,500 acres granted Darnall 7 Oct 1684; located on the west side of Eastern Branch of the Potomac River; containing 250 acres; /s/ Richard Evans (mark); wit. G. Hamiltone, William Thomson
      Liber R, Page 189

Court of 9 Jun 1691:
 George Plater, Gent., presents a woman servant named **Margarett Nicholson**, judged age 22 years; a man servant named **John Symmes**, judged age 9 years
 Catherine Wakelin, wife of **Richard Wakelin, Jr.**, binds her son, **Richard Wakelin** age 4 years on 18 Aug next, to live with and serve **John Godshall** to age 21

Liber R, Page 193

12 Jul 1690; Agreement in 2 documents; from **Edward Turner** to Gilbert Marsh; regarding land where Marsh has lived for 7 years; mentions one share of plantation where Turner now lives and a 15 foot dwelling house and 30 foot tobacco house and a 20 foot tobacco house; /s/ Edward Turner, **Mary Turner** (mark), Gilbert Marsh (mark; wit; Robert Clark and William Williams, Martha Middleton (mark)

Liber R, Page 194

9 Jun 1691; Indenture from **John Cornish**, surgeon, and **Martha** his wife, and **Robert Smallpage**, planter, and **Elinor** his wife, of one part, to **Joshuah Graves**, planter; for 6,000# tobacco a tract called *Moore's Fishing Place*; bounded by Matthias OBryan's land and parcels called *Hopewell* and *Howland*; located in *Zachia Manor*; containing 254 acre; /s/ Robert Smallpage, John Cornish; wit. Joseph Cornell, John Allward (mark); ack. by Martha Cornish and Elinor Smallpage

Liber R, Page 196

9 Jun 1691; Indenture from **Ninian Beall**, Gent., holding letter of atty. from **Benjamin Hadduck**, to sell his estate; from Ninian Beall to **Michaell Ashford**, carpenter, a tract called *Hadducks Hill* in the freshes of the Potomac; bounded by Hadduck's *Seaman's Delight*; containing 500 acres; /s/ Ninian Beall; wit. Henry Hardy, John Godshall, Will. Hutchison

Liber R, Page 197

10 Jun 1691; Indenture from **Michaell Ashford**, carpenter, and **Rachell** his wife, to **Thomas Hussey**, Gent.; for 35,000# tobacco; a parcel of land called *Moore's Ditch*; located on the west side of Zachia Swamp, adjoining land of George and Robert Gooderick, planters; laid out for 500 acres; /s/ Michaell Ashford (mark), Rashell Ashford (mark); wit. Robert Thompson, Cleborne Lomax, Wm. Stone

Liber R, Page 230

17 Jul 1689; Indenture from **William Blankenstein**, Gent., atty. of **John Peirse**, merchant, to **Charles Evens** of St. Mary's Co., merchant; patent dated 1 Jun 1687 granted Peirse; a tract called *Jemaire* [or *Jamaica*] in the freshes of the Potomac on

Broad Creek; containing 500 acres; for 10,000# tobacco; /s/ Wm. Blankenstien; wit. Jno. Wooderike, Wm. Nuthed, W. Taylard

Liber R, Page 232

27 May 1689; Indenture from **William Hutchison** to **John Swallwell** of Anne Arundel Co.; for £45; a tract called *Fortune* on the south side of the Eastern Branch of the Potomac; bounded by William Tannehill; containing 500 acres; /s/ Will Hutchison; wit. John Addison, James Thomson, G. Hamiltone

Liber R, Page 234

25 Dec 1690; Indenture from **James Cottrell**, planter, to **Nicholas Wise**, planter; 100 acres adjoining land of Anne Burford; for 15 years; /s/ James Cottrell; wit. Ralfe Gwyn (mark), Tho. Burford

Liber R, Page 234

Cattle Marks: **Mary Dickison**, d/o Thomas Dickison of Piscataway; **Thomas Marsh**, s/o Gilbert Marsh; **John Marsh**, s/o Gilbert Marsh; **Alexander Smith Turner**, s/o Edward Turner; **Anne Nicholas**, d/o William Nichols of Pickawaxen

Liber R, Page 239

11 Aug 1691; Indenture from **Charles Evens**, Gent., to **Henry Hawkins**, Gent.; for 10,000# tobacco; a parcel of land called *Jamaica* [or *Jamaira*]; containing 500 acres; (see Liber R, Page 230); /s/ Charles Evens, **Ann Evens**; wit. John Addison, Jon. Bayht, Cleborne Lomax

Liber R, Page 241

11 Aug 1690; Indenture from **Thomas Smoote**, carpenter, to **John Wilder**, Gent.; for 8,000# tobacco; a parcel of land called *Smootes Discovery*; bounded by Thomas Smootes usual landing, Cabbin land, land of Richard Harrisson, Wicomico River; containing 200 acres of land; /s/ Thomas Smoote, **Elizabeth Smoote**; wit. Henry Hawkins, Randolph Hinson (mark), Cleborne Lomax

Liber R, Page 267

Cattle Marks: Sep 1691; **Thomas Cofer; John Cofer, George Bateman, Benjamin Duglas**, s/o John Duglas, planter; **John**

Stewart, Elizabeth Stewart
> Liber R, Page 271

Nov 1691; Cattle Marks: **Buckley Witter**; Dr. **William Hall**, **Henry Quando, Onsley Hill**; **John Cuemey**; **Nicholas Couch**; **Thomas Browne**

> Liber R, Page 276

10 Nov 1691; Indenture from **Richard Harrison** of St. Mary's Co., planter, to **Jeffry Cole**, tailor; for 3,000# tobacco; a parcel of land formerly in possession of Richard Harrisson, dec'd, father of afsd. Richard; called *Harrissons Venture*; containing 50 acres; /s/ Richard Harrisson; wit. John Boarcroft, Dennis Lenden (mark), John Martin

> Liber R, Page 277

10 Nov 1691; Indenture from **Henry Moore**, son and heir of Henry Moore, dec'd, to **Robert Smallpage**, planter; for 6,000# tobacco; a tract called *Maismire*; bounded by Daniel Mathena, Mattawoman Creek, and George Howe; containing 200 acres; /s/ Henry Moore (mark); wit. Joshuah Graves, John Godshall, Edward Till

> Liber R, Page 279

25 Sep 1691; Indenture from **Anthony Smith**, planter, and **Martha** his wife, to **William Dent**; for 6,500# tobacco; a parcel of land laid out of land of Thomas Baker, dec'd, due Martha, d/o Thomas Baker; known as *Lott Number Three*; containing 181 acres; /s/ Anthony Smith (mark), Martha Smith (mark); wit. Charles Shepherd, Robert Smallpage, William Roddery (mark). [It appears Anthony Smith left his wife destitute and the court ordered William Dent to pay Joyse Garrett, wife of Charles Garrett, part of the afsd. tobacco for the maintenance of Martha Smith.]

> Liber R, Page 281

9 Nov 1691; Indenture from **John Bayne** of St. Mary's Co. to his daughter **Anne Bayne**; for fatherly love; half a parcel called *Lonist? Thickett*; containing 1,060 acres; /s/ Jon. Bayne; wit. Jo. Courts, Jr., Thos. Whichaley

> Liber R, Page 332

17 Aug 1690; From **Charles Shepherd** to **Henry Ward**, youngest

son of John Ward, dec'd; a slave; /s/ Charles Shephert; wit.
Wm. Surgeant, James Finley
Liber R, Page 333

16 Jan 1691; From **Charles Shepherd** to **James Speake**, s/o John Speake; a heifer; /s/ Charles Shepherd; wit. Wm. Surgeant, Bowling Speake

Cattle Marks; **John Athey**, s/o George Athey; **Jeremy Snell**; **Edward Marloe**; **Penelope Martin**; **Henry Robins**; **William Robins**, s/o Henry Robins
Liber R, Page 337

Thomas Mattox, servant to William Dent, judged age 12

David Mattox, judged age 156, servant to George Plater

John Neale, servant to Humphrey Warren; petitions for freedom
Liber R, Page 338

James Thorneborrow, servant to Philip Lynes; requesting freedom

William Smith, servant to Richard Land, runaway

Thomas Mannister, son of John Mannister, dec'd, bound to John Raines to age 21
Liber R, Page 338

10 Mar 1690; Indenture from **George Austrey** of Stafford Co., Virginia, to **Thomas Mitchell**, planter; for 5,000# tobacco; a parcel of land called *Abberdeen*; taken up by Alexander Gallant who conveyed to George Austrey; bounded by John Wheeler's *Exiter*; containing 100 acres; /s/ George Austrey (mark); wit. Geo. Godfrey, Willm. Frost
Liber R, Page 340

14 Jan 1691; Indenture from **John Addison**, Gent., to **William Dent**, attorney; for 2,000# tobacco; a parcel called *Boat Sail*; surveyed for Capt. Nicholas Gwither, now in possession of John Barker at Nanjemy; laid out for 60 acres; /s/ John Addison; wit. Wm. Stone, Robt. Thompson
Liber R, Page 372

Anne Thomas petitions the court for freedom of her dau. **Elizabeth Thomas**; Thomas Mitchell, master

Elizabeth Moris, orphan of **Thomas** and **Anise Moris**; petitions for her freedom

Grace Thompson, servant of John Stone; had bastard

Margaret Swettnam, servant of Gerrard Fowlkes; had bastard
Peter Hayes, servant of Robert Thompson, Jr., judged to be age 13
Daniell Mahoune, servant of Thomas Craxstone, runaway
Elizabeth Rue bound her dau., Temperance Rue, to James Finley
Francis Hanby bound his son, John Hanby, which he had by
    Elizabeth Harleton, to Edward Millsteade
James Burchner, servant to Philip Lynes; petition for freedom
Deusman Walker, servant to Henry Hawkins
               Liber R, Page 376
10 Dec 1690; Indenture from **William Huchison**, Gent., to **William Walson**, planter; a tract called *Vineyard*; bounded by Rock Creek and the Potomac River; laid out for 70 acres; lease for life of Walson or 20 years from this date; wife **Jane Walson**, **Elizabeth** his dau.; /s/ Will Hutchison, William Walson (mark); wit. John Stewart, ? Hamillone
               Liber R, Page 411
Cattle Marks; **Thomas Whithaley**; **Ignatius Wheeler**; **John Mankin**, s/o Stephen Mankin
               Liber R, Page 418
Anne Doulton, servant to Thomas Lindsey; runaway
Anne Elswood, servant to James Neal, runaway
Charles Smith, servant to Marke Lampton, runaway
Samuell Sigley, servant to Mitchell Ashford
               Liber R, Page 421
10 Jul 1691; Indenture from **Randolph Henson**, Gent., **Barbarah** his wife, and **Richard Wade**, planter, and **Anne** his wife, to **John Bayne** of St. Mary's Co.; for 52,000# tobacco [27,000# from each couple]; a tract called *Lonist Thickett* containing 1,060 acres; by patent to Maj. Thomas Brookes dated 3 Aug 1668; to Zachery Wade, father of Richard Wade, and Randolph Henson on 12 Nov 1672; /s/ Randolph Hinson (mark), Barbara Hinson, Richard Wade, Anne Wade (mark); wit. John Addison, Cleborne Lomax, George Plater, William Dent, William Marshall, Lewis Jones (mark), Thomas Hatton, Henry Bath (mark)
               Liber R, Page 432
1 Jul 1692; Indenture from **William Cash** and **Rebeckah** his wife

of Westmoreland Co., Virginia, to **Henry Key**, planter; for a certain sum of tobacco; 25 acres part of 100 acres called *Dosey Lane* in possession or Thomas Maris at this decease; now in possession of Henry Key; land belonging to the 4 daus. of Thomas Maris; /s/ William Cash (mark), Rebeckah Cash (mark); wit. Thomas Lileard (mark); Mary Boughton (mark)
Liber R, Page 464

14 Sep 1692; Indenture from **Thomas Moore**, planter, to **James Barrett**; for 2,000# tobacco; remainder of a parcel called *Whiteland* on the north side of Piscataway River and south side of Mattawoman Creek; containing 450 acres; /s/ Thomas Moore (mark); wit. Cleborne Lomax, William Dent
Liber R, Page 466

13 Sep 1692; **Thomas Baker** and **William Dent**, guardian to **Andrew Baker**, request division of a parcel called *Harrisson's Guift* of 250 acres being in joint ownership between Thomas and Andrew Baker; bounded by the Potomac River; /s/ Will Hutchison, Dennis Rueland (mark), Richard Edgar
Liber R, Page 466

14 Sep 1692; Indenture from **Thomas Baker**, planter, and **Elizabeth** his wife, to **William Dent**, Gent.; for 16,500# tobacco; a parcel of land being part of *Hanstone?* containing 550 acres patented for Thomas Baker, father of afsd. Thomas Baker, and Andrew Baker; divided between Thomas and Andrew 13 Sep; now in occupation of Thomas Orrell?; bounded by *Baker's Rest, Baker's Hollow*; containing 109 acres 2 leagues above Cedar Point and known as *Lot #2*; also 118 acres; /s/ Thomas Baker (mark), Elizabeth Baker (mark); wit. Robert Yates, Antho. Neale
Liber R, Page 502

26 Sep 1692; Cattle Marks: **John Knight; Anne Knight**, d/o John Knight
Liber R, Page 507

31 Oct 1692; Indenture from **Anthony Neale**, Gent., to **Gilbert Clarke**; for 2,000# tobacco; Lot #12 in Charles Town; /s/ Anthony Neale; wit. Robert Duglas, Thomas Nation

Liber R, Page 509

4 Nov 1692; Indenture from **Thomas Lynsey**, planter, to **Peirse Neeland**; for 300 acres of land already delivered; a parcel called *Galleys Discovery*; bounded by *Wheeler's Palme, St. Barbary*; containing 100 acres; /s/ Thomas Lynsey (mark), Peirse Neeland (mark); wit. William Moss, Griffith Davis (mark), John Athersith (mark)

Liber R, Page 534

1692; Cattle Mark: **William Hutchison**

Liber R, Page 536

10 Jan 1692; Gift from **Henry Thompson**, planter, to **Margarett Mankin**, d/o Stephen and Mary Mankin; a filly

Liber R, Page 537

10 Jun 1688; Indenture from **William Barton**, Gent., to **William Hungerford**, planter, of Stafford Co., Virginia, and **Margaret** his wife, d/o William Barton; for fatherly love; a parcel called *Barton Woodyard*; containing 100 acres; also a tract called *Capell*; bounded by Daniell Johnson's *Lyons Denn*; containing 100 acres; /s/ Wm. Barton, Mary Baton (mark); wit. Rando. Hinson (mark), John Addison

Liber R, Page 538

20 Feb 1690; Indenture from **William Dent**, attorney-at-law, and **Elizabeth** his wife, to **Thomas Warner**, planter; for 200 acres of land at Pope's Creek; a plantation tract where John Barker now lives; located on Burdetts Creek at Nanjemy; a tract containing 70 acres bounded by Queen's Creek Branch; also a parcel called *Baltimore County* containing 70 acres; also *Boatsail* adjoining *Baltimore County*; surveyed for John Addison; containing 200 acres; /s/ William Dent, Elizabeth Dent; wit. Francis Harrisson, John Barker (mark)

Liber R, Page 541

13 Dec 1692; Cattle Marks: **John Thomas**; **Sarah Cassock**, d/o John Cassock

Liber R, Page 542

23 Jan 1692; Indenture from **Simon Nicholls** and **William Younge** to **John Chittam**, planter; for 3,000# tobacco; a parcel called *Blackash*; bounded by Potomac River; containing 146 acres in

Calverton Manor; /s/ Simon Nicholls (mark), William Young (mark); wit. John Addison, Will Hutchison
Liber R, Page 543
31 Jan 1692; Indenture from Col. Ninian Beall of Calvert Co., atty. for **Benjamin Haddock**, to **John Emmett**, carpenter; for 6,000# tobacco; a tract called *Seaman's Delight*; bounded by land of Richard Evans; containing 500 acres; /s/ Ninian Beall; wit. Hugh Moor, Wm. Stone, Will Hatton
Liber R, Page 548
Cattle Marks: **Jane Onell**, d/o Thomas and Isabell Onell; **John Harisson**; **Luke Wheeler**, s/o Ignatius Wheeler; 10 Jan 1692/3

Liber S
1692 to 1694

Liber S, Page 12

16 Dec 1692; Indenture from **Thomas Lugar** to **William Dent**; for 6,000# tobacco; a parcel on the north side of Piscataway River called *St. Barbaries Manor*; on the south side of a great swamp called Beaver Dam that falls into a marsh called Great Marsh; containing 1,000 acres; granted John Lugar, Gent., grandfather to Thomas Lugar; to his son John Lugar; to his son Thomas Lugar; portion excepted; /s/ Thomas Lugar (mark) wit. Cleborne Lomax, Wm. Stone

Liber S, Page 47

Cattle Marks: **Mary Saunders**, d/o John Saunders

Liber S, Page 48

19 Jul 1692; Indenture from **Philip Mason**, planter, and **Mary** his wife, to **Thomas Lewis**; for 6,000# tobacco; 1/2 part of tract called *Battessey*; bounded by Cash Creek; laid out for 250 acres; /s/ Philip Mason (mark), Mary Mason (mark); wit. John Addison, Wm. Hall, Will Hutchison

Liber S, Page 49

1 Aug 1692; Original warrant from His Lordship surveyed for **Anthony Neale**, s/o Capt. James Neale; bounded by land of Arthur Turner, by a marsh that falls into St. Raphaell's Creek, land of Christopher Russell and land surveyed for Benjamin Gill; containing 494 acres; /s/ Rando. Brandt, Depty. Surveyor

Liber S, Page 50

3 Jan 1692; Indenture from **Walter Story**, Gent., to **James Cox**, blacksmith; for 3,500# tobacco; a parcel of land being part of *The Store* plantation on the Potomac River; adjoining land of Philip Lynes, Hampton Creek; containing 50 acres; /s/ Walter Story, **Mary Story** (mark); wit. Wm. Hatch, James Latemar

Liber S, Page 56

14 Mar 1692; Indenture from **William Hutchison** to **Luke Read** of Anne Arundel Co.; for £50; a parcel called *Aaron* now in occupation of Luke Read; located a little above Anacostin

Fort; bounded by Luke Green; laid out for 300 acres according to certificate dated 17 Mar 1687; /s/ Will Hutchison; wit. Thomas Hussey, John Swallwell (mark)

Liber S, Page 59

12 Sep 1692; Indenture from **John Raines**, planter, to **Edward Ford**; for 100 acres of land called *Wellford* in Nanjemy; bounded by John Posey's land called *St. James*; located in *Zachia Manor*; for 2,000# tobacco; /s/ John Raines (mark); wit. George Clemmons, Benj. Pocter

Liber S, Page 65

Cattle Marks: **John Cox; William Williams**, s/o John Williams

Liber S, Page 108

24 Apr 1693; Cattle Marks: **Allward Hardy Ashman; John Dawson; Richard Combes; George Kingerley**

Liber S, Page 109

18 Feb 1692; Indenture from **William Reeves**, planter, and **Anne** his wife, to **John Courts**, Gent.; for 8,000# tobacco; half part of a tract of 200 acres called *Harguesse's Hope*; bounded by *Zachia Manor* and *Zachia Swamp*; /s/ William Reeves (mark), Anne Reeves (mark); wit. Robert Yates, William Hanton, Wm. Hatch

Liber S, Page 110

24 Apr 1693; Deposition of Willliam Williams, age 53; for purpose of conveyance of land from **Thomas Mudd** to **John Saunders** in right of his wife **Sarah**, d/o Maj. William Boarman: In 1673 deponent was a tenant to Major, then Capt. Wm. Boarman on his tract of land where Thomas Mudd now dwells; deponent was retainer of Boarman for 18 years more or less prior to that date; he heard Boarman say that 400 acres of the 800 acres in the patent went to his dau. Sarah in marriage to Mr. Joseph Piles; the match was broken by disagreement of parents of Mr. Piles; then a match was proposed between Dr. Thomas Matthews of Portobacco and his eldest son Thomas Matthews and Sarah; when deponent returned from 5-6 months in England, Sarah and Thomas were living on land where Thomas Mudd now lives; deponent asked how Capt. Boarman "would do by ye son George to

whom you have promised this land now given your daughter;" Boarman replied other provision had been made for George....; /s/ Wm. Williams; wit. James Smallwood
> Liber S, Page 112

Cattle Marks: **Christopher Whittymore; Anne Whittymore,** d/o Christopher; **William Pattison**
> Liber S, Page 119

13 Jun 1693; Indenture from **Nicholas Beade,** planter, to **John Allen,** planter; for 5,000# tobacco; a parcel of land called *The Adventure*; surveyed by Owen Jones 20 Jan 1668; conveyed to Edward Knight by indenture 4 Sep 1669; conveyed to Nicholas Beade 2 Jan 1670; containing 70 acres; /s/ Nicholas Beade (mark); wit. Thomas Lewis, Cleborne Lomax
> Liber S, Page 125

28 Jun 1690; Warrant granted to **James Thompson** 6 Apr 1690 by assignment to **Robert Middleton** for 164 acres part of *Mount Pleasant* in *Zachia Manor*; /s/ Will. Hutchison, dep'y surveyor
> Liber S, Page 126

18 Apr 1690; From **James Thompson** to **Robert Middleton**; assignment of above; /s/ James Thompson; wit. Wm. Hutchison

13 Jun 1693; From **Robert Middleton** to **William Hutchison**; rights in above 164 acres of *Mount Pleasant*

Cattle Marks: **Edward Musgrove; Dennis Doyne**
> Liber S, Page 127

18 Jul 1692; recorded 16 Jun 1693; Indenture from **Robert Middleton,** planter, and **Mary** his wife, to **John Clement**; for 8,000# tobacco; a parcel of land called *Wickham* in *Piscataway Manor*; bounded by Francis Adames' *Primar*, John Wheeler; containing 112 acres; /s/ Robert Middleton, Mary Middleton; wit. John Addison, Will Hutchison
> Liber S, Page 128

Tymothy Mahawney, servant to Humphrey Warren, judged age 17

Catherine Ivery, servant to Anne Neale (mother of Anthony Neale), judged to be age 15
> Liber S, Page 129

John Cole, servant to Robert Benson, judged age 18

Hans Herrickson, s/o Hans and Judith, age 4; to serve Robert Benson to age 21

Bryan Farrell, servant to John Speake; runaway

Elizabeth Heselden, servant to Robert Thompson; had bastard

                    Liber S, Page 133

19 Apr 1689; Warrant of 1,000 acres of land granted **William Hutchison**; assigned to **Robert Middleton** for 176 acres called *Turkey Thickett* on the west side of Hinson's Branch; /s/ Will Hutchison

24 Dec 1692; **Robert Middleton** assigns rights in above to **John Addison**; /s/ Robert Middleton; wit. James Miller, Will. Hutchison

Cattle Mark: **Thomas Onell**

                    Liber S, Page 168

12 Sep 1693; Cattle Marks: **Gerrard Marshall; Elizabeth Cornish; Edward Cornish; Elizabeth Nicholls**, d/o William Nichols

                    Liber S, Page 169

14 Nov 1693; Cattle Marks: **Henry Hawkins**, s/o Henry Hawkins; **Francis Sheiffeild; Charles Guy; John Payne; Mary Wilkinson**, d/o Lancelott and Mary; **Elizabeth Smith**, d/o Richard Smith; **John Jackson; Arthur Smith**; s/o Richard Smith

                    Liber S, Page 170

14 Feb 1692; enrolled 14 Nov 1699; Indenture from **James Connoway** of Stepney Parish, Stebunheath, Middlesex Co., mariner, to **John Addison** of Potomac River, Gent.; by indenture dated 4 Nov 1692 between John Meekes and John Addison; for £70; to John Addison a parcel called *St. Elizabeth* on the east side of Piscataway River about 8 miles from Piscataway Creek; bounded by land of the late George Thompson, a swamp, St. John's Creek; containing 600 acres; /s/ James Conaway; wit. Tobyah Winne, Sr., Robert Coleman, ___, Wm. Smith, Jr.; attested in London 17 Feb 1692 in the Lord Mayor's Count in the Mayoralty of St. John Fleet Knight

Liber S, Page 174
Cattle Marks: **Michaell Wallis**; **Benoni Fanning**; **Sarah Newman**, d/o George Newman; **Mary** and **Elizabeth Newman**; d's/o George Newman

Liber S, Page 187

17 Apr 1693; Indenture from **William Dent**, planter, to **John Higdon** of St. Mary's Co., planter; for 2,000# tobacco; a parcel of land called *Hallyfax*; located on the north side of Oxon Runn; containing 90 acres; /s/ William Dent (mark); wit. Ralph Shaw, Cleborne Lomax

Liber S, Page 189

14 Nov 1693; Indenture from **John Sheerman**, planter, to Nicholas Cooper, planter; for 2,000# tobacco; a 50 acre parcel called *Watson's Purchase* of 300 acres; bounded by Nanjemy Creek and land of Robert Downes; /s/ John Sheereman (mark); wit. Peter Achilles, Cleborne Lomax

Liber S, Page 191

13 Jun 1693; Indenture from **Thomas Warner**, planter, to **Peter Achilles**, planter; for a parcel called *The Gift* of 50 acres and a parcel called *Oakington* of 100 acres and "four hundred pounds;" plantation where John Barker lives or did live of 70 acres; bounded by a marsh on Burdett's Creek at Nanjemy, 200 acres of John Barker and Queenes Creek; land called *Baltimore's Bounty*; containing 70 acres; also tract called *Boatsayle* of 60 acres joining *Baltimore Bounty*; surveyed by John Addison conveyed to William Dent; containing 60 acres; the said 3 parcels containing 200 acres; /s/ Thomas Warner (mark); wit. Nicholas Cooper (mark), John Sheerman (mark), Cleborne Lomax

Liber S, Page 193

13 Jun 1693; Indenture from **Peter Achilles**, planter, to **Thomas Warner**; a parcel where John Barker lives or did live containing 70 acres; also a parcel called *Baltimore's Bounty* containing 70 acres; also a parcel called *Boatsaile* of 60 acres; total 200 acres at Nanjemy; for *The Gift* on the north side of Piscataway River and Chingamuxon Creek; bounded by John Hatch; containing 50 acres; also *Oakington* of 100 acres on the

north side of the Potomac at the head of Chingamuxon Creek; /s/ Peter Achilles; wit. Nicholas Cooper (mark), John Sheerman (mark), Cleborne Lomax
                    Liber S, Page 205
2 Jan 1693; Indenture from **Thomas Austin**, planter, and **Susanna** his wife, to **Michaell Martin**; for 5,000# tobacco; a parcel of land called *Habnabala Venture*; bounded by Daniell Johnson's land called *Johnsons Choice* and *Smootes Choice*; laid out for 250 acres; /s/ Thomas Austin (mark), Susanna Austin (mark); wit. Wm. Barton, Henry Hawkins
                    Liber S, Page 211
John Jones, servant to John Wilder, judged age 14
Richard Newton, servant to Capt. Ignatius Causin, judged age 14
Elizabeth Forster, servant to Samuell Luckett; runaway
George Witter, s/o Thomas Witter, dec'd; apprenticed for 4 years to John Martin, boatwright, and Demaris his wife; with consent of John Duglas, cooper, his father-in-law [step-father]
                    Liber S, Page 212
William Witter, s/o Thomas Witter, chooses his father-in-law [step-father] John Duglas, cooper, as guardian
                    Liber S, Page 239
16 Feb 1693; Cattle Mark: **Rebeckah Turling**, d/o Isable Onell
21 Feb 1693; **Mary Ashforth**, d/o Michaell and Rachell Ashforth, swears **Christopher Gregory** is the father of the child she now goes with
                    Liber S, Page 240
Cattle Marks: **George Brett**; **Susanna Brett**; **Thomas Smallwood**; **Thomas Wheeler**, s/o Thomas; **Ignatius Wheeler**, s/o Thomas; **Anne Wheeler**, d/o Thomas
                    Liber S, Page 241
Cattle Marks: **Thomas Allrook**; **Frances Frampton**
                    Liber S, Page 242
Susannah Blizard, d/o Giles Blizard, dec'd, to remain in custody of her mother-in-law [step-mother] Mary Thompson
William Gray, servant to Joseph Manning; runaway

Liber S, Page 245

13 Mar 1693; Indenture from **William OBryan** to **Peter Fernandis**; for 7,000# tobacco; a parcel of land called *Archlough* on the south side of the main fresh of St. Thomas Creek; bounded by his own land called *Quernson*; containing 200 acres; /s/ William OBryan; wit. Thomas Jenkins, William Woodard (mark)

Liber S, Page 275

26 Apr 1694; Indenture from **Thomas Love** to **Philip Hoskins**, Gent.; for 5s; a parcel of land on the west side on Portobacco Creek where his father William Love did live; containing 100 acres; /s/ Thomas Love (mark); wit. Wm. Barton, Henry Hawkins, Cleborne Lomax; in return Philip Hoskins to care for Thomas Love for the rest of his natural life; Hoskins also to receive cattle, horses, chattel, and other possessions

Liber S, Page 278

Cattle Marks: **John Shacker**; **Sarah Shacker**, d/o John; **John Swellwell**; **Elinor Warren**, d/o Thomas

Liber S, Page 279

Cattle Marks: **Abraham Warren**, s/o Humphrey; **Humphrey Warren**, s/o Humphrey

Liber S, Page 284

John Barefoot, s/o John Barefoote, dec'd; to serve Richard Boughton to age 21

James Geer, servant to Capt. William Barton, judged age 12

John Cooke, servant to Richard Newton, runaway

Liber S, Page 286

16 Oct 1684; Indenture from **Edward Sanders**, Gent., admn. to **Henry Brayne**, dec'd, and **Jane** his wife, to **Giles Blizard**; obligation of Henry Brayne dated 2 Jul 1674 unto John Cane for use of his daughter **Susanna Cane**, assigns on the day of marriage of Susanna 20,000# tobacco; marriage was 21 Aug 1684 between Giles Blizard and Susanna Cane. Now this Indenture for 20,000# tobacco Edward and Jane Sanders convey a parcel dated 8 April 1683 called *Bowplain* on the east side of the Anacostia River on St. John's Creek; bounded by John Meekes; laid out for 1,000 acres bearing date of 12

Feb 1660; /s/ Edward Sanders, Jane Sanders; wit. Wm. Wells, Richard Conner (mark), Mary Wells (mark)
> Liber S, Page 288

4 Jun 1694; Resurvey at request of **Robert** and **Francis Greene** of *Greene's Inheritance* on Portobacco Branch; patented in the names of Leonard, Robert and Francis Greene; divided into 3 parts; 1st part to Francis Greene; 2nd part of Robert Greene; 3rd part divided into 4 lots for the children of **Leonard Greene**; Lot # 1 to **Francis Wheeler** and **Winnifried** his wife; Lot # 2 to **Thomas Green**; Lot # 3 to **Mary Greene**, Lot # 4 to **Margaret Greene**
> Liber S, Page 313

1694 Cattle Marks: **Ignatius Matthews; Henry Smith; Thomas Smith**, s/o Henry Smith; **William Smith**, s/o William Smith; **Thomas Wakefield**, s/o Abell Wakefield
> Liber S, Page 319

William Forbis, servant to William Dent, judged age 17
> Liber S, Page 329

Cattle Marks: **John Anderson; Edward Anderson**, s/o John
> Liber S, Page 330

25 Aug 1694; Indenture from **Thomas Baker**, planter, and **Elizabeth** his wife, to **Thomas Onell**; for 18,000# tobacco; part of the tract which Thomas Baker, father of afsd. Thomas, and moiety of tract called *Harrisson's Gift* containing 250 acres patented by Thomas Baker and his brother Andrew Baker; now in tenure of Thomas Onell; bounded by *Baker's Rest* and the Potomac; laid out for 109 acres; also land from the same source called *Lot # 2* containing 118 acres; also a parcel purchased by Thomas Baker, Sr., from John Jarboe of St. Mary's Co., part of a patent of 300 acres which Jarboe sold Barker, Sr. excepting an assignment to John Nevill; /s/ Thomas Baker (mark), Elizabeth Baker (mark); wit. Cleborne Lomax, William Hawton, Robert Yates
> Liber S, Page 333

Cattle Mark: **John Sanders**

Liber S, Page 334

Cattle Marks: **Mary Saunders**, d/o John and Sarah; **Mary Maston**, d/o Richard and Mary; **Henry Maston; Elizabeth Maston; John Maston; John Leete; William Leete;** Elizabeth Teares; d/o Hugh; **Francis Adames, Jr.**; Richard Nelson; Elizabeth Davis, d/o Griffith Davis, **Valentine Hill; Robert Marris; Francis Bullarie; Robert Greene**

Liber S, Page 342

Thomas Hills, servant to Robert Smallpage, runaway

Mary Davis, servant to George Plater; requesting freedom

Joan Fitzgerald, servant to William Sarjeant; complaints about her master

Liber S, Page 344

13 Aug 1694; Indenture from **William Griffin** to **James Smallwood, Sr.**; for 10,000# tobacco; a parcel called *The Hills*; bounding Smallwood's land called *Porke Hall*; containing 113 acres; /s/ William Griffin; wit. Robert Smallpage, John Parker (mark)

Liber S, Page 345

28 Apr 1694; Indenture from **Joseph Harrisson** of Nanjemy to **John Stone**, Gent., together with his brother vestrymen of Nanjemy Parish; for 200# tobacco; a parcel of land about 1/4 mile from Nanjemy Run on the upper side of a deep branch between plantations of Francis Harrison and Joseph Harrisson; one acre of land for the building of a Protestant Church called St. Joseph's; /s/ Joseph Harrisson (mark); wit. John Suratt, John _____

Liber S, Page 348

11 Sep 1694; Indenture from **Marke Lampton**, planter, and **Elizabeth** his wife, to **William Hutchison**, Gent.; for 7,000# tobacco; a parcel called *Jeamind* containing 371 acres; bounded by *Wade's Adventure*; /s/ Marke Lampton (mark), Elizabeth Lampton (mark); wit. Cleborne Lomax, Wm. Barton

Liber S, Page 350

22 Jun 1694; Indenture from **Thomas Wicherly**, planter, to **Joshuah Guibert** of St. Mary's Co.; for 10,000# tobacco; a parcel called *Cedar Tower Hill*; bounded by John Nevill's

land on the Wicomico River; /s/ Thomas Wicherly; wit.
Cleborne Lomax, Jon. Bayne; acknowledged by **Elizabeth Wicherly**

Liber S, Page 388

Gift from **Elizabeth Barton**, wife of William Barton of Mattawoman, to her Goddaughter **Elizabeth Parker**, d/o John Parker; a cow calfe

Liber S, Page 389

14 May 1692; Articles of Pease and Amity with **Ornatomaquate**, the Emperor of the Piscataway [10 pages barely legible]

Liber S, Page 400

_ Dec 1694; **Lilias Boyd**, relict and executrix appointed by the deceased **Hugh Moore**, sometime Doctor of Humanity in the City of Glasgow; hereby appoints William Mounteith, merchant of Glasgow, and James Knox, merchant, admns. of Moore's will dated 7 Dec 1691 for **Hugh** and **Jennett Moore**, children of my sd. dec'd husband; /s/ Lyllias Boyd; wit. William Boyd, James Lashlan; certified in Glasgow

Liber S, Page 404

11 Nov 1694; Indenture from **John Smith** of Calvert Co., planter, and **Elizabeth** his wife, to **Jervis Windsor**, planter; for 4,800# tobacco; a parcel called *Smith's Chance* on the south side of Mattawoman Runn; bounded by Richard Brightwell; located in *Manor of Zachia*; containing 144 acres; /s/ John Smith, Elizabeth Smith; wit. Sam. Peter, Edw. Potter

Liber S, Page 405

13 Nov 1694; Indenture from **Emmannuell Ratclife**, planter, to **James Coghill** and **William Coghill**; for 1,600# tobacco; called *Pentealey? Folly*; bounded by Giles Blizard on the south side of Oxon Run; laid out for 100 acres; /s/ Emmannuell Ratelife; wit. Gerrard Fowke, Thomas Stone

Liber S, Page 407

7 Jan 1694; Indenture from **William Clarkson** to **Robert Clarkson**; for 7,000# tobacco; [very dim]; a parcel called *Clarksons Purchase*; containing 122 acres; /s/ William Clarkson; wit. Thomas Addison, Andrew Hurd, William Rothery (mark)

Liber S, Page 410

29 Dec 1694; Indenture from **Samuell Boughton**, planter, to **Morris Loyd**; for 4,000# tobacco; a parcel called *Eatons Delight*; [very dim]; containing 200 acres; /s/ Samuell Boughton; wit. Christopher Gregory; Thomas Jenkins

Liber S, Page 412

12 Feb 1694; Indenture from **John Gaines** of Talbott Co. to **Edward Fitzgerald**; for 8,000# tobacco; a parcel of land called *Chesnutt Point* on the west side of Wicomico River; bounded by Edward Swann, Edward Philnutt, and William Marshall; containing 200 acres; /s/ John Gaines; wit. Gerard Fowke, Cornelius Haddock, John Smith

Liber S, Page 414

11 Mar 1694; Indenture from **James Makey**, planter, to **William Dent**, Gent.; for 5,000# tobacco; parcel called *Thompkinsons Long Looked For*; [very dim]; on the north side of the Potomac; containing 200 acres; /s/ James Makey; wit. Christopher Gregory, Samll. Boughton

Liber S, Page 418

8 Nov 1694; Indenture from **Walter Evans**, planter, to **Benjamin Berry**, planter; for 1,800# tobacco; a parcel called *Evans His Range*; [very dim]; containing 100 acres; /s/ Walter Evans; wit. Thomas _____; Andrew Hurd

Liber S, Page 420

17 Jul 1694; Indenture from **Thomas Gibson** to **Henry Gifford**; for 12,000# tobacco; a parcel called *Gibson's Close*; [very dim]; /s/ Thomas Gibson (mark); wit. Jno. Harrison, Ralph Smith (mark); ack. by **Elizabeth Gibson**

Liber S, Page 423

8 Mar 1694; Indenture from **Thomas Gibson** to **Henry Gifford**, carpenter; for 6,000# tobacco; a parcel...[very dim]; /s/ Thomas Gibson (mark), **Elizabeth Gibson** (mark); wit. George Tubman, John Wilson

Liber S, Page 424

27 Mar 1695; Indenture from **William Hutchison** to **Jeremiah Snell**; for 5,600# tobacco; a parcel called *?Contented Acres*;

[very dim]; /s/ Will Hutchison; wit. James Smallwood, John Hanson

Liber S, Page 430

17 Jul 1694; Indenture from **James Ward,** son of John Ward, dec'd, and Deamaris, his wife, alias Damaris Sarjeant ye natural mother of James Ward, bound to **Robert Edmondson;** /s/ James Ward (mark); wit. John Stone, Thomas Stone

Liber S, Page 431

13 Nov 1695; Indenture from **Francis Hanby** and **Alise** his wife; Alise binds her son **Samuell Barker,** now age 7 years, to Samuell Luckett; /s/ Francis Hanby (mark), Alise Hanby (mark); wit. Gilbt. Clarke, Tho. Burford

Index

Aaron, 144
Abberdeen, 139
Abbot, Thomas, 85
Abbott, Edward, 33, 38, 51
Abbott, Susanne, 90
Abis, Matthew, 90
Achilles, Peter, 23, 24, 25, 43, 148, 149
Acres, John, 90
Adames, Edwd., 90
Adames, Francis, 10, 14, 20, 21, 72, 75, 85, 146
Adames, Francis, Jr., 152
Adames, Henry, 14, 56, 85, 92, 96, 98, 99, 106, 108
Adames, John, 85
Adams, Mr., 99, 100
Addison, John, 114, 133, 135, 137, 139, 140, 142, 144, 146, 147, 148
Addison, Rebecca, 117
Addison, Thomas, 153
Addition, 61
Adventure, The, 15, 21, 146
Agambra, Domindego, 99, 104
Ailer, Elizabeth, 90
Aix, 133
Akerden, 31
Alcock, Thom., 81, 85
Alden, Mary, 90
Aldgate, 65
Aldis, William, 90
Aldred, Theophilus, 5
Allanson's Folly, 20, 47, 52, 64, 67, 81
Allanson's Manor, 29
Allanson, John, 51

Allanson, Mary, 30
Allanson, Thomas, 1, 2, 5, 6, 8, 9, 11, 12, 18, 20, 24, 25, 29, 30, 37, 42, 54, 59, 66, 67, 85, 96
Allcock, Mary, 85
Allcock, Thomas, 1, 20, 47, 53, 63, 66
Allcock, Thomas, Jr., 85
Allen, John, 22, 27, 41, 49, 52, 85, 94, 146
Allen, Martha, 16
Allen, Mary, 4
Allen, William, 4, 6, 9, 10, 11, 13, 16, 69
Allerton, Elizabeth, 16
Allerton, Isaac, 16, 17
Allinson, Annabella, 90
Allison, Charles, 133
Allrook, Thomas, 149
Allward, John, 15, 17, 36, 65, 85, 92, 102, 121, 124, 125, 136
Allward, Margarett, 125
Allward, Mary, 124, 125
Ambrose, Richard, 26
Anderson, Edward, 151
Anderson, John, 151
Anderson, Lawrence, 90
Anderson, Ralph, 90
Anglish, John, 90
Antwerp, 26, 34, 116
Archiball, John, 105
Archlough, 150
Armstrong, Richard, 90
Asborough, Thomas, 122
Ashanan, Richard, 55
Ashbrooke's Rest, 27, 34, 57
Ashbrooke, James, 73, 85

Ashbrooke, John, 122
Ashbrooke, Lettise, 23, 27
Ashbrooke, Thomas, 14, 23, 27, 75, 85
Ashen Swamp, 116
Ashford, Michael, 17, 52, 76, 83, 121, 136, 140, 149
Ashford, Rachell, 52, 76, 136, 149
Ashforth, Mary, 149
Ashman, Allward Hardy, 127, 145
Ashman, Anne, 127
Ashman, Elizabeth, 85, 127
Ashman, Mary, 127
Ashman, Richard, 59, 67, 85, 127
Ashman, Standidge, 127
Ashton, James, 73
Askins, John, 106
Askins, Rebekah, 106
Asobrey, John, 41
Aspenall's Chance, 64, 67
Aspinall, Elizabeth, 64
Aspinall, Henry, 9, 11, 12, 15, 24, 39, 42, 52, 53, 54, 60, 62, 64, 85, 96
Aspinall, Henry, Jr., 85
Aspinall, Humphrey, 81
Aspinall, Mary, 9
Athee, see Athey
Athersith, John, 142
Athey's Hopewell, 46
Athey, Ann, 75
Athey, George, 35, 46, 50, 73, 75, 85, 109, 120, 139
Athey, John, 139
Athey, Sarah, 120
Athman, Richard, 52
Atkins, Anne, 21
Attchison, George, 90
Attkins, William, 90

Attwicks, Humphrey, 77
Attwood Purchase, 134
Attwood, John, 134
Aunley, James, 90
Aushish, William, 90
Austin, Susanna, 149
Austin, Thomas, 149
Austrey, George, 139
Austria, George, 31

Bacoke, John, 90
Bailey, Grace, 90
Bailies, Tho., 85
Baily, William, 90
Baiteman, Patrick, 90
Baker's Addition, 52
Baker's Hollow, 141
Baker's Rest, 141, 151
Baker, Andrew, 124, 141
Baker, Elizabeth, 134, 141, 151
Baker, John, 59, 115
Baker, Martha, 124
Baker, Thomas, 2, 6, 10, 13, 14, 26, 33, 37, 52, 59, 85, 91, 95, 108, 124, 138, 141, 151
Baker, Thomas, Sr., 151
Baker, William, 15, 27
Baldwin, Robert, 59
Balfe, Oliver, 6
Ball, Margaret, 90
Ball, Thomas, 90
Ball, Walter, 78
Ballaine, John, 27
Ballis, James, 115
Baltimore County, 142
Baltimore's Bounty, 148
Banckes, Mary, 132
Banckes, Richard, 132
Banckes, Samuel, 132
Banckes, Sarah, 132

Bankes, George, 9, 10, 32
Barber, Luke, 40
Barbour, Nathaniel, 81
Barbous, Wm., 85
Bard, Peter, 90
Barefoot, John, 114, 150
Barker's Englargement, 50
Barker's Rest, 84
Barker, Joan, 50, 84, 90
Barker, John, 77, 84, 106, 115, 129, 139, 142, 148
Barker, Margaret, 122
Barker, Robert, 90
Barker, Samuell, 155
Barker, Sarah, 46
Barker, Will, Jr., 85
Barker, William, 85
Barlow, Joel, 90
Barnabis, 116
Barnaby, 133, 135
Barnehill, 65, 73
Barnes, Edward, 90
Barnes, Elizabeth, 130
Barnes, Godshall, 130
Barnes, Henry, 32, 33, 43, 85
Barnes, Matthew, 130
Baron, Richard, 90, 122
Barrett, Elizabeth, 103, 112
Barrett, James, 103, 112, 132, 141
Barrett, John, 90
Barrett, Robert, 132
Barrett, William, 90
Barrett, William, Jr., 41
Barrett, William, Sr., 41
Barron, John, 110
Barrott, Robert, 38
Barrow, Charles, 121
Barrow, John, 91
Barthelo Harbor, 78
Bartlett, Ralph, 82, 85

Barton Woodyard, 142
Barton, Elizabeth, 123, 153
Barton, George, 85, 91
Barton, Grace, 121
Barton, Margaret, 142
Barton, Martha, 20, 21
Barton, Mary, 114
Barton, Nathan, 8, 12, 17, 20, 21, 72, 85, 101, 122
Barton, Robert, 91
Barton, William, 12, 20, 39, 69, 76, 77, 81, 83, 85, 90, 92, 93, 94, 95, 96, 97, 98, 104, 114, 119, 121, 122, 142, 149, 150, 152, 153
Barton, William, Jr., 8, 21, 25, 32, 69, 85, 95, 104, 122, 123
Bartonzee, 115
Batchelor's Agreement, 19
Batchelor's Harbour, 6, 16, 63
Batchelor's Hope, 14, 40, 72
Batchelor's Horne, 133
Bateman, Elizabeth, 129
Bateman, George, 129, 137
Bath, Henry, 140
Batherton, John, 91
Batker, Thomas, 141
Batterzee, 118, 144
Battle, Anthony, 91
Batts, Richard, 80
Bawlding, Mary, 91
Bawlding, Robert, 91
Bayht, Jon, 137
Bayly, John, 59, 125
Bayly, Mary, 125
Bayly, Nicholas, 91
Bayly, Thomas, 85
Bayne, Anne, 138
Bayne, Elinor, 48, 73

Bayne, John, 81, 101, 120, 138, 140
Bayne, Walter, 74
Beade, Mary, 69
Beade, Nicholas, 69, 85, 146
Beade, Sarah, 69
Beall, Charles, 113
Beall, Ninian, 113, 135, 136, 143
Beamont, John, 105, 106
Beamont, Thomas, 105, 106
Beane, Elenor, 2, 99
Beane, Mr., 91, 102
Beane, Walter, 2, 47, 71
Beaumont, Richard, 74
Beck, Elizabeth, 124
Beck, Margarett, 124
Beck, Mary, 124
Beck, Richard, 92, 100, 38, 39, 124
Bedford, Henry, 28, 29, 30, 31
Belaine's Hill, 60
Belaine, Elizabeth, 130
Belaine, Grace, 69
Belaine, Jemima, 130
Belaine, John, 42, 65, 69, 70
Belaine, Mary, 130
Belaine, Nicholas, 60, 65, 69, 117, 130
Belayne, see Belaine
Bell, Bridgett, 91
Bell, Charles, 113
Bell, Elizabeth, 91
Bell, Ninian, 113
Bellingham, Alise, 91
Bene, Thomas, 91
Bennett, John, 91
Bennett, Mary, 91
Bennett, Thomas, 13, 14, 115
Benson, John, 91
Benson, Robert, 85, 146, 147
Berke, Richard, 45

Berkenhead, Rupert, 9
Berry, Benjamin, 154
Berry, Elizabeth, 91
Berry, John, 91
Betties Delight, 43, 45
Bewplaine, 1, 150
Beyerwood, 105
Bezick, John, 85
Binningham, Mary, 91
Bishop, William, 91, 116
Bissell, Mary, 85
Bissick, John, 30
Blackash, 142
Blake, Francis, 61
Blankenstein, William, 136, 137
Bleu Plane, 79, 80
Blizard, Giles, 79. 80, 104, 108, 149, 150, 153
Blizard, Susannah, 149
Blooksitch, 56
Blumstead, John, 50, 85
Blumsted, Katherine, 50
Boarcroft, John, 138
Boarde, Nicholas, 21
Boareman's Content, 40
Boareman, Capt, 92
Boarman, George, 145, 146
Boarman, Sarah, 5
Boarman, William, 5, 11, 39, 49, 53, 56, 74, 90, 91, 94, 100, 102, 145
Boarman, William, Jr., 74
Boatsail, 139, 142, 148
Boise, Elinor, 104
Bollier, Giles, 67
Bonard, Henry, 93, 95
Bond, John, 14, 85
Bonner, Elizabeth, 38, 65
Bonner, Henry, 12, 14, 15, 16, 19, 30, 31, 38, 47, 48, 52, 55, 58,

59, 60, 65, 69, 70, 77, 85, 94, 95, 97, 103
Bonners Retirement, 65
Book, Richard, 94
Booker, John, 91, 103
Booth, John, 85
Boswell, John, 39, 85, 111
Boswell, Marie, 111
Boswell, Martha, 111, 121
Boswell, Mathew, 85, 111
Boswell, Michael, 111, 121
Boswell, William, 111, 121
Bouge, Thomas, 108
Boughton, Mary, 141
Boughton, Richard, 8, 12, 13, 25, 28, 78, 80, 82, 104, 132, 150
Boughton, Samuell, 82, 154
Bouke, Ann, 14
Bourd, Jane, 91
Bowing, William, 91
Bowles, John, 16, 48, 95, 96, 101, 102
Bowles, William, 48
Bowling, Capt., 108
Bowling, James, 70, 99, 101
Bowman, John, 113
Boyce, Eleanor, 105
Boyce, James, 105
Boyce, John, 105
Boyce, William, 105
Boyd, Lilias, 153
Boyden, Anne, 22
Boyden, Elinor, 54
Boyden, Elizabeth, 43, 54, 68, 132
Boyden, Francis, 36
Boyden, John, 4, 5, 10, 22, 23, 27, 29, 30, 31, 32, 34, 37, 54, 85

Boyden, Mary, 54, 85, 105
Boyden, Roger, 38

Boyden, William, 1, 2, 4, 5, 6, 9, 10, 22, 23, 24, 29, 30, 31, 38, 43, 68, 105, 132
Boyer, Jno., 82
Boyse, Elenor, 69
Boyse, Elizabeth, 85
Boyse, John, 69
Boyse, William, 69, 85
Bozer, Benj., 124
Bracener, Henry, 85
Bracher, John, 110, 118
Bradbree, Anthony, 29
Bradshaw, John, 108
Bradshaw, Thomas, 91
Brandt, Mary, 103
Brandt, Randolph, 47, 49, 51, 52, 56, 57, 58, 60., 63, 64, 72, 73, 74, 76, 78, 85, 103, 112, 119, 144
Branner, Edward, 107
Branner, Henry, 107, 113
Bransoner, Henry, 112
Brant, Robert, 132, 133
Brasher, John, 85
Brayne, Henry, 150
Brayne, Jane, 69, 150
Brayner, Henry, 85
Breade, Jane, 56
Breade, John, 102
Breame, Christopher, 21, 26, 34, 106, 107
Breckeridge, Thomas, 46
Breeden, Elizabeth, 23
Breeden, Gerrard, 9, 10, 23
Breeden, John, 132
Breedens Neck, 132
Brett's Beginning, 57
Brett, George, 57, 58, 149
Brett, Susanna, 149
Brewer, William, 17

Bridges, Antho., 96
Bridges, Joseph, 116
Bridges, Theophen, 105
Bridgets, Elizabeth, 91
Bright, Edward, 91
Bright, Thomas, 65, 91
Brightwell, Richard, 153
Brimins, Christopher, 98
Britton, William, 21, 30
Broadhead, Anne, 91
Brooke, Ellinor, 28
Brooke, John, 104
Brooke, Richard, 27, 46
Brooke, Thomas, 28, 41, 91
Brookes, Hen., 91
Brookes, Thomas, Maj., 140
Brookesbanck, Abraham, 110
Broonely, Thomas, 91
Brown, see Browne
Browne, Elizabeth, 69, 121, 122
Browne, Garrard, 2, 6, 9, 11, 14, 17, 18, 19, 20, 24, 25, 26, 30, 34, 37, 43, 67, 69, 85
Browne, James, 58, 104, 105
Browne, John, 122
Browne, Mary, 69
Browne, Philip, 45
Browne, Robert, 48
Browne, Thomas, 77, 91, 128, 138
Browne, William, 69, 121
Bruxbanke, Abraham, 91
Bryan, Mathias, 14
Bryant, Thomas, 51
Bull, William, 91
Bullarie, Francis, 152
Bullett, Benjamin, 131
Bullett, Elizabeth, 103, 131
Bullett, Joseph, 33, 38, 39, 53, 85, 94, 103, 131
Bunney, John, 56

Burchner, James, 140
Burdette, Thomas, 60
Burdit's Nest, 8
Burdit's Rest, 8
Burdit, Elizabeth, 8, 69
Burdit, Francis, 8, 69
Burdit, Parthenia, 8, 69, 78
Burdit, Sarah, 8, 69, 78
Burdit, Thomas, 8, 69, 77
Burdit, Verlinda, 8, 69
Burford, Anne, 137
Burford, Thomas, 64, 65, 66, 73, 74, 77, 85, 114, 118, 133, 137, 155
Burkhaine, John, 91
Burloyne Hill, 83
Burnam, William, 85
Burnband, William, 117
Burnham, Jno., 85
Burnham, Sam, 85
Burnham, William, 105
Burrowes, Paul, 72
Burton, 68, 119
Bushere, John, 85
Buskeridge, Thomas, 47
Busklow, Benjamin, 92
Butcher, Jno., 76, 80
Butcher, Mary, 80
Butler, Eliza, 119
Butler, John, 48
Butler, Peter, 45
Butterfield, Jno., 79
Buttler, John, 101
Butwell, Cornelius, 108
Byers, Terlaugh?, 103
Byfield Close, 25

Cabioge, Jno, 64
Cable, John, 69, 85
Cable, William, 121

Cage, John, 2, 93, 99, 101, 107, 122
Cage, William, 120
Caine, John, 1, 11, 19, 33, 35, 36, 37, 59, 69, 85
Caldwell, George, 85
Calvert, Charles, 17, 116, 134
Calvert, Elizabeth, 79, 116, 134
Calvert, Philip, 12
Calvert, William, 20, 79, 116, 134
Calverton Manor, 143
Campton, Christopher, 92
Cane, John, 76, 79, 80, 150
Cane, Susanna, 79, 80, 150
Canland, John, 92
Capell, 142
Capshaw, Francis, 92
Car, John, 25
Carey, Hugh, 92
Carey, Philip, 46
Carnell, Christopher, 2
Carney, Jno., 84
Carpenter, Christopher, 92
Carpenter, Henry, 92
Carpenter, Richard, 31, 32, 85

Carr, Grace, 69, 123
Carr, Peter, 58, 85, 91, 94, 95, 97, 98
Carreddale, Thomas, 92
Carrill, Daniell, 116
Carson, Sarah, 85
Cartee, Charles, 121
Cartie, Demud Mack, 92
Cary, John, 17
Caryl, Richard, 92
Cash, Rebeckah, 140, 141
Cash, William, 140, 141
Casleton, Mary, 21, 33

Casleton, Robert, 11, 21, 29, 33, 58
Cassock's Lopp, 29, 44
Cassock, Benjamin, 111
Cassock, John, 29, 33, 44, 58, 78, 81, 85, 111, 142
Cassock, Margaret, 121
Cassock, Sarah, 142
Castleton, Robert 78
Cathew, Christopher, 92
Causine, Ignatius, 6, 11, 19, 20, 23, 24, 32, 38, 48, 51, 66, 83, 90, 91, 101, 102, 106, 149
Causine, Nicholas, 23
Cayne, James, 92
Cedar Tower Hill, 152
Chaireman, John, 85
Chandler, Anne, 73
Chandler, Jane, 124
Chandler, Jobe, 14, 16, 19, 24, 33, 35, 36
Chandler, Mary, 66, 104, 126
Chandler, Richard, 28, 65, 66, 73, 78, 85, 93, 98, 99
Chandler, William, 28, 37, 51, 58, 65, 66, 70, 73, 85, 90, 97, 98, 124, 126
Chaplin, Thomas, 92
Chapman, Barbara, 25
Chapman, George, 92
Chapman, Richard, 22, 25
Charles Towne, 30
Charleson, Charles, 126
Charman's Purchase, 6
Charman, John, 6, 13, 19
Cherrybub, Elizabeth, 130
Cherrybub, John, 130
Cherrybub, Mary, 130
Cheshire Thickett, 33
Cheshire, 65, 66

Chesson, Barbary, 56
Chesson, John, 48, 56
Chesson, Mary, 56
Chestnut Point, 3, 133, 154
Chew, Edith, 92
Chittam, John, 142
Chomley, Francis, 92
Chosen, 19
Christian Temple Manor, 37, 133
Chummey, Francis, 113
Chysham, Thomas, 94
Clarke's Inheritance, 66, 75
Clarke, Ambros, 122
Clarke, Anne, 92
Clarke, Beteres, 92
Clarke, Gilbert, 106, 108, 141, 155
Clarke, James, 92
Clarke, Jane, 48
Clarke, John, 8, 26, 47, 66, 67, 86, 99, 100, 101, 122
Clarke, Mary, 92
Clarke, Robert, 47, 59, 69, 92, 98, 115, 136
Clarke, Samuel, 33, 53, 120
Clarke, Susanna, 38, 92
Clarke, Thomas, 66, 86, 95, 100, 105
Clarke, Veteres, 69, 86
Clarkson, Robert, 153
Clarkson, William, 112, 153
Clarksons Purchase, 153
Clary, Morris, 92
Clement, John, 52, 58, 86, 105, 146
Clemmons, George, 145
Clipsham, Susannah, 77, 107
Clipsham, Thomas, 45, 77, 93, 101, 112
Clipshawe, Thomas, 61

Coates, Bartholomew, 21, 37, 96
Coates, John, 27, 30, 62, 100
Coates, Mr., 99
Coates, Ralph, 23, 27, 31, 33, 34, 37, 40
Coates, Thomas, 13, 86
Cobb, John, 19
Cobb, Sam., 92
Cocker, Will, 24
Coddington, Elizabeth, 104
Coffer, Thomas, 122, 137
Coffers, John, 33, 122, 137
Coghill, Christian, 130
Coghill, James, 130, 153
Coghill, William, 130, 153
Colborne, Nicholas, 119
Colchester, 41, 65
Cole, Giles, 24
Cole, Henry, 3
Cole, Jeffery, 115, 120, 138
Cole, John, 125, 146
Cole, Mary, 125
Cole, Nicholas, 108
Cole, Phillip, 80, 125
Cole, Thomas, 11
Coleman, Robert, 147
Coll, John, 105
Colley, Joseph, 26
Colliar, Gyles, 86
Collier, Thomas, 116
Collingwood, Robert, 92
Collins, Alise, 92
Combe's Purchase, 62
Combes, Richard, 145
Comer, Richard, 116
Conner, Richard, 112, 151
Connoway, James, 147
Contented Acres, 154
Cooke, John, 105, 150
Cooksey, Samuell, 104

Coolidge, John, 60
Coomes' Purchase, 27
Coomes, Eliza., 86
Coomes, Philip, 27
Cooper, Anne, 126
Cooper, Edward, 86
Cooper, John, 92, 126
Cooper, Joseph, 86
Cooper, Mary, 86
Cooper, Nicholas, 86, 126, 148, 149
Cooper, Penellopy, 126
Cooper, Roger, 92
Cooper, Thomas, 92
Cooper, Walter, 23, 86
Cooper, ____, 78
Corker's Hogg Hole, 40
Corker's Hoghole, 31
Corker, Thomas, 30, 31, 32, 33, 34, 35, 36, 37, 39, 40, 42, 43, 45
Cormack, Margarett Mark, 93
Cornall, Joseph, 103, 111, 112, 114, 136
Cornall, Margaret, 111, 114
Corner, Gilbert, 3, 69, 86
Corner, Jobe, 23, 30, 35, 36, 42, 43, 45, 133
Cornish, Edward, 127, 147
Cornish, Elizabeth, 127, 147
Cornish, John, 86, 127, 136
Cornish, Margarett, 127
Cornish, Martha, 127, 136
Cornish, Richard, 127
Cornute, Hendrick, 92
Cornwall, Francis, 92
Corsley, Thomas, 24
Corvell, Joseph, 83
Cosleton, Marie, 69
Cosleton, Robert, 69

Coslinton, Jno., 86
Cosner, Jobe, 24
Cottell, James, 137
Cottwell, James, 92
Couch, Nicholas, 138
Couffer, John, 8
Coulchester, 29
Court, Cleat, 92
Court, Elizabeth, 123
Courts Palace, 3
Courts, Charity, 128
Courts, John, 3, 39, 42, 65, 73, 96, 98, 99, 105, 117, 118, 123, 128, 145
Courts, John, Jr., 50, 59, 73, 105, 138
Courts, Margaret, 3, 123
Cow Land, 73
Cow Springs, 57
Cox, James, 86, 144
Cox, John, 145
Craxon, Sarah, 86
Craxon, Thomas, 25
Craxstone, Thomas, 140
Craystone, Thomas, 98
Credwell, George, 45, 86
Cressey, Mary, 47
Cressey, Samuel, 2, 6, 11, 13, 14, 17, 22, 23, 26, 27, 33, 37, 40, 43, 44, 47, 86, 93, 99
Crips, Nicholas, 92
Crouch, Anne, 105
Crouch, Edward, 86
Crumpe, Garvis, 15
Cuckold's Delight, 117
Cuemey, John, 138
Culles, Charles, 50, 86
Cullin, James, 116
Cumpton, William, 92
Cunney, John, 86, 106

Cunningham, George, 92
Curtis, John, 92
Cutler, Elizabeth, 86
Cutler, Samuel, 86
Cuttler, Margaret, 86

Dallyson, Mary, 93
Damer, Thomas, 93
Daniell Mount, 21
Dansy, Jane, 119
Dansy, John, 119
Darnall, Henry, Col., 135
Daverill, Thomas, 93
Davies, Alexander, 13, 15, 16
Davies, Alise, 93
Davies, Griffith, 93
Davies, James, 93
Davies, Walter, 57, 86
Davies, William, 53, 93
Davis, Elizabeth, 152
Davis, Griffith, 142, 152
Davis, John, 30, 62, 63, 86, 93, 112
Davis, Mary, 152
Davis, Wm., 81
Dawson, Elizabeth, 128
Dawson, John, 128, 145
Dawson, Mary, 128
de Creyger, John, 93
Deakes, Henry, 117
Deakons, Tho., 93
Deane, Edward, 6, 8, 53
Deane, John, 51
Deane, William, 37, 51
Deberell, Ann, 73
Deberell, Elizabeth, 73
Deberell, Thomas, 62, 73
Decosta, Mathias, 84
Degregor, Jno., 86
Delahahy Chance, 83
Delehay, George, 76, 83, 116

Delehay, John, 27, 64, 82, 83
Delehay, Thomas, 116
Dennie, Edmond, 53, 54, 56, 58, 59, 61, 62
Dennis,, edm'd, 83
Dent, Anne, 130
Dent, Elizabeth, 106, 126, 127, 130, 142
Dent, George, 117, 127
Dent, John, 55, 86, 90, 97
Dent, Mary, 55
Dent, Peter, 114, 115
Dent, Thomas, 40, 93, 99, 117, 126, 144
Dent, William, 73, 74, 75, 78, 80, 82, 84, 106, 115, 118, 126, 127, 130, 138, 139, 140, 141, 142, 148, 151, 154
Deverall, Anne, 125
Deverell, Elizabeth, 86, 125
Deverell, Thomas, 125
Dickenson, Roger, 5, 6, 78
Dickeson, Jeremiah, 4, 5, 6, 10, 13, 18, 66, 69, 90, 91, 95, 99
Dickeson, Thomas, 69, 93
Dickinson, Anne, 66
Dickinson, Mr., 98
Dickison, Mary, 137
Dickson, Elizabeth, 93
Dickson, John, 112
Dickson, William, 15, 16
Diggs, William, 74, 126
Dike, Elizabeth, 120
Dike, Mary, 120
Dike, Matthew, 93, 120
Dine, Mary, 59
Divell, James, 93
Dixon, Thomas, 86, 111, 128
Dobson, Jeremiah, 28
Dobson, Samuel, 12, 27, 40, 44, 53

Docker's Delight, 45
Dod, Anne, 128
Dod, Jane, 128
Dod, John, 124
Dod, Mary, 59, 122, 124
Dod, Richard, 2, 59, 122, 124, 128
Dods, Thomas, 93
Dodson, Rich., 80
Dog's Neck, 1, 5, 6, 9, 11, 39, 57, 58
Dolton, Richard, 93
Doniphen, Alexander, 33
Donohau, Cornelius, 93
Donohau, Fincene, 93
Dorkers Delight, 120
Dosett, Edward, 93
Dosey Lane, 141
Doughty, Francis, 2, 14
Doughty, Robert, 93
Douglas Adventure, 63
Douglas, Benjamin, 137
Douglas, Charles, 86
Douglas, Elizabeth, 69, 86, 123
Douglas, John, 19, 28, 47, 53, 55, 56, 57, 60, 63, 69, 86, 98, 99, 128, 137, 149
Douglas, Joseph, 86
Douglas, Mary, 128
Douglas, Robert, 86, 117, 141
Douglas, Sarah, 86
Doulton, Anne, 140
Douraslet, 76
Dove, Wm., 79
dover, 83
Dover, Christopher, 93
Dowell, George, 41
Downes, Elizabeth, 93
Downes, Robert, 57, 101, 102, 125, 148
Doyne, Dennis, 146

Doyne, Joshua, 79, 97, 106, 116, 117
Doyne, Robert, 38, 45, 63, 97, 106, 119
Drury Lane, 19
Dublin, 32
Dunn, Isaac, 93
Dunnington, Francis, 104
Dunshaw, John, 33
Dunstan, John, 86
Duppe, Thomas, 93
Durham, 32
Dulsstatway, Jacob, 84
Dutton, Elizabeth, 129
Dutton, Matthew, 129
Dutton, Thomas, 129
Dymossa, ____, 84
Dyzer, Philip, 135

Earle, John, 113
Eason, John, 93
Eaten, Samuel, 94
Eathyes, Arther, 116
Eathyes, Nathaniel, 116
Eaton, Nathaniel, 8
Eaton, Samuel, 8
Eaton, Thomas, 93
Eatons Delight, 154
Edelen, Richard, 11, 12, 15, 26, 27, 28, 29, 30, 32, 35, 39, 42, 49, 50, 52, 55, 58, 62, 66, 83, 92, 94, 97, 110, 115
Edgar, Richard, 141
Edge, Thomas, 93
Edgerton, Charles, 134
Edmondson, Robert, 155
Edwards, John, 93
Effton Hills, 11
Eglin, Richard, 116
Elizabeth and Mary (ship), 113

Elkins, Ralph, 82
Elliot, William, Jr., 107
Elliot, William, Sr., 107
Ellis, Hugh, 93
Ellis, James, 111
Ellis, Thom., 93
Ellison, John, 93
Elsey, Thomas, 86
Elswood, Anne, 140
Emanson, Elizabeth, 22, 27
Emanson, Nicholas, 11, 14, 22
Emenson, Mrs., 48
Emerson, Elizabeth, 107
Emerson, Nicholas, 95, 107, 122
Emerson, William, 122
Emmett, John, 143
Enibruson, Drick, 93
Eniburson, Christopher, 93
Ennis, David, 93
Estep, 57
Eure, Christopher, 93
Evans His Range, 154
Evans, Anthony, 66
Evans, Edward, 104, 110
Evans, Elizabeth, 110
Evans, Joan, 93
Evans, Peter, 80
Evans, Richard, 135, 143
Evans, Walter, 114, 154
Evens, Ann, 137
Evens, Charles, 136, 137
Everite, Francis, 86
Exeto, 31
Exiler, 117, 139

Faelor, Ambrous, 86
Fair Fountaine, 66
Faning, Elizabeth, 64
Faning, John, 38, 43, 59, 64, 73, 75, 78, 86, 91

Faning, Mary, 64
Fanning, Benoni, 148
Far, Peter, 56
Farlor, see Farlowe
Farlowe, Ambros, 69, 86, 124
Farlowe, William, 69, 124
Farmer, Chriso., 82
Farmer, Rice, 94
Farnandis, Elizabeth, 107
Farnandis, Peter, 107
Farrell, Bryan, 147
Farrow, James, 94
Father's Gift, The, 40
Faulkner, Jno., 86
Fearnley, John, 118
Fearson, John, 99
Fendall's Delight, 46
Fendall, Brigett, 115
Fendall, Henry, 74
Fendall, Josias, 12, 21, 44, 66, 69, 70, 74, 93, 95, 96, 97, 100, 101, 102
Fendall, Mary, 74
Fendall, Samuel, 4, 21, 45, 69, 81, 86, 97, 98, 102
Fendall, Tho., 86
Fenner, Thom., 94
Ferenley, John, 47
Fernandez, Pedro, 94
Fernandis, Peter, 150
Fernandos, Peter, 86
Fernandos, Wenefrett, 86
Ferneley, Francis, 46
Fernleys Rest, 118
Fernson, John, 86
Fershing, Jno., 86
Field, Charles, 94
Finley, James, 66, 108, 139, 140
Fire, Ralph, 94
Fish, Elinor, 94

Fisher, Elisabeth, 94
Fitzgerald, Edward, 154
Fitzgerald, Joan, 152
FitzJames, Dominick Bodkin, 61
Fletcher's Addition, 53, 67
Fletcher, Henry, 15, 47, 51, 53, 86

Fletsher, Catherine, 94
Flowers, Elizabeth, 119
Flowers, Richard, 119
Fockes, Thomas, 42
Foote, Richard, 61
Forbins, William, 151
Ford, Edward, 133, 145
Ford, John, 21, 26, 42
Forster, Elizabeth, 149
Forster, Will, 113
Fortas, Margrett, 94
Fortune, 137
Fowke, Anne, 28, 90, 98, 100, 126
Fowke, Elizabeth, 28, 126
Fowke, Gerrard, 3, 8, 17, 28, 82, 99, 100, 105, 126, 140, 153, 154
Fowke, Hallaleujah, 108, 120
Fowke, Mary, 126
Fowke, Maryland, 28
Fowke, Richard, 2, 12, 15, 26, 36, 38, 39, 92, 94, 108, 115, 118, 120, 135
Fowke, Roger, 60
Fowler, William, 94, 133
Fowtrell, George, 94
Fox, James, 86
Frampton, Frances, 149
Francis, John, 73, 103
Francisson, Francis, 94
Francklin, Henry, 130
Francklin, Jane, 130
Francklin, Mary, 130

Franckum, Francis, 94
Francom, Amie, 9, 12
Francom, Elizabeth, 12
Francom, Henry, 9, 11, 12, 72, 118
Franklings, Henry, 112
Fransom, John, 74
Frawver, Edward, 81
Frawners, Henry, 86
French Lewis, 18
French, Hugh, 16, 50, 63, 64, 78, 91
Frost, Jeremiah, 25, 37
Frost, Willm., 139
Fr__ner, Edward, 112
Furnase, Elizabeth, 86
Furnice, Francis, 29, 41
Furnis, Mary, 41

Gaines, John, 154
Galey's Venture, 33
Galey, Edward, 94
Galey, Loranso, 94
Galey, Martha, 33
Galey, Thomas, 33
Gallant, Alexander, 16, 23, 31, 139
Gallaway, James, 57
Galleys Discovery, 116, 142
Gambra, Richard, 112, 115
Gannett, Thomas, 114
Garbor, Jno., 84
Gardener, William, 31
Gardiner, Edward, 121
Gardiner, Hugh, 86, 121
Gardiner, Luke, 6
Gardner, Jno., 86
Gardner, Richard, 50
Garrett, Charles, 78, 126, 138
Garrett, James, 94

Garrett, Joyse, 126, 138
Gaskoyne, Sam., 94
Gateley, Edward, 94
Gaven, Thomas, 82
Geer, James, 150
Geniers' Swamp, 55
Geniers, John, 55
German, Geo., 94
Gerrard, Thomas, 56, 62, 91, 92, 97, 98, 99, 100, 102, 105
Ghogh, Jane, 94
Gibbens, Thomas, 104
Gibbon, Philip, 19, 22, 31, 32, 35, 36
Gibbs, John, 94
Gibson's Close, 154
Gibson, Dorothy, 94
Gibson, Elizabeth, 154
Gibson, Richard, 54
Gibson, Thomas, 68, 94, 119, 132, 154
Gifford, Henry, 154
Gift, The, 2, 24, 25, 148
Gilbard, James, 94
Gilbert, Jane, 105
Gill, Benjamin, 144
Gills Land, 74
Gilpinge, Sylvanus, 54
Ginney, John, 94
Gisbrough, 117, 133
Gleine, George, 108
Glosse, John, 5
Glover's Point, 22, 27, 107
Glover, George, 94
Glover, Giles, 22, 25
Glover, Mary, 94
Glyn, Francis, 86
Goat, Robert, 111
Goates Lodge, 21, 44
God's Gift, 120

Goddard, George, 94
Godfrey, George, 22, 24, 26, 30, 32, 42, 43, 52, 58, 64, 69, 70, 101, 102, 139
Godfrey, George, Jr., 86
Godfrey, Mary, 69
Godfrey, Thomas, 69
Godfrey, William, 69, 86
Godshall, John, 8, 10, 18, 19, 25, 27, 30, 51, 53, 59, 66, 67, 75, 76, 77, 113, 133, 135, 136, 138
Godshall, Sarah, 75
Godson, John, 66, 75, 86
Golbard, James, 94
Golden, Thomas, 15
Goldsmith, John, 75
Gooch, John, 115, 120
Gooderick, Elizabeth, 79
Gooderick, Francis, 36, 93, 95, 101
Gooderick, George, 15, 17, 36, 45, 48, 80, 115, 136
Gooderick, Henry, 95, 134
Gooderick, Mary, 124
Gooderick, Robert, 52, 79, 136, 124
Goodge, John, 86, 100
Goodwicks, Mr., 59
Goomes, John, 86
Goos, Anne, 127
Goos, George, 127
Goos, Mary, 127
Goos, Sarah, 127
Goose Bay, 107
Goose Creek, 28
Goosh, John, 91
Gordian, Daniell, 6
Gosh, Richard, 94
Gosling, John, 20

Gough, William, 34
Goureleg, Barbary, 130
Goureleg, John, 130
Graces, Geo., 104
Gramboe, Domingoe, 86
Grant, William, 30
Graves, George, 55, 80, 84, 106
Graves, Joshia, 120
Graves, Joshua, 61, 65, 80, 82, 86, 111, 114, 132, 136, 138
Graves, Sam'll, 86
Graves, Thomas, 94
Gray, John, 48, 58, 73, 86
Gray, Joseph, 119
Gray, Ruth, 94
Gray, William, 149
Graydon, Margaret, 48
Grayner, Richard, 12
Greane, Henry, 84
Greenah, 45
Green Chase, 73
Greene's Inheritance, 151
Greene's Purchase, 28, 35, 43, 55, 58
Greene, Francis, 86, 151
Greene, James, 94, 133
Greene, John, 29, 51, 94
Greene, Leo, 2
Greene, Leonard, 151
Greene, Luke, 4, 6, 10, 18, 19, 27, 28, 29, 31, 32, 34, 35, 41, 43, 46, 86, 145
Greene, Margaret, 151
Greene, Mary, 151
Greene, Richard, 94
Greene, Robert, 86, 98, 101, 151, 152
Greene, Thomas, 117
Greenhalgh, Edw., 77
Gregory, Christopher, 149, 154

Gregory, Jacob, 65
Greyden, Margaret, 95
Gridmore, Nicholas, 47
Griffin, Robert, 95
Griffin, William, 111, 114, 152
Grisbrough, 116
Grosser, Mary, 95
Groube, Richard, 95
Groves, Alise, 130
Groves, Elizabeth, 130
Groves, George, 67, 83, 86, 130
Grubb's Venture, 27
Grubb, John, 26, 27, 47, 78, 87, 117
Grunion, Tho., 134
Grunwin, Thomas, 74, 116
Gryer, John, 95
Gubbins, Mary, 105
Guesse, Richard, 108
Guibert, Joshua, 47, 152
Gutridge, James, 95
Guy, Charles, 147
Gwin, John, 111
Gwirlye, Jno., 87
Gwither, Nicholas, Capt., 139
Gwyn, John, 31., 63, 64
Gwyn, Ralfe, 137
Gwynn, Anne, 128
Gwynn, Christopher, 128
Gwynn, Susanna, 128
Gwyther, William, 66

Habnabala Venture, 149
Hackister, John, 19, 23, 35, 39
Hacorte, William, 107
Haddock, Benjamin, 117, 120, 136, 143
Haddock, Cornelius, 154
Hadducks Hill, 136
Hagar, Mary, 84

Hagar, robt., 83, 84
Hagar, Wm., 95
Haggetts Priory, 120
Haggister's Addition, 35
Half Way Tree, 64, 82
Halford, John, 50
Hall Spring, 116
Hall, Charles, 95
Hall, Isaac, 67, 95
Hall, John, 95, 129
Hall, Margrett, 95
Hall, Mary, 87, 70, 125, 129
Hall, Matthew, 91
Hall, Rebecca, 103
Hall, Richard, 70, 87, 125
Hall, Walter, 2, 39
Hall, William, 79, 95, 105, 111, 129, 138, 144
Hallyfax, 148
Halse, John, 59
Halton, William, 110
Hambye, Francis, 104
Hamer, Susannah, 87
Hamillone, ___, 140
Hamilton, Gaven, 114
Hamilton, Gowan, 134, 135, 137
Hamilton, John, 44, 45, 47, 48, 57, 60, 63, 77
Hammersley, Francis, 133
Hammond, John, 46, 87, 95
Hanby, Alise, 155
Hanby, Francis, 140, 155
Hanby, John, 140
Haneland, William, 113
Hanns, Jno., 95
Hanson, Anne, 130
Hanson, Hans, 84
Hanson, John, 19, 45, 50, 53, 87, 130, 155
Hanson, Mary, 130

Hanson, Randolph, 28, 61, 111, 134
Hanstone, 141
Hanton, William, 145
Harbut, Wm., 107
Harcutt, Wm., 81
Hard Frost, 59, 63, 66
Hardshift, 78, 118, 132
Hardwick, Thomas, 133
Hardy, Henry, 48, 51, 57, 73, 78, 91, 97, 108, 116, 117, 136
Hargess Hope, 28, 31
Hargesse, Thomas, 21, 26, 28, 29
Hargesse, William, 28, 29, 31
Harguess, Jom., 94
Harguess, Tho., 87
Harguesse's Hope, 145
Harguesse, Ann, 121
Harguesse, William, 121
Harison, Catherine, 122
Harison, Joseph, 122
Harison, Martha, 106
Harisson, John, 143
Harleton, Elizabeth, 140
Harmon, John, 52
Harmon, Matthew, 40, 78
Harrington, John, 87
Harris, George, 6, 8, 11
Harris, Jane, 95
Harris, John, 11, 20, 76, 130
Harris, Mary, 60, 130
Harris, Richard, 69, 70
Harris, Roger, 116
Harris, Samuel, 87
Harris, Susanna, 69
Harris, Thomas, 60, 70, 94, 130
Harris, Will, 26
Harrison, Anne, 95
Harrison, Benjamin, 34
Harrison, Catherine, 34

Harrison, Elizabeth, 122
Harrison, Francis, 54, 109, 121, 152
Harrison, John, 53, 81, 100, 106, 108, 115, 154
Harrison, Joseph, 4, 13, 18, 24, 25, 27, 28, 34, 95, 109, 121, 152
Harrison, Margaret, 121
Harrison, Mary, 121
Harrison, Oliver, 116
Harrison, Richard, 18, 82, 83, 107, 121, 137, 138
Harrison, Robert, 95
Harrison, Thomas, 93, 101
Harrisson's Gift, 141, 151
Harrissons Venture, 138
Hart, Robert, 44
Harvey, John, 58, 59, 63
Haselton, Elizabeth, 95
Hatch, John, 2, 5, 24, 25, 37, 42, 43, 54, 67, 92, 93, 101, 148
Hatch, Sarah, 110
Hatch, William, 91, 101, 104, 105, 110, 144, 145
Hatherton, John, 95
Hatton's Point, 41
Hatton, Thomas, 77, 87, 140
Hatton, William, 39, 100, 117, 143
Haughton, Joseph, 87
Hawking, Henry, 126
Hawking, Henry, Jr., 126
Hawking, Mary, 126
Hawking, William, 126
Hawkins, Elizabeth, 87, 107, 119
Hawkins, Henry, 8, 17, 20, 21, 44, 54, 55, 60, 66, 81, 87, 92, 96, 98, 101, 102, 104, 107, 108, 113, 119, 137, 140, 147, 149, 150

Hawkins, John, 83, 84, 95, 107
Hawkins, Josias, 82
Hawton, William, 110, 151
Hay, James, 87
Hayden, Francis, 65
Hayes, James, 23, 26
Hayes, Peter, 140
Hayes, Thomas, 41
Hayles, Mary, 95
Hayward, John, 95
Hayward, Samuell, 20
Haywood, Mary, 95
Headlow, Edith, 122
Heard, John, 55
Heard, William, 28, 30, 35, 39
Helgar, Anne, 56, 57
Helgar, Thomas, 56, 57, 87
Helme, John, 12, 37, 87
Hely, Roby., 76
Hendall, Francis, 95
Henley, Henry, 51, 72, 87
Henley, Robert, 17, 73, 75, 90, 91, 93, 96, 98, 102
Hensely, Edward, 95
Hensey, William, 17
Henshall, Thomas, 87
Hensly, William, 95
Henson, Barbarah, 140
Henson, Geo., 79
Henson, Randolph, 140
Henson, Thomas, 87
Hensy, Thomas, 14
Herbert, Catherine, 129
Herbert, Elizabeth, 126
Herbert, John, 95, 126
Herbert, Mary, 129
Herbert, William, 77, 95, 129, 132, 134
Hereman, John, 87
Heroitt, Robert, 48

Herrickson, Hans, 147
Herrickson, Judith, 147
Hes, Richard, 115, 118
Heselden, Elizabeth, 147
Hey, Charles, 95
Heydon, Francis, 15, 17, 56, 61, 87
Heydon, Thomasine, 56, 61
Hibert, Saml., 103
Hicks, Thomas, 64, 95
Hickson, Henry, 108
Hickson, James, 108
Higdon, John, 148
Hill Port, 133
Hill, And., 32
Hill, Charles, 2
Hill, Edward, 113
Hill, John, 26, 30, 34
Hill, Mathew, 16
Hill, Onsley, 124, 138
Hill, Thomas, 95, 108, 124, 152
Hill, Valentine, 152
Hill, Walt, 95
Hills, Clement, 50
Hills, Edee, 12
Hills, Susanna Marea, 12
Hills, The, 77, 108, 152
Hills, William, 12, 70, 122
Hinch, Mathew, 95
Hincks, Dorothy, 95
Hinde, William, 95
Hindle, Joshua, 95
Hinsey, William, 70, 92
Hinson, George, 25, 87
Hinson, Randolph, 114, 137, 142
Hinton, Zachary, 95
His Excellency's Gift, 37
His Lordship's Manor, 135
Hiscok, Robert, 12
Hispanola, 81

Hitchinson, John, 14
Hithersall, Thomas, 119
Hitt, Matthew, 48
Hobart, Richard, 120, 133
Hobb, Isable, 133
Hobb, Thomas, 133
Hodgly, John, 95
Hodgson, Johannah, 97
Hodgson, Richard, 57, 63, 73, 78
Hodgson, William, 57
Hog Quarter, 8, 39
Hogdin, Johnathan, 96
Hoggin, Henry, 96
Holgar, Thomas, 41, 51, 54
Holland, Phillip, 103
Holmes, George, 27
Holmes, Grace, 96
Holmes, John, 42, 87
Holton, Joseph, 48, 96
Homefaire, 78
Hooke Norton, 50
Hooks, Peirsy, 42
Hope, Robert, 133
Hope, Walter, 120
Hopewell, 75, 103, 111, 113, 136
Hopkins, Robert, 117
Hopkins, Thomas, 3
Hopper, Thomas, 9
Horton, Alise, 128
Horton, Joseph, 30, 47, 59
Hosking, Thomas, 96
Hoskins, Elizabeth 72
Hoskins, Jeremi, 96
Hoskins, John, 78, 81
Hoskins, Lauran, 96
Hoskins, Philip, 23, 26, 64, 72, 80, 81, 113, 150
Houghton, James, 96
How, Richard, 87
Howard, John, 96

Howe, George, 11, 16, 138
Howell, Alexander, 96
Howell, Thomas, 42, 93
Howell, William, 65, 67, 79, 110, 112
Howes, Thomas, 96
Howland, 9, 11, 14, 103, 111, 113, 114, 132, 136
Howland, George, 113
Howling, Mary, 120
Howling, William, 120
Howse, George, 9
How___, George, 68
Hoyle, Samuell, 96
Huchison, William, 140
Huckleberry Swamp, 6
Hudlestone, Thomas, 26
Hudson, Robert, 34, 96
Hulse, James, 87
Hulse, Meverall, 17, 26, 39, 46, 50, 54, 68, 111
Hulse, Wm., 76
Humble, Barbary, 96
Humerton, Mary, 96
Humfray, Tho., 77
Hungerford's Branch, 56
Hungerford, 57
Hungerford, Margaret, 142
Hungerford, William, 76, 77, 142
Hunley, Robert, 100, 101
Hunt, Alice, 70, 122
Hunt, John, 96
Hunt, Mary, 122
Hunter, Richard, 96
Hunter, William, 87, 96
Huntsman, Samuell, 96
Hurd, Andrew, 153, 154
Hurly, Daniel, 33
Huscoula, Dennis, 99
Hussey, Ho., 65

Hussey, James, 2, 4, 23
Hussey, Joane, 17
Hussey, Johanna, 3, 52, 87
Hussey, Thomas, 1, 2, 3, 6, 15, 17, 22, 24, 32, 36, 43, 50, 52, 58, 61, 64, 65, 67, 70, 72, 76, 81, 82, 83, 87, 93, 94, 96, 97, 99, 101, 102, 107, 118, 136, 145
Hutchins, Elianor, 96
Hutchinson, John, 6, 87
Hutchison, William, 112, 114, 120, 134, 136, 137, 141, 142, 143, 144, 145, 146, 147, 152, 154, 155
Hutton Lorkrue, 50
Huytinge, Francis, 120
Hu___, Elianor, 96
Hyatt, Thomas, 35, 46, 47

Ingham, John, 76, 113
Inglesby, Bridgett, 47
Ingolsby, Robert, 35
Ingothorpe, 57
Ipswich, 113
Irish Damm, 49
Ivarson, Alise, 96
Ivery, Catherine, 146

Jackson, James, 96
Jackson, John, 147
Jackson, Mary, 96
Jackson, William, 87
Jamaica, 136, 137
Jamaira, 136, 137
James, John, 133
James, William, 11
Jarboe, John, 13, 14, 33, 115, 151
Jeamind, 152
Jeffrey, Tho., 96
Jeffs, John, 96

Jenkins, Anne, 43
Jenkins, Daniell, 117
Jenkins, Eliz., 87
Jenkins, Josias, 116
Jenkins, Mary, 87
Jenkins, Thomas, 15, 16, 22, 26,
    38, 40, 43, 46, 52, 53, 76, 87,
    92, 95, 108, 150, 154
Jenkins, William, 21, 87
Jenkinson, Mary, 44
Jenkinson, William, 44
Jerricoe, 30
Jobe's Comfort, 30, 35, 39
Johnson's Choice, 120
Johnson's Retirement, 21
Johnson's Town, 21
Johnson, Cornelius, 96
Johnson, Daniel, 1, 4, 8, 22, 25, 26,
    41, 46, 47, 52, 90, 92, 97, 114,
    142, 149
Johnson, Elisabeth, 4
Johnson, Jemimima, 96
Johnson, John, 64, 96
Johnson, Thomas, 96
Johnsons, 76, 77
Johnsons Choise, 77, 80149
Johnstone, Anne, 87
Johnstone, Henry, 87
Jones, Anne, 126
Jones, Edward, 96
Jones, Elizabeth, 34, 87, 96, 124
Jones, Humphery, 2, 9, 10, 32, 36, 57
Jones, Jane, 126, 129
Jones, Joanna, 2, 87
Jones, John, 35, 36, 38, 40, 41, 44,
    47, 119, 121, 149
Jones, John, Sr., 35
Jones, Katherine, 108
Jones, Lewis, 62, 63, 76, 140

Jones, Margarett, 124
Jones, Mary, 96
Jones, Morgan, 6, 111, 118
Jones, Moses, 96, 112, 113, 119, 129
Jones, Owen, 2, 5, 8, 9, 10, 11, 15,
    25, 32, 34, 45, 87, 90, 146
Jones, Owen, Jr., 35, 87
Jones, Philip, 96
Jones, Richard, 2, 10, 14, 34, 72,
    87, 95, 97, 124, 126
Jones, Robert, 97
Jones, Thomas, 72, 87
Jones, Walter, 87
Joyod, Richard, 8
Judd, Mich'll, 72

Kanedagh, Jeremy, 97
Karnes, Henry, 127
Karnes, Mary, 127, 128
Karnes, Robert, 127, 128
Karnes, William, 128
Keane, John, 14
Keech, James, 42, 50
Keech, William, 110
Keelby, John, 97
Keene, Francis, 51
Keett, Elizabeth, 111
Keett, William, 110
Keewan, Peter, 61
Kekley, William, 97
Kemp, Roger, 119
Kennedie, Jeremie, 87
Kent, Robert, 97
Kersey, Thomas, 87
Key, Henry, 141
Killcart, John, 104
Kimberton, John, 35
Kimbrow, John, 30

King, Thomas, 9, 10, 13, 15, 16, 17, 23, 35, 72, 87, 92, 98, 100
Kingerley, George, 145
Kingsbury, George, 104
Kingstone, Thomas, 97
Kirby, Paul, 97
Kirkley, Christopher, 87
Kirley, Catherine, 129
Kirley, Christopher, 129
Kirten, Zachary, 97
Knight, Anne, 141
Knight, Edward, 15, 21, 23, 87, 109, 119, 146
Knight, Elinor, 119
Knight, Hannah, 97
Knight, John, 119, 141
Knight, Rebecca, 119
Knowlwater, John, 115
Knox, James, 153
Korkbey, William, 97
Kue, John, 108
Kylborne, Eliza, 70
Kylborne, Francis, 32, 70
Kymborough, Mary, 26

Lakemore, James, 97
Lamaster Beginnings, 43
Lambare, John, 30
Lambe, Richard, 2
Lambert, Edmund, 4, 5
Lambert, Eleanor, 4, 8, 21, 63
Lambert, Elizabeth, 87, 123
Lambert, Ellen, 18
Lambert, Ellinor, 87
Lambert, John, 4, 5, 6, 8, 18, 21, 29, 42, 46, 63, 67, 87, 91, 96, 99, 100, 123
Lambert, John, Jr., 63
Lambert, Josias, 87
Lambert, Richard, 87
Lambert, Samuel, 123
Lambert, Sarah, 67
Lambert, William, 63, 123
Lambeth, Edmund, 87
Lambton, Marke, 87
Lampton, Elizabeth, 125, 152
Lampton, Marke, 125, 140, 152
Lampton, Mary, 125
Lampton, William, 125
Lancaster, 45
Land, Elizabeth, 130
Land, John, 82, 130
Land, Mary, 56
Land, Penelope, 130
Land, Richard, 130, 139
Land, Philip, 34, 106
Lane, Elizabeth, 123
Lane, William, 123
Langham, George, 18, 19, 21, 25, 26, 27, 34, 56
Langham, William, 121
Langhly, Mary, 70
Langworth, James, 61
Langworth, William, 61
Lanham, John, 110, 121
Lans, William, 97
Lashlan, James, 153
Latemar, James, 144
Lawrence, Jno., 83
Lawrence, Thomas, 97
Layhay, 73
Layron Stone, 41
Leads, 112
Leah, Jacob, 34, 40
Lee's Purchase, 51
Lee, Jacob, 31
Lee, James, 58, 64, 82
Lee, John, 87
Lee, Margaret, 97
Lee, Thomas, 116, 117

Lee, William, 51, 57, 63
Leech, James, 104
Lees, Eleanor, 108
Leesh, James, 97
Leet, George, 112
Leete, John, 152
Leeter, William, 152
Legate, Bridet, 115
Legatt, Bridgett, 16
Lemaire's Purchase, 29, 44
Lemaire, John, 29, 44, 45, 48, 51, 56, 81, 82, 87, 105, 106
Lemaire, Margaret, 45, 51, 82
Leman, Jno., 87
Lenden, Dennis, 138
Lenham, John, 97
Lenox, Catharine, 112
Lewgar, John, 3, 12, 33, 41, 87, 113, 144
Lewgar, Martha, 3
Lewgar, Thomas, 113, 114, 116, 132, 133, 144
Lewis, David, 129
Lewis, Henry, 129
Lewis, Jane, 129
Lewis, Mary, 129
Lewis, Thomas, 144, 146
Lewis, William, 14, 16, 60, 77
Lileard, Thomas, 141
Lilly, Henry, 58
Lindsey's Project, 31
Lindsey, 8, 53
Lindsey, Edmond, 5, 16, 17, 20, 22, 28, 31, 33, 37, 45, 51, 53, 55, 70, 87, 91, 96, 111, 112, 114
Lindsey, Eleanor, 22
Lindsey, Elizabeth, 53

Lindsey, James, 2, 5, 6, 8, 9, 10, 13, 14, 15, 16, 18, 19, 23, 37, 48, 118, 119, 122
Lindsey, Thomas, 111, 116, 140
Lines, Philip, 16, 19, 27. 34, 37, 40, 41, 42, 43, 44, 45, 46, 47, 48, 50, 51, 55, 57, 80, 88, 90, 92, 94, 95, 96, 97, 98, 99, 100, 102
Ling, Francis, 64, 87, 125
Ling, Mary, 64, 125
Ling, Michaell, 87, 125
Ling, William, 64, 70, 87, 125
Little Crayner, 78
Little Ease, 120, 134
Little Marsh, 120
Littlepage, James, 11, 51
Littlepage, Robert, 11, 97
Liwes, Thomas, 112
Lloyd, Headrick, 97
Loathbury, 42, 47
Locust Thickett, 25, 28, 38, 134
Lodge, George, 21, 34
Loman, Richard, 135
Lomax, Blanch, 46, 70, 121, 124, 125
Lomax, Cleborne, 36, 38, 48, 49, 50, 43, 44, 46, 52, 55, 59, 60, 62, 63, 64, 65, 66, 68, 70, 72, 77, 81, 83, 84, 87, 93, 103, 107, 110, 111, 113, 115, 116, 117, 118, 119, 120, 121, 124, 125, 132, 135, 136, 137, 140, 141, 144, 146, 148, 149, 150, 151, 152
Lomax, John, 125
Lomax, Katherine, 70, 124
Lomax, Ralph, 124
Lomax, Susanna, 124

Lomax, Thomas, 9, 27, 29, 30, 39, 44, 46, 50, 58, 61, 62, 64, 87, 125
London, 56
Long, Jemima, 87, 123
Long, John, 16, 84
Long, Robert, 88, 123
Lonish Thickett, 138, 140
Loodgham, Charles, 97
Lord Baltimore, 40
Lot # 12, 141
Lot #2, 151
Lott Number Three, 138
Lourey, William, 119
Love, Thomas, 150
Love, William, 15, 88, 101, 150
Loveday, Joan, 52, 53
Loveday, William, 43, 46, 52, 53
Lovelace, Frances, 17
Low Land, 78, 117
Lowe, John, 117
Lowe, William, 113
Lower Poole, 110
Loyd, Morris, 121, 134, 154
Loyde, Morris, 134
Luckett, Elizabeth, 125, 126, 128
Luckett, Ignatius, 128
Luckett, Samuel, 80, 104, 125, 126, 107, 128, 149, 155
Luckett, Thomas, 126
Lues, Thomas, 97
Lugar, see Lewgar
Luke, John, 21
Lumber Street, 40
Lumbroso, John, 22, 26, 70
Lybscome, Dorothy, 97
Lyndsey, Edmund, 76, 88
Lynes, Philip, 75, 77, 78, 80, 108, 115, 116, 117, 118, 120, 132, 139, 140, 144

Lynsey, Thomas, 142
Lyon's Den, 26, 45, 142
Lyon's Hole, 26, 38, 135

Mackenhine, John, 97
Mackewen, J., 134
Mackey, Jacobi, 32
Mackey, James, 10, 32, 97
Mackmere, Jeremiah, 96
Mackmere, John Howard, 97
Mackmere, Phillis, 96
Mackmillion, George, 25, 69, 123
Mackmillion, Grace, 123
Mackmillion, Peter, 123
Macknew, Jeremiah, 30, 42
Macoy, Esther, 106
Macoy, James, 8, 106
Maddock's Folly, 47
Maddock, Cornelius, 80, 82, 114
Maddock, Edward, 25, 26, 28, 35, 39, 42, 43, 45, 46, 47, 48, 58, 65, 66, 72, 82, 88, 135
Maddock, Margery, 65, 82
Maddock, Mary, 103, 114
Maddock, William, 105
Maddox, David, 44
Madgely, Richard, 19, 88
Maglockery, Elizabeth, 106
Maglockery, William, 106
Maglocklin, Kellam, 53, 56, 88

Magniell, Daniell, 134
Mahawney, Tymothy, 146
Mahoune, Daniell, 140
Maisemore, 9, 16, 68, 132, 138
Makey, James, 73, 154
Makhenie, Daniel, 3
Manhew, John, 97
Mankin, Elizabeth, 120, 125
Mankin, John, 125, 140

Mankin, Margaret, 142
Mankin, Mary, 120, 125, 126, 130, 142
Mankin, Stephen, 58, 120, 125, 126, 130, 140, 142
Mann, Cristentempell, 25
Mannexley, Margaret, 97
Manning, Joseph, 95, 96, 149
Mannister, John, 70, 139
Mannister, Thomas, 139
Manwarren, Walter, 97
Marberry, Francis, 121, 134
Marchagay, Benjamin, 12
Marchall, Richard, 97
Marchantailor's Hall, 29
Marden, John, 97
Maris, Sarah, 70, 88, 97
Maris, Thomas, 19, 21, 70, 141
Marken, John, 97
Markeneard, Elinor, 97
Marler, Jonathan, 2, 6, 10, 13, 27, 28, 35, 41
Marloe, Edward, 139
Marloe, John, 88
Marlow, Anthony, 97
Marlow, Bur., 75
Marlow, Eliza., 75
Marlow, John, 105
Marlow, Jonathan, 26
Marlow, Susanna, 75
Marly, Jonathan, 13
Marris, Robert, 152
Marsh Land, 37, 52
Marsh, Gilbert, 88, 136, 137
Marsh, John, 137
Marsh, Michaell, 107
Marsh, Thomas, 137
Marsh, William, 97
Marshagay, Bennett, 42, 55, 102
Marshagay, Benj., 88

Marshall, Barbary, 128
Marshall, Elizabeth, 122, 128
Marshall, Gerrard, 147
Marshall, Tho, 65
Marshall, William, 3, 16, 47, 55, 59, 70, 91, 93, 99, 101, 122, 128, 133, 140, 154
Martin, Demaris, 128
Martin, James, 116
Martin, John, 112, 120, 128, 138, 149
Martin, Joseph, 125
Martin, Katherine, 125
Martin, Mary, 120, 125
Martin, Michael, 149
Martin, Penelope, 128, 139
Martin, Ruth, 112, 120
Martine, James, 17, 75
Maryes, Thomas, 88
Mary & Ann (ship), 76
Mary, The (ship), 76
Maryland Point, 6, 106
Maskey, James, 133
Maskey, John, 133
Maslee, Jonathan, 72
Mason, Elizabeth, 125
Mason, Francis, 73, 75
Mason, Jno., 97
Mason, Mary, 127, 144
Mason, Philip, 112, 115, 118, 125, 127, 144
Mason, Richard, 78, 115
Mason, Samuell, 125
Mason, Thomas, 93
Mason, William, 97, 127
Massey, John, 97
Massey, Thomas, 57
Maston, Elizabeth, 152
Maston, Henry, 152
Maston, John, 152

Maston, Mary, 117, 152
Maston, Richard, 88, 117, 152
Maston, Robert, 88
Mathena, Daniel, 9, 16 , 22, 29, 62, 68, 72, 73, 88, 138
Mathena, Elizabeth, 70, 88
Mathena, George, 70
Mathena, Sarah, 73, 88
Matthews, Anne, 49, 56
Matthews, Ignatius, 49, 133, 151
Matthews, Jane, 49, 56
Matthews, Thomas, 6, 17, 49, 52, 58, 79, 93, 94, 105, 145
Matthews, Victoria, 49, 56
Matthews, William, 49, 56
Mattox, David, 139
Mattox, Thomas, 139
Maud, Isaac, 88
Maybanck, Elizabeth, 98
Maycocke, Seabright, 70, 94
Mayday, 51
Mayers, Christopher, 116
Mayrook, Mary, 72
Mayrook, Seabright, 72
Mayrook's Rest, 72
Meekes, Francis, 103, 106, 116, 133
Meekes, John, 1, 147, 150
Merdilla, 114
Meredith, John, 15
Meriton, Jos., 103
Mershantayless Hall, 41
Michels, Thomas, 2
Middleton, Edward, 107
Middleton, Martha, 136
Middleton, Mary, 81. 118, 146
Middleton, Robert, 42, 46, 57, 81, 88, 90, 117, 118, 134, 146, 147
Middleton, William, 1

Midgely, Richard, 23, 36, 88, 92, 96
Milerne, 52, 54, 67
Milersie, 64
Miles, Elizabeth, 98
Miles, Morrise, 53
Miles, Nathaniel, 98
Mill Dam, The, 61
Mill Land, The, 61
Miller, Francis, 88
Miller, George, 48, 73, 135
Miller, Grase, 127
Miller, James, 118, 147
Miller, John, 88, 112, 127
Miller, Peter, 127
Millgeate, 41
Milshaw, John, 98
Milstead, Edward, 98, 126, 140
Milstead, Susanna, 126
Milstead, William, 126
Ming, Edward, 76, 83, 113, 36, 95, 107, 116
Ming, Jane, 76, 113, 116
Mingoe, Charles, 127
Mingoe, Elizabeth, 127
Mingoe, Lewis, 127
Mings his Chance, 107
Minork, Michael, 28, 33, 88, 90
Mirandy, Andrew, 98
Mires, Christopher, 98
Mitchell, Anthony, 98
Mitchell, Joan, 46, 47
Mitchell, Robt., 139
Mitchell, Thomas, 73, 77, 92, 98, 101, 111, 139
Montague Addition, 64
Montague, Mr., 122
Montague, Stephen, 4, 5, 6, 10, 13, 14, 16, 18, 22, 24, 25
Moody, Anne, 130

Moody, Jane, 130
Moody, William, 130
Moore's Branch, 1
Moore's Ditch, 52, 136
Moore's Fishing Place, 103, 111, 112, 114, 136
Moore's Folly, 113
Moore's Hope, 15, 36
Moore's Lodge, 22, 40, 41
Moore's Rest, 17
Moore, Elisabeth, 1, 17, 22, 54, 82, 123
Moore, Henry, 1, 14, 15, 16, 17, 22, 36, 54, 61, 82, 88, 100, 103, 112, 113, 115, 123, 132, 138
Moore, Hugh, 143, 153
Moore, Jennett, 153
Moore, John, 54, 123
Moore, Thomas, 123, 141
Moore, _____, 27
Morecraf's Friendship, 32
Moredick, 80
Morgan, Elizabeth, 47
Morgan, Frances, 98
Moris, Elizabeth, 139
Moris, Thomas, 139
Morrell, Christopher, 98
Morren, John, 13
Morris, Annas, 98, 139
Morris, Christopher, 104
Morris, Elinor, 56
Morris, Ellice, 98, 108
Morris, Jacob, 90
Morris, John, 50, 56, 88, 98
Morris, Mary, 104, 130
Morris, Penelope, 104, 130
Morris, Richard, 8, 9, 22, 25, 41, 52, 70, 77, 97, 98, 99, 104, 130

Moss, William, 142
Mould, Barbara, 88
Mould, John, 32, 59, 88
Moulton, Margaret, 98
Moungurrah, Hugh, 82
Mount Clipsham, 77
Mount Nabo, 116
Mount Pleasant, 146
Mountague Mountaines, 67
Mountagues Addition, 67
Mountaigne, 52
Mounteith, William, 153
Mouraster, James, 98
Mouraster, Wm., 98
Move, Peter, 98
Mudd, Thomas, 98, 102, 105, 145
mulatto, Susanna, 73
Mulgraves, Dorothy, 126
Mullikin, James, 117
Munkister, James, 88
Munn, Edward, 26
Munn, John, 4, 11, 12, 13, 23, 24, 25, 32, 37, 62, 78, 88, 96, 100, 101, 102
Murfrey, Dennie, 122
Murphy, Daniell, 78, 98
Murraine, Nicholas, 98
Murty, Stephen, 39
Musgrove, Cuthbert, 40, 60, 67, 88
Musgrove, Edward, 146

Napping, 11
Nash, Samuell, 98
Nation, Thomas, 141
Neale, Anne, 74, 79, 146
Neale, Anthony, 48, 65, 74, 88, 141, 144, 146
Neale, Elizabeth, 74, 79
Neale, Henry, 28, 46, 98

Neale, James, 48, 65, 74, 75, 79, 84, 88, 93, 94, 98, 99, 108, 134, 140
Neale, James, Jr., 79, 90
Neale, John, 139
Neale, Mr., 56, 57
Neale, Robert, 105
Neeland, Peirse, 142
Neeves, Mary, 98
Nelson, Richard, 132, 152
Nelson, Simon, 45
Nevill, Joane, 6, 70
Nevill, Johannah, 1
Nevill, John, 3, 13, 14, 18, 33, 70, 115, 151, 152
Nevill, William, 3, 6, 13, 14, 29, 31, 78
New Exchange, 24
Newby, Jno, 88
Newen, Owen, 64, 92, 126
Newman, Ann, 98
Newman, Elizabeth, 148
Newman, George, 101, 148
Newman, Hannah, 104
Newman, Mary, 148
Newman, Richard, 105
Newman, Sarah, 148
Newman, William, 75, 112, 119
Newport, 17
Newton, Jane, 131
Newton, Jo., Jr., 88
Newton, John, 95, 97, 98, 119, 131, 149, 150
Nibbs, Edw., 67
Nicholas, Anne, 137
Nicholas, William, 120
Nicholls, Elizabeth, 147
Nicholls, Simon, 142, 143
Nichols, Rachell, 98
Nichols, William, 137, 147

Nicholson, Esther, 98
Nicholson, John, 98
Nicholson, Margarett, 135
Nicholson, William, 98
Nicolls, Christobell, 98
Nolinn, Patrick, 98
Nonesuch, 4, 29, 30, 32, 41, 55, 58
Norman, Tho., 98
Normansell, Thomas, 105
Norton, Amy, 98
Norton, Hamond, 34, 88, 98
Norwood, William, 50
Notley, Thomas, 41
Nuthed, Wm., 137

Oakes, Francis, 108
Oakington, 43, 148
Oard, Peter, 98
Obryan, Elizabeth, 123
Obryan, Ellener, 70, 122
Obryan, Magdalen, 124
Obryan, Mathias, 3, 32, 70, 112, 114, 123, 124, 132, 136
Obryan, William, 124, 150
Ofaine, John, 48
Okeane, John, 91, 92
Oneale, Daniell, 14
Oneale, Hugh, 14
Oneale, Joy, 14
Oneale, Winifrett, 14
Ord, Anne, 127
Ord, James, 127
Ord, Mary, 127
Ord, Peter, 121, 127
Orme, Andrew, 42
Ornatomaquate, Emp., 153
Orrell, Isabell, 143, 149
Orrell, Jane, 143
Orrell, Thomas, 143, 147, 151
Orson, Bearer, 98

Oulson, John, 98
Oversee, Simon, 14, 16
Owen's Purchase, 23, 26
Owen, Hugh, 133
Owen, John, 21, 23, 26, 98

Paine, John, 71, 90, 91, 122
Pake, Walter, 5, 6, 9, 24, 25, 37
Palmer, Ambros, 121
Palmer, Samuel, 11
Paris, John, 65
Parke, John, 88
Parker, Ann, 99
Parker, Elizabeth, 153
Parker, James, 99
Parker, John, 99, 152, 153
Parker, Jos., 88
Parker, Thomas, 53, 88
Parker, Wm., 88
Parkes, Robert, 99
Parrett, Jo., 133
Partnership, 36, 56, 61, 62, 65
Pattison, John, 99
Pattison, William, 146
Pauding, Wm., 99
Payne, John, 19, 21, 32, 64, 70, 88, 147
Payne, Mary, 64
Peacocke, Wm., 99
Peake, Walter, 54
Pearson, John, 99
Pearson, Nathaniell, 99
Pearson, Thomas, 133
Peart, James, 12
Peeso, Comape, 99
Peircy, Thomas, 122
Peirse, John, 136
Pembrooke, Jane, 110
Pembrooke, John, 110
Pembrooke, Mary, 99

Pencott, James, 112
Penn, Marke, 129
Penn, Mary, 129
Penn, William, 88, 129, 133
Pennington, Francis, 119
Pentealey Folly, 153
Perfect, William, 97
Perkins, Robert, 88
Perrie, Mathew, 108
Persivall, Charles, 99
Pery, Robert, 116
Peter, Sam., 153
Peterson, Jacob, 1, 43, 54, 88
Petit's Creek, 60
Petits, Thomas, 60
Phillips, Edward, 99
Phillips, John, 99
Phillips, Thomas, 99, 111, 114
Philnutt, Edward, 154
Philpott, Charles, 122
Philpott, Edward, 3, 116, 122, 128
Philpott, Johannah, 47
Philpott, John, 128
Philpott, Susanna, 128
Phogg, Charles, 99
Phyllips, Hugh, 99
Picherd, Robert, 99
Pigott, Bartholomew, 104
Pigott, Sarah, 104, 112
Piles, John, 100
Piles, Joseph, 74, 145
Pinnar, Amos, 88
Pinnar, Ann, 76, 88
Pinnar, Richard, 12, 21, 26, 34, 40, 41, 44, 88, 101, 103
Pinnar, William, 20, 21, 40, 41, 44, 76, 88
Pinner, 38, 40
Piper, James, 99
Piper, John, 12, 47

Piscataway Manor, 146
Planter's Delight, 15, 32, 42
Plater, George, 135, 139, 140, 152
Plea, Jacob, 88
Plymouth, 83, 104
Plynkes, Thomas, 113
Pocter, Benj., 145
Poirsefield, 59
Polter, Matthew, 88
Pomfrett, 52, 58, 79
Poore, Peter, 99
Pope's Hallow, 60
Pope, Francis, 3, 10, 12, 16, 41, 70
Pope, John, 59, 70, 73
Pope, Thomas, 3, 33, 70
Porfit, William, 92, 101
Porke Hall, 152
Posey, Anne, 59
Posey, Benjamin, 130
Posey, Humphrey, 130
Posey, John, 30, 39, 60, 62, 65, 59, 69, 88, 99, 120, 130, 145
Posey, Mary, 130
Posey, Susanna, 130
Potter, Edward, 104, 112, 113, 116, 117, 118, 119, 153
Potter, George, 121
Potter, Robert, 121
Potts, John, 108
Potts, Robert, 88
Potts, Thomas, 99
Pouncy, George, 111
Pouncy, Mary, 111, 121
Powcher, Thomas, 105
Powell, Edward, 10, 13
Powell, George, 4, 41, 88
Powell, Robert, 99, 111, 129
Power, Mary, 103
Poynton Manor, 4, 5, 8, 10, 15, 16, 18, 19, 27, 39, 65

Pratt, Henry, 52
Price's Adventure, 36, 81
Price, Edward, 20, 23, 24, 25, 29, 30, 36, 38, 88, 91, 92, 95, 99
Price, John, 88
Price, Richard, 45
Price, Samuell, 16
Price, William, 1, 2, 3, 4, 5, 6, 9, 10
Prichard, David, 11, 12, 13, 23, 24, 43, 75
Prichard, Thomas, 42, 47
Primar, 146
Prince, Abigall, 99
Prise, Anne, 129
Prise, Edward, 134
Prise, Mary, 129
Prise, Robert, 129
Prises Adventure, 118
Prodday, Nicholas, 88, 93
Proddy, Jane, 133
Proddy, Nicholas, 133, 135
Proddy, Thomas, 135
Promise, 55, 59, 67
Prouce, Mr., 91
Prouse, Robert, 2, 24, 25
Pryor, Marie, 107
Pryor, Mary, 107, 113
Pryor, William, 107, 113
Purchase, 115
Purnie, John, 104
Pye, Col., 108
Pye, Edw., 79

Quando, Henry, 138
Quernson, 150

Raines, Elizabeth, 121, 127
Raines, Henry, 127
Raines, John, 121, 127, 139, 145

Raines, Lucy, 121, 127
Raley, 21
Ramos, John, 60
Randall, Richard, 6, 24, 26, 88, 92, 122
Ranford, William, 99
Raspin, Samuel, 61, 88
Ratcliffe, Emmannuell, 111, 119, 153
Ratcliffe, Mullenex, 111
Ratelife, Bathsheba, 129
Ratelife, John, 129
Ratelife, Richard, 129
Ratliff, William, 36
Ray, Edward, 99
Raylor, Richard, 99
Read, John , 99
Read, Luke, 144
Reason, Elizabeth, 70
Reddick, John, 58
Reddick, Margery, 58
Redding, Isabel, 99
Redish, John, 96, 97
Reeves, Anne, 145
Reeves, Richard, 103
Reeves, William, 145
Rennicke, Anne, 99
Resnsh, Hugh, 78
Rich Hill, 9, 50, 81, 106
Richards, John, 61, 64, 65, 67, 76, 80, 83
Richardson, Bernard, 99
Richardson, Joseph, 99
Rigg, Mary, 105
Rigg, Thomas, 80, 104, 105
Right, Ellino., 125
Rights, George, 125
Rigon, James, 106
Ring, Ralph, 99
River's Spring, 2, 4, 9, 23, 37

Rivers, Christopher, 9, 23
Robbins, see Robins
Roberts, Anne, 99
Roberts, Edward, 20, 25
Roberts, John, 88
Roberts, William, 100
Robertson, Marie, 100
Robey, John, 114
Robins, Henry, 100, 139
Robins, John, 64
Robins, Robert, 8, 14, 17, 22, 28, 32, 34, 46, 92, 95
Robins, William, 139
Robinson, Ann, 100
Robinson, Elizabeth, 6, 22, 43
Robinson, Jno. Jr., 88
Robinson, John, 6, 14, 15, 22, 26, 34, 43, 69, 88, 122
Robinson, Joyse, 126
Robinson, Ma_, 73
Robinson, Mary, 100, 126
Robinson, Richard, 62, 88, 126
Robinson, Samuell, 100
Robinson, Susanna, 54, 126
Robinson, Thomas, 20, 31, 54, 60, 76
Robinson, William, 13, 14
Robods, Richard, 100
Roddery, William, 138
Rogers, Mary, 100
Rome, 41
Rookerd, Edward, 61, 64
Rookerd, Mary, 61
Rookewood, Mary, 129
Rookwood, Edward, 53, 67, 73, 102, 110, 129
Roolants, Dinah, 128
Roolants, Margery, 128
Roolants, Robert, 128
Rose, John, 100

Roser, Benjamin, 96
Rosewell, Elizabeth, 74
Rosewell, William, 50, 74, 75
Rothery, William, 153
Rought, Anne, 121
Rought, Sarah, 121
Rought, William, 121
Rouse, John, 122
Rouze, Anne, 100
Rower, Samuel, 11
Rowland, Robert, 95, 98, 99
Rowles, Elizabeth, 108
Rozer, Benjamin, 1, 10, 13, 15, 16,
　　17, 19, 32, 36, 38, 40, 41, 44,
　　45, 48, 51, 53, 56, 57, 58, 59,
　　61, 70, 88, 94, 95, 96 97 99,
　　100, 102, 123
Rozer, Col., 108, 135
Rozer, Johannah, 57
Rozer, Madam, 98
Rozer, Mary, 124
Rozer, Mr., 95, 96, 101, 102
Rozer, Notley, 70, 123
Rue, Elizabeth, 140
Rue, Temperance, 140
Rueland, Dennis, 141
Russell, Charl., 52
Russell, Christopher, 144
Russell, Daniel, 24
Russell, Thomas, 49, 51
Russell, Walter, 41
Russell, William, 41, 42, 48

Sackimore, Edward, 104
Salt, Mary, 100
Sander, Mathew, 75
Sanders, Edward, 150, 151
Sanders, Jane, 151
Sanders, John, 151
Sapercote, Abram, 126

Sapercote, Elizabeth, 126
Sapercote, Rachel, 126
Sapwate, Abraham, 57
Sarjeant, Damaris, 155
Sarjeant, William, 152
Saunders, Edward, 100, 106
Saunders, John, 41, 42, 49, 55, 88,
　　121, 130 144, 145, 152
Saunders, Mary, 130, 144, 152
Saunders, Matthew, 22, 29, 51,
　　88, 121
Saunders, Sarah, 130, 145
Scarlett, Martin, 73
Scarry___, Richard, 100
Scotland Yard, 6, 32
Scutt, Edward, 134
Scutt, Mary, 134
Seaman's Delight, 136, 143
Seawell, Rebekah, 100
Seer, Thomas, 100
Sees, Thomas, 105
Selby, Nicholas, 89
Seney, Daniell, 100
Sennett, see Sinnett
Serdmore, Nicholas, 50
Serewitt, Tho., 100
Sergant, William, 110
Shabrooke, John, 4
Shacker, John, 150
Shacker, Sarah, 150
Shaw, John, 100
Shaw, Ralph, 24, 80, 90, 91, 99,
　　114, 115, 118, 148
Sheereman, John, 135, 148, 149
Sheffield, Francis, 72, 147
Shelton, Mary, 100
Shenstone, George, 38, 40
Shenstone, Mary, 38, 40
Shepherd, Charles, 138, 139
Sherrell, Samuel, 34, 44

Sherwood, Francis, 89
Shoreman, Jno., 100
Short, Amos, 33
Short, George, 100
Shrewsbury, 23, 25, 37, 42, 54, 60, 67
Shuttleworth, Edw., 78
Shuttleworth, Lydia, 78
Shuttleworth, Thomas, 34, 76, 78, 89, 109
Sigeloy, Samuell, 100
Sigley, Samuel, 140
Simes, Margaret, 90
Simes, Philip, 90
Simmes, Francis, 104
Simpson's Delight, 31, 34, 36, 40, 44
Simpson's Supply, 25, 29, 46, 67
Simpson, Alexander, 14, 31, 40, 43, 56
Simpson, Samuel, 100
Simpson, Sander, 33, 56
Simpson, William, 110
Simscon, Richard, 105
Simson, Geo., 89
Singleton, Elizabeth, 103
Singleton, Richard, 100
Sinnett, Alexander, 6
Sinnett, Alise, 100
Sinnett, Anne, 26, 51
Sinnett, Catherine, 89
Sinnett, Garrett, 11, 33, 43, 48, 51, 70, 92, 122, 123
Sinnett, Gerrard, 26
Sinnett, Margarett, 123
Sinnett, Mary, 89
Sinnett, Robert, 89
Skidmore, Anne, 83, 133
Skidmore, Nicholas, 65, 67, 78, 83, 133

Skidmores Hope, 67
Skidmore Rest, 83, 84
Skinner, Thomas, 100
Skipton, 33, 58
Slater, John, 57, 100
Sly, Gerrard, 57
Slye, Robert, 6, 33
Small Hopes, 115
Small, John, 47
Smallpage, Elinor, 136
Smallpage, Robert, 136, 138, 152
Smallwood, James, 21, 44, 53, 76, 80, 91, 92, 94, 103, 108, 111, 114, 123, 124, 146, 155
Smallwood, James, Sr., 152
Smallwood, John, 123
Smallwood, Mary, 123
Smallwood, Mathew, 124
Smallwood, Thomas, 149
Smith's Chance, 153
Smith's Hope, 49
Smith, Alexander, 25, 39, 62, 63, 70, 92, 95, 97, 105
Smith, Anne, 117
Smith, Anthony, 138
Smith, Arthur, 147
Smith, Charles, 140
Smith, Daniel, 38, 134, 135
Smith, Elizabeth, 100, 135, 153
Smith, George Geer, 89
Smith, Henry, 151
Smith, James, 104
Smith, John, 89, 121 153, 154
Smith, Martha, 138
Smith, Ralph, 60, 100, 154
Smith, Richard, 17, 70, 117, 147
Smith, Robert, 100
Smith, Samuel, 57
Smith, Sarah, 60
Smith, Thomas, 151

Smith, William, 56, 57, 78, 90, 99, 100, 102, 106, 113, 118, 139, 151
Smith, Wm., Jr., 147
Smmes, John, 135
Smolare, John, 103
Smoote, Anne, 108, 112
Smoote, Edward, 81, 108, 119
Smoote, Elizabeth, 122, 137
Smoote, Grace, 122
Smoote, Richard, 50, 70, 97, 101, 108, 122
Smoote, Thomas, 75, 89, 108, 137
Smoote, William, 50, 75, 76, 66, 78, 80, 100, 108, 112, 119, 122, 132
Smootes Choise, 121, 149
Smootes Discovery, 137
Smoots Putchase, 81
Smoots, 76
Smyth, Alexander, 93, 101
Smyth, John, 8, 122
Snell, Jeremiah, 139, 154
Snell, Margaret, 100
Snoggin, Elizabeth, 129
Snoggin, George, 129
Snoggin, John, 129
Snoggin, Mary, 129
Snoggin, Susanna, 129
Snow, Christopherv
Snowden, Wm., 100
Solby, Nick, 26
Solley, Edward, 35
Soute, Wm., 89
Southbury, 65
Southrisk, 109
Speake, Bowling, 139
Speake, James, 139
Speake, John, 83, 104, 139, 147
Speake, Winnifred, 83, 104

Speeke, Thomas, 90, 95, 100
Spicer, Absolon, 100
Spring Plaine, 48
Spurling, Jeremiah, 104
Square Adventure, 80, 132
St. Barbara, 113
St. Barbarie Manor, 114, 144
St. Barbary, 142
St. Bridgetts, 76
St. David's, 53
St. Edmonds, 28, 55
St. Edmundsberry, 48
St. Edward, 113
St. Elizabeth's, 19, 38, 45, 147
St. Ignatius, 19, 35, 36
St. Inigoes Manor, 119
St. James, 79, 145
St. John's, 30, 61, 62
St. Joseph's Church, 152
St. Joseph's, 19
St. Margaret's, 22, 29, 41
St. Nicholas, 20, 23, 24
St. Patrick's, 48
St. Peter's, 51
St. Thomas Manor, 5682,
St. Thomas, 116
Standish, Alexander, 50, 89
Standover, William, 58
Stannard, William, 51
Steede, Thomas, 89, 100
Stephens, Mary, 100
Stephens, Richard, 100
Stephens, Simon, 29, 31, 57, 89

Steward, John, 140
Stewart, Elizabeth, 138
Stewart, John, 138
Stidman, Edward, 101
Stoake Hill, 15, 16, 42
Stone Hill, 39, 60

Stone's Delight, 20
Stone, Elizabeth, 116
Stone, John, 4, 10, 11, 13, 36, 46, 93, 96, 98, 102, 139, 152, 155
Stone, Mathew, 19, 20, 38, 65, 66, 93
Stone, Mathias, 101
Stone, Richard, 5, 10, 13
Stone, Thomas, 4, 10, 13, 19, 20, 44, 93, 153, 155
Stone, Verlinda, 11, 50
Stone, William, 5, 15, 16, 19, 58, 82, 116, 136, 139, 143, 144
Stonehill, Mathew, 92
Stonehouse, Thomas, 101
Stonestreet, Thomas, 100
Store, The, 144
Story, Elizabeth, 69, 70
Story, Mary, 144
Story, Walter, 69, 144
Stringer, George, 101
Stump Neck, 57
Sudberie, Gregorie, 101
Sunley, William, 121
Suratt, John, 152
Surgeant, Wm., 139
Surling, Robert, 106
Swaine, George, 101
Swallwell, John, 137, 145
Swan Harbor, 116
Swan, Edward, 3, 12, 55, 59, 102
Swan, Susannah, 3, 12
Swann, Edward, 154
Swanson, Francis, 6
Sween, Sarah, 101
Swellwell, John, 150
Swettnam, Margaret, 140
Swinborne, Eliz., 81
Swinborne, Nicholas, 78
Symons, Elizabeth, 121

Sympson, Alexander, 97, 122
Sympson, Thomas, Jr., 104
Synett, Garrett, Jr., 76

Tallor, William, 43
Tannehill, William, 114, 137
Tanshall, Edward, 89
Tanshall, Jno., 89
Tanshall, Thos., 89
Tarkington, John, 9
Tatshall, 76, 80
Taylard, W., 137
Taylor, Anne, 129
Taylor, Edmond, 15, 16, 42, 48, 89, 97
Taylor, Elinor, 24
Taylor, Elizabeth, 38, 101
Taylor, George, 24, 71, 101
Taylor, John, 38, 102, 129
Taylor, Susannah, 71
Taylor, Thomas, 38, 48, 94, 97, 101, 129
Taylor, William, 75, 89
Teares, Elizabeth, 152
Teares, Hugh, 121, 152
Thatryer, Mary, 101
Theobalds, Clement, 31, 32, 34, 36, 40, 42, 43, 45, 63, 100
Theobalds, William, 59, 66, 68, 72, 80, 82, 89, 103, 111, 112, 114
Thirst, Elizabeth, 128
Thomas His Chance, 35, 134
Thomas Street, 34, 56
Thomas Town, 78, 103
Thomas's Addition, 81, 106
Thomas, Anne, 101   , 139
Thomas, David, 12, 24, 29, 36, 41, 43, 72, 75, 81, 89, 118, 120
Thomas, Edward, 101

Thomas, Elizabeth, 139
Thomas, Hugh, 9, 39, 46, 81
Thomas, John, 121, 142
Thomas, Susanna, 35
Thomas, William, 15, 35, 55, 61, 89, 105
Thomas, William, Jr., 112
Thompkins, Giles, 129
Thompkins, Sarah, 129
Thompkinson, Jane, 28
Thompkinson, John, 6, 10, 12, 20, 28, 33, 44, 91
Thompkinsons Long Looked For, 154
Thompson's Rest, 39
Thompson, Anne, 64
Thompson, George, 1, 2, 5, 6, 10, 11, 13, 14, 15, 25, 32, 36, 42, 59, 60, 79, 80, 120, 121, 132, 147
Thompson, Grace, 139
Thompson, Henry, 101, 120, 142
Thompson, James, 116, 146
Thompson, John, 75, 101, 104, 133
Thompson, Mary, 149
Thompson, Robert, 38, 41, 60, 73, 75, 89, 92, 96, 132, 136, 139, 147
Thompson, Robert, Jr., 64
Thompson, Susanna, 120
Thompson, William, 104, 118
Thompson, ____, 76
Thomson, James, 134, 137
Thomson, William, 135
Thorneborrow, James, 139
Thorneton, Jermett, 101
Thornton, Francis, 24, 29, 31
Thornton, James, 117
Tibbett, John, 101

Tiblee, Thomas, 101
Tigner, Richard, 101
Till, Edward, 138
Tillsey, Mabella, 101
Tinkerell, Thomas, 62
Tipton, Edward, 101
Tiskerell, Anne, 61
Tiskerell, Thomas, 61, 89
Tod, Thomas, 101
Tofle, Thomas, 132
Tolson, Thomas, 93
Tomkins, Gyles, 14
Tomkinson, John, 106
Tompkins, Joan, 111
Tompkinson's Long Looked For, 10
Tompkinson, Giles, 50
Towell, David, 51, 53, 89
Tower Dock, 34
Tower Hills, 62
Towne, Henry, 90
Trench, Ann, 101
Trenn, Henry, 133
Trew, Priscilla, 89
Trew, Richard, 11, 17
Troope's Rendezvous, 6, 24, 26, 46, 53
Troope, Robert, 6, 18
True, Anne, 4, 29
True, Richard, 4, 5, 18, 29
Tubb, Thomas, 47, 101
Tubman, George, 154
Tukerell, Thomas, 56
Turkey Thickett, 147
Turling, Rebeckah, 149
Turlinge, John, 126
Turner, Alexander Smith, 137
Turner, Anne, 70
Turner, Arthur, 70, 71, 90, 144
Turner, Edward, 70, 136, 137
Turner, James, 71

Turner, Mary, 136
Turner, William, 101
Twigges, John, 17, 29, 30, 31, 89

Tyler, James, 47, 65
Tylly, James, 89
Tymothie, Will, 101
Typton, Edward, 101, 120
Tyre, James, 48, 90, 97

Vainall, 26, 38, 135
Vaine, Henrie, 101
Vandry, Elizabeth, 23
Vandry, John, 20, 23, 24
Vanse, Joseph, 108
Vassall, Elizabeth, 125
Vassall, Leny, 89, 89
Vassall, Lewis, 125
Vassall, Thomas, 125
Vaudry, Jno., 94, 100
Venture Beginning, 27
Veren, Nathaniel, 59
Verritt, John, 101
Vineyard, 140
Vos, Richard
Voyall, Mitholob, 33

Wade's Adventure, 152
Wade's Land, 107
Wade, Anne, 140
Wade, Edward, 123
Wade, Mary, 121
Wade, Mr., 95
Wade, Richard, 92, 107, 140
Wade, Sarah, 122
Wade, William, 124
Wade, Zachary, 26, 28, 30, 38, 51,
   62, 71, 75, 91, 93, 96, 100,
   101, 107, 110, 111, 121, 122,
   123, 124, 140

Wadestone Inlargement, 62, 111
Wadestones, 107
Wahope Purchase, 51
Wahope, Archibald, 11, 13, 31,
   45, 51, 72, 91, 97, 98, 100,
   101
Wahope, Elizabeth, 48
Waineman, Rise, 19
Wainman, Richard, 23
Wakefield, 50
Wakefield, Abell, 151
Wakefield, Thomas, 35, 72, 151
Wakelin, Catherine, 135
Wakelin, Mary, 73
Wakelin, Richard, 73, 89, 135
Wakelin, Richard, Jr., 135
Walker's Runn, 12
Walker, Alise, 45, 120
Walker, Deusman, 140
Walker, James, 2, 12, 13, 45, 91,
   120
Walker, Robert, 120
Wallis, Michaell, 148
Wallwort, Isaac, 101
Walson, Elizabeth, 140
Walson, Jane, 140
Walson, William, 140
Walter, John, 8, 12, 20, 89
Walter, Samuel, 58
Walton, Samuel, 67
Want Water, 72
Ward, Anne, 122
Ward, Deamaris, 155
Ward, Henry, 101, 116, 138
Ward, James, 155
Ward, John, 6, 23, 27, 30, 52, 58,
   71, 93, 94, 98, 122, 123, 139,
   155
Ward, Katherine, 116
Ward, Mary, 122

Ward, Richard, 101
Ward, Robert, 43
Ward, William, 12, 13, 35, 60 89

Ward, Zachary, 38
Wardner, Thomas, 14
Ware, Robert, 39
Warner, Christopher, 36, 71, 101

Warner, Elizabeth, 89
Warner, Margaret, 71
Warner, Tho., Jr., 89
Warner, Thomas, 108, 115, 142, 148
Warrell, Robert, 30
Warren, Abraham, 150
Warren, Charles, 128
Warren, Elinor, 89, 150
Warren, Elizabeth, 89, 115, 128
Warren, Humphrey, 41, 75, 77, 81, 89, 93, 95, 96, 100, 101, 102, 108, 112, 115, 117, 118, 119, 122, 128, 139, 146, 150
Warren, Humphrey, Jr., 89, 90, 101
Warren, John, 128
Warren, Margery, 128
Warren, Mary, 114
Warren, Notley, 128
Warren, Thomas, 77, 81, 108, 114, 120, 134, 150
Wassell, 34, 43, 56
Waters, Esther, 47
Waters, John, 20, 47
Waterworth, Catherine, 101
Waterworth, John, 101
Watkins, William, 110
Watridge, Anne, 101
Watson's Addition, 20
Watson's Marsh, 20, 76

Watson's Purchase, 148
Watson, Andrew, 6, 11, 12, 15, 17, 21, 25, 44, 133
Watson, John, 113
Watson, ____, 83
Waye, Jane, 112
Waye, Joan, 120
Waye, Richard, 89, 98, 100, 112, 120
Wayman, Rise, 58
Wayne, Richard, 135
Wayneman, Rice, 89
Webb, Michael, 76, 115
Webber, Thomas, 89
Weeks, Elizabeth, 96
Wellcome, 33, 53
Wellford, 145
Wells, Henry, 89
Wells, Mary, 151
Wells, Thomas, 47
Wells, William, 52, 54, 55, 58, 59, 63, 66, 80, 89, 98, 151
Welsh, Jason, 89
Wentworth's Rest, 30
Wentworth's woodhouse, 72
Wentworth, 12
Wentworth, Francis, 89
Wentworth, Thomas, 3, 22, 29, 30
West, Mary, 76
Wharton's Rest, 31
Wharton, Elizabeth, 71, 89
Wharton, Jesse, 43
Wharton, Margaret, 54, 71, 89
Wharton, Thomas, 31, 32, 64, 71, 75, 89
Wheeler's Adventure, 58, 79
Wheeler's Choice, 5, 6
Wheeler's Hope, 81
Wheeler's Palme, 3, 34, 116, 142

Wheeler's Rest, 40
Wheeler, Anne, 149
Wheeler, Benjamin, 110
Wheeler, David, 101
Wheeler, Francis, 151
Wheeler, Ignatius, 104, 120, 123, 132, 133, 140, 143, 149
Wheeler, James, 89, 123
Wheeler, John, 2, 13, 15, 23, 31, 42, 58, 72, 79, 80, 81, 83, 91, 92, 94, 95, 97, 103, 105, 117, 119, 122 123, 139, 146
Wheeler, Luke, 143
Wheeler, Mary, 51, 60, 117, 123
Wheeler, Richard, 110
Wheeler, Robert, 51, 54, 60, 67, 89
Wheeler, Thomas, 89, 108, 110, 123, 149
Wheeler, Winnifred, 104, 123, 151
Wheeler, ____, 118
Whichaley, see Wicherly
Whilden, John, 102
White, Alexander, 6, 20, 91
White, Marie, 71, 122
Whitehorne, Jno., 102
Whiteland, 6, 22, 141
Whitlocke, Jno, 63
Whitt, Samuell, 102
Whittaker, Mary, 132
Whittymore, Anne, 146
Whittymore, Christopher, 146
Wicherly, Elizabeth, 153
Wicherly, Thomas, 103, 112, 115, 118, 133, 134, 138, 140, 152
Wickham, 146
Wicomico Fields, 77, 108, 112, 119
Wicksall, 81
Wiggs, David, 102

Wilder, Edward, 46, 128
Wilder, Ever Elay, 128
Wilder, John, 112, 128, 135, 137, 149
Wilder, Robert, 102
Wilfray, Lusi, 102
Wilkenson, William, 71
Wilkinson, John, 76, 89, 102, 116
Wilkinson, Lancelott, 89, 147
Wilkinson, Mary, 147
Willbee, Mishael, 102
William, John, 118
William, Peter, 102
William, Richard, 105
Williams, Edward, 102, 120
Williams, Hugh, 102
Williams, Jane, 102
Williams, John, 89, 102, 126, 145
Williams, Katherin, 102
Williams, Rise, 95
Williams, Sarah, 126
Williams, William, 1, 5, 102, 126, 136, 145, 146
Williamson, Lancelot, 102
Willman, Henry, 102
Wills, William, 99
Willson, Thomas, 89
Wilson, Giles, 59
Wilson, John, 154
Wilson, Lawrence, 102
Wilson, Robert, 102
Windson, Jervis, 153
Wine, Elizabeth, 67, 68
Wine, Francis, 8, 22, 27, 43, 44, 56, 68, 89, 90, 92, 107, 119
Wine, Henry, 68, 119
Wine, Jno, 68
Winne, Tobyah, 147
Winter, John, 102
Wise, Nicholas, 121, 137

Withsall, 52
Witten, 115
Witter, Bulkeley, 125, 138
Witter, George, 127, 149
Witter, Mary, 44, 125, 127
Witter, Mrs., 108
Witter, Thomas, 32, 36, 40, 44, 64, 89, 125, 127, 149
Witter, William, 125, 149
Wolfe, Joseph, 34, 53, 58
Wolleston Manor, 74
Wolph, Mary, 89
Wood, John, 89, 91, 98
Wood, Mary, 89
Woodard, John, 56, 89
Woodard, William, 150
Woodberrie, 59
Woodberries Hope, 64, 82
Wooderike, John, 137
Woodgard, Henry, 103
Woodgard, Richard, 103
Woolaston Manor, 48, 74
Woolley, Charles, 30
Word, John, 45
Worland, John, 45, 89, 103, 120
Worrall, Edward, 41, 83
Worrell, Margaret , 71
Worrell, Robert, 71
Worthington, Joseph, 102
Wright, George, 102
Wright, Joannes, 12
Wright, John, 3, 30, 33, 89, 93, 96, 114, 133
Wyck, Thomas, 103
Wynne, Elizabeth, 71
Wynne, Thomas, 71
Wyott, John, 102
W____, Margaret, 102

Yappe, Roger, 104

Yates, Charles, 129
Yates, Rebeckah, 129
Yates, Robert, 129, 132, 141, 145, 151
Yeabsley, Thomas, 33
Yorkshire, 120
Young, Charles, 102
Young, Eliz., 83
Young, Jane, 102
Young, John, 124
Young, Lawrence, 52, 59, 124
Young, Mr, 90, 91
Young, Mrs., 95
Young, Sarah, 52, 124
Young, Thomas, 59, 124
Young, William, 142

Zachia Manor, 21, 22, 31, 42, 120, 121, 133, 136, 142, 145, 146, 153

____, Edward, 46, 102
____, James, 41
____, Robert, 102
____, Ruth, 102

Other Heritage Books by Elise Greenup Jourdan:

The Greenup Family

Abstracts of Charles County, Maryland Court and Land Records:
Volume 1: 1658-1666
Volume 2: 1665-1695
Volume 3: 1694-1722

Colonial Records of Southern Maryland:
Trinity Parish & Court Records, Charles County; Christ Church Parish & Marriage Records, Calvert County; St. Andrew's & All Faith's Parishes, St. Mary's County

Colonial Settlers of Prince George's County, Maryland

Early Families of Southern Maryland:
Volume 1 (Revised) and Volumes 2-10

Settlers of Colonial Calvert County, Maryland

Settlers of Colonial St. Mary's County, Maryland

The Land Records of Prince George's County, Maryland:
1702-1709
1710-1717
1717-1726
1733-1739
1739-1743

with Francis W. McIntosh

1840 to 1850 Federal Census: Tazewell County, Virginia

1860 Federal Census: Tazewell County, Virginia

1870 Federal Census: Tazewell County, Virginia

www.ingramcontent.com/pod-product-compliance
Lightning Source LLC
Chambersburg PA
CBHW051055160426
43193CB00010B/1186